AUTODESK® 3DS MAX® 2016

ESSENTIALS

AUTODESK® 3DS MAX® 2016

ESSENTIALS

Randi L. Derakhshani

Dariush Derakhshani

Acquisitions Editor: Stephanie McComb
Development Editor: Clark David
Technical Editor: Jon McFarland
Production Editor: Joel Jones
Copy Editor: Kathy Grider-Carlyle
Editorial Manager: Mary Beth Wakefield
Production Manager: Kathleen Wisor
Associate Publisher: Jim Minatel
Proofreader: Kathryn Duggan
Indexer: Nancy Guenther
Project Coordinator, Cover: Brent Savage
Cover Designer: Wiley
Cover Image: Courtesy of Dariush Derakhshani; Back Cover Images: Courtesy of Randi L. Derakhshani

ISBN: 978-1-119-05976-9
ISBN: 978-1-119-05990-5 (ebk.)
ISBN: 978-1-119-05989-9 (ebk.)

For general information on our other products and services or to obtain technical support, please contact our Customer Care Department within the U.S. at (877) 762-2974, outside the U.S. at (317) 572-3993, or fax (317) 572-4002.

Wiley publishes in a variety of print and electronic formats and by print-on-demand. Some material included with standard print versions of this book may not be included in e-books or in print-on-demand. If this book refers to media such as a CD or DVD that is not included in the version you purchased, you may download this material at http://booksupport.wiley.com. For more information about Wiley products, visit www.wiley.com.

Library of Congress Control Number: 2015943414

ACKNOWLEDGMENTS

Education is an all-important goal in life and should always be approached with eagerness and earnestness. We would like to show appreciation to the teachers who inspired us; you can always remember the teachers who touched your life, and to them we say thanks. We would also like to thank all of our students, who taught us a lot during the course of our many combined academic years.

Special thanks go to Stephanie McComb, David Clark, Joel Jones, and Mary Beth Wakefield, our editors at Sybex who have been professional, courteous, and ever patient. Our appreciation also goes to technical editor Jon McFarland, who worked hard to make sure this book is of the utmost quality. We could not have done this revision without their help.

In addition, many thanks to our son, Max, our motivation and our inspiration.

WRITING ON THE HP ELITEBOOK

Having a good computer system is important with this type of work, so a special thank you goes to HP for keeping us on the cutting edge of workstation hardware by providing us with a fully decked-out EliteBook 8760w, which was our primary computer in writing this book. What struck us about the laptop was that it was not only portable, making it easy for a writing team to collaborate; it was also powerful enough to run truly demanding tasks. It takes a special machine to run graphics-intensive applications, such as the Autodesk® 3ds Max® 2016 software, and we were thrilled to write this book on the HP EliteBook.

Running an Intel i7 CPU with 16GB of RAM and an NVIDIA Quadro 5010M (with a whopping 6 GB of memory) gave us the muscle we needed to run multiple applications alongside 3ds Max splendidly. Dual 320 GB hard drives gave us plenty of space for Windows 7 Professional and its applications, and still left lots of room for renders. We opted out of the RAID option to mirror the drives (you can also stripe them for performance), but that doesn't mean we neglected our backup duties with this machine! The 8760w was easily integrated into a gigabit network in the home office, and on fast Wi-Fi everywhere else, so we had constant access to the home network and the hundreds upon hundreds of files (and all their backups!) necessary to write this book.

And since we are so very image-conscious (as in the screen!), we wondered if the images we created and captured for this book would be done justice on "just a laptop screen." The EliteBook has a stunning 17-inch, 30-bit IPS display panel that put those questions to rest very quickly! The EliteBook screen is professionally accurate and calibrated for optimum image clarity and correct color. Barely a handful of high-end mobile workstations could even come close to meeting the demands that image professionals put on their gear. But this notebook HP DreamColor display is remarkable—there's just no other way to put it—going as far as besting any of our desktop screens in color and vibrancy.

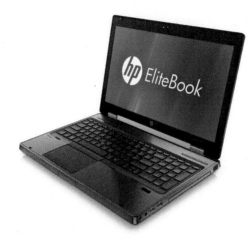

With performance at such a high level, and in a nice portable form, we were easily convinced that we should perform all of our intensive work for this book on the EliteBook. Going back to a desk-bound tower quickly became a non-option. Thanks, HP!

About the Authors

Randi L. Derakhshani is an Autodesk-Certified Instructor. She began working with computer graphics in 1992 and was hired by her instructor to work at Sony Pictures Imageworks, where she developed her skills with the Autodesk® 3ds Max® program and Apple's Shake image-compositing program among many other programs. A teacher since 1999, Randi enjoys sharing her wisdom with young talent and watching them develop. Currently, she is teaching at Exceptional Minds, a school where individuals on the autism spectrum learn through customized instruction the fields of multimedia, computer animation, and post-production. She also teaches a wide range of classes, from Autodesk 3ds Max, Autodesk® Maya®, and ZBrush to compositing with The Foundry's Nuke. Juggling her teaching activities with caring for a little boy makes Randi a pretty busy lady.

Dariush Derakhshani is an Autodesk-Certified Instructor and Certified Evaluator, a visual-effects supervisor, a writer, and an educator in Los Angeles, California, as well as Randi's husband. Dariush used Autodesk® AutoCAD® software in his architectural days and migrated to using 3D programs when his firm's principal architects needed to visualize architectural designs in 3D on the computer. Dariush started using Alias PowerAnimator version 6 when he enrolled in USC Film School's animation program, and he has been using Alias/Autodesk animation software for the past 14 years. He received an MFA in film, video, and computer animation from the USC Film School in 1997. He also holds a BA in architecture and theater from Lehigh University in Pennsylvania. He worked at a New Jersey architectural firm before moving to Los Angeles for film school. He has worked on feature films, music videos, and countless commercials as a 3D animator, as a CG/VFX supervisor, and sometimes as a compositor.

Contents at a Glance

CONTENTS

CHAPTER 13   **Introduction to Lighting: Interior Lighting**   **315**

CHAPTER 14   **3ds Max Rendering**   **341**

INTRODUCTION

Welcome to Autodesk® 3ds Max® 2016 Essentials. The world of computer-generated (CG) imagery is fun and ever changing. Whether you are new to CG in general or are a CG veteran new to 3ds Max designing, you'll find this book the perfect primer. It introduces you to the Autodesk 3ds Max software and shows how you can work with the program to create your art, whether it is animated or static in design.

This book exposes you to all facets of 3ds Max by introducing and plainly explaining its tools and functions to help you understand how the program operates—but it does not stop there. This book also explains the use of the tools and the ever-critical concepts behind the tools. You'll find hands-on examples and tutorials that give you firsthand experience with the toolsets. Working through them will develop your skills and the conceptual knowledge that will carry you to further study with confidence. These tutorials expose you to various ways to accomplish tasks with this intricate and comprehensive artistic tool. They should give you the confidence you need to venture deeper into the feature set in 3ds Max, either on your own or by using any of the software's other learning tools and books as a guide.

Learning to use a powerful tool can be frustrating. You need to remember to pace yourself. The major complaints CG book readers have are that the pace is too fast and that the steps are too complicated or overwhelming. Addressing those complaints is a tough nut to crack, to be sure. No two readers are the same. However, this book offers the opportunity to run things at your own pace. The exercises and steps may seem confusing at times, but keep in mind that the more you try and the more you fail at some attempts, the more you will learn how to operate the 3ds Max engine. Experience is king when learning the workflow necessary for *any* software program, and with experience comes failure and aggravation. But try and try again. You will find that further attempts will always be easier and more fruitful.

Above all, this book aims to inspire you to use the 3ds Max program as a creative tool to achieve and explore your own artistic vision.

Who Should Read This Book

Anyone who is interested in learning to use the 3ds Max tools should start with this book.

If you are an educator, you will find a solid foundation on which to build a new course. You can also treat the book as a source of raw materials that you can adapt to fit an existing curriculum. Written in an open-ended style, *Autodesk® 3ds Max® 2016 Essentials* contains several self-help tutorials for home study as well as plenty of material to fit into any class.

What You Will Learn

You will learn how to work in CG with Autodesk 3ds Max 2016. The important thing to keep in mind, however, is that this book is merely the beginning of your CG education. With the confidence you will gain from the exercises in this book, and the peace of mind you can have by using this book as a reference, you can go on to create your own increasingly complex CG projects.

What You Need

Hardware changes constantly and evolves faster than publications can keep up. Having a good solid machine is important to production, although simple home computers will be able to run the 3ds Max software quite well. Any laptop (with discrete graphics, not a netbook) or desktop PC running Windows XP Professional, Windows 7, or Windows 8 (32- or 64-bit) with at least 2 GB of RAM and an Intel Pentium Core 2 Duo/Quad or AMD Phenom or higher processor will work. Of course, having a good video card will help; you can use any hardware-accelerated OpenGL or Direct3D video card. Your computer system should have at least a 2.4 GHz Core 2 or i5/i7 processor with 2 GB of RAM, a few GBs of hard-drive space available, and a GeForce FX or ATI Radeon video card. Professionals may want to opt for workstation graphics cards, such as the ATI FirePro or the Quadro FX series of cards. The following systems would be good ones to use:

- ▶ Intel i7, 4 GB RAM, Quadro FX 2000, 400 GB 7200 RPM hard disk
- ▶ AMD Phenom II, 4 GB RAM, ATI FirePro V5700, 400 GB hard disk

You can check the list of system requirements at the following website: www.autodesk.com/3dsmax.

FREE AUTODESK SOFTWARE FOR STUDENTS AND EDUCATORS

The Autodesk Education Community is an online resource with more than five million members that enables educators and students to download—for free (see website for terms and conditions)—the same software used by professionals worldwide. You can also access additional tools and materials to help you design, visualize, and simulate ideas. Connect with other learners to stay current with the latest industry trends and get the most out of your designs. Get started today at www.autodesk.com/joinedu.

What Is Covered in This Book

Autodesk® 3ds Max® 2016 is organized to provide you with a quick and essential experience with 3ds Max to allow you to begin a fruitful education in the world of computer graphics.

Chapter 1, "The 3ds Max Interface," begins with an introduction to the interface for 3ds Max 2016 to get you up and running quickly.

Chapter 2, "Your First 3ds Max Project," is an introduction to modeling concepts and workflows in general. It shows you how to model using 3ds Max tools with polygonal meshes and modifiers to create a retro alarm clock.

Chapter 3, "Modeling in 3ds Max: Architectural Model Part I," takes your modeling lesson from Chapter 2 a step further by showing you how to use some of the Architecture Engineering and Construction (AEC) tools to build an interior space using a room from an image.

Chapter 4, "Modeling in 3ds Max: Architectural Model Part II," continues with the interior space from Chapter 3 by adding some furniture. The main focus of this chapter is the Graphite Modeling Tools tab and its many tools.

Chapter 5, "Introduction to Animation," teaches you the basics of 3ds Max animation techniques and workflow by animating a bouncing ball. You will also learn how to use the Track View - Curve Editor to time, edit, and finesse your animation.

Chapter 6, "Animation Principles," rounds out your animation experience by showing the animation concepts of weight, follow-through, and anticipation when you animate a knife thrown at a target.

Chapter 7, "Character Modeling Part I," introduces you to the creation of polygon mesh character model of an alien. In this chapter, you begin by blocking out the primary parts of the body.

Chapter 8, "Character Modeling Part II," continues the alien model, focusing on using the Editable Poly toolset. You will finish the body details, head, hands, and feet.

Chapter 9, "Introduction to Materials," shows you how to assign textures and materials to your models. You will learn to texture the couch, chair, and window from Chapter 4 as you learn the basics of working with 3ds Max materials and UVW mapping.

Chapter 10, "Textures and UV Workflow: The Alien," furthers your understanding of materials and textures, and introduces UV workflows in preparing and texturing the alien.

Chapter 11, "Character Studio: Rigging," covers the basics of Character Studio in creating a biped system and associating the biped rig to the alien model.

Chapter 12, "Character Studio: Animation," expands on Chapter 11 to show you how to use Character Studio to create and edit a walk cycle using the alien model.

Chapter 13, "Introduction to Lighting: Interior Lighting," begins by showing you how to light a 3D scene with the three-point lighting system. It then shows you how to use the tools to create and edit 3ds Max lights for illumination, shadows, and special lighting effects. You will light the furniture to which you added materials in Chapter 9.

Chapter 14, "3ds Max Rendering," explains how to create image files from your 3ds Max scene and how to achieve the best look for your animation by using proper cameras and rendering settings when you render the interior scene.

Chapter 15, "mental ray," shows you how to render with mental ray. Using Final Gather, you will learn how to use indirect lighting.

The companion web page to this book at www.sybex.com/go/ 3dsmax2016essentials provides all the sample images, movies, and files that you will need to work through the projects in *Autodesk® 3ds Max® 2016*.

 N O T E   This book is a great primer for Autodesk 3ds Max. If you're interested in taking the Autodesk Certification exams for 3ds Max, go to www.autodesk .com/certification for information and resources.

The Essentials Series

The Essentials series from Sybex provides outstanding instruction for readers who are just beginning to develop their professional skills. Every Essentials book includes these features:

▶ Skill-based instruction with chapters organized around projects rather than abstract concepts or subjects

▶ Downloadable tutorial files showing the start and end state of each exercise

▶ Digital files (via download) so you can work through the project tutorials yourself. Please check the book's web page at www.sybex .com/go/3dsmax2016essentials for these companion downloads.

You can contact the authors through Wiley or on Facebook at www.facebook .com/3dsMaxEssentials.

CHAPTER 1

The 3ds Max Interface

The Autodesk® 3ds Max® 2016 software interface is where you view and work with your scene. This chapter explains its basic operations and tools. You can use this chapter as a reference as you work through the rest of this book, although the following chapters and their exercises will orient you to the 3ds Max user interface (UI) quickly. It's important to be in front of your computer when you read this chapter, so you can try out techniques as we discuss them in the book.

In this chapter, you will learn to

▶ **Navigate the workspace**

▶ **Transform objects using gizmos**

▶ **Use the Graphite Modeling Tools set**

▶ **Use the command panel**

▶ **Use the time slider and track bar**

▶ **Manage files**

Navigating the Workspace

The following sections present a brief rundown of what you need to know about the UI and how to navigate in the 3D workspace.

User-Interface Elements

Figure 1.1 shows the 3ds Max UI. (See Table 1.1 for explanations of the UI elements.) At the top left of the application window is an icon called the Application button ( ); clicking it opens the Application menu, which provides access to many file operations. Running along the top is the

Quick Access toolbar, which provides access to common commands and the InfoCenter, which in turn offers to access many product-related information sources. In this version of the program, they have rolled out a new Enhanced Menus workspace that defines the look of the interface. When you first open the program, you will see the Default workspace. To switch to a different workspace, go to the Quick Access toolbar located at the top of the interface. In the Workspaces drop-down list, choose the desired workspace. Some of the most important commands in the Quick Access toolbar are file-management commands such as Save File and Open File. If you do something and then wish you hadn't, you can click the Undo Scene Operation button (⟵ ▾) or press Ctrl+Z. To redo a command or action that you just undid, click the Redo Scene Operation button (⟶ ▾) or press Ctrl+Y.

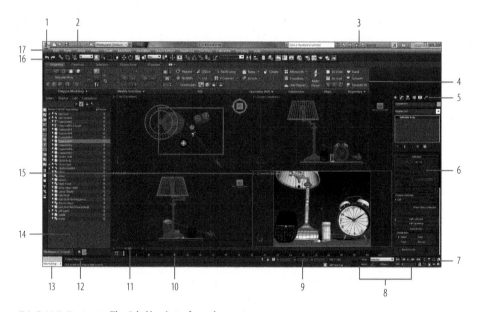

FIGURE 1.1   The 3ds Max interface elements

TABLE 1.1   The 3ds Max interface elements*

Element	Function	Description
1	Application button	Opens the Application menu, which provides file management commands.
2	Quick Access toolbar	Provides some of the most commonly used file management commands as well as Undo Scene Operation and Redo Scene Operation.

Element	Function	Description
3	InfoCenter	Provides access to 3ds Max product-related information.
4	The ribbon	Provides access to a wide range of tools to make building and editing models in 3ds Max fast and easy.
5	Command panel tabs	Where all the editing of parameters occurs; provides access to many functions and creation options; divided into tabs that access different panels, such as the Create panel, Modify panel, etc.
6	Rollout	A section of the command panel that can expand to show a listing of parameters or collapse to just its heading name.
7	Viewport navigation controls	Icons that control the display and navigation of the viewports; icons may change depending on the active viewport.
8	Animation Time/Keying controls	Controls for animation keyframing and animation playback controls.
9	Coordinate display area	Allows you to enter transformation values.
10	Track bar	Provides a timeline showing the frame numbers; select an object to view its animation keys on the track bar.
11	Time slider	Shows the current frame and allows for changing the current frame by moving (or scrubbing) the time bar.
12	Prompt line and status bar controls	Prompt and status information about your scene and the active command.
13	MAXScript Mini Listener	A command prompt window for the MAXScript language. The window is useful for performing interactive work and developing small code fragments.
14	Scene Explorer	Scene Explorer is a dialog for viewing, sorting, filtering, and selecting objects. This dialog can also rename, delete, hide, and freeze objects. It can create and modify object hierarchies and access object properties.

(Continues)

TABLE 1.1 *(Continued)*

Element	Function	Description
15	Viewports	You can choose different views to display in these four viewports, as well as different layouts from the viewport label menus.
16	Main toolbar	Provides quick access to tools and dialog boxes for many of the most common tasks.
17	Menu bar	Provides access to commands grouped by category.

*The numerals in the first column refer to labels in Figure 1.1.

Just below the Quick Access toolbar is the menu bar, which runs across the top of the interface. The menus give you access to a ton of commands—from basic scene operations, such as Duplicate and Group under the Edit menu, to advanced tools such as those found under the Modifiers menu. Immediately below the menu bar is the main toolbar. It contains several icons for functions, such as the four transform tools: Select and Move, Select and Rotate, Select and Uniform Scale, and Select and Place (⊹ ↻ 🖼 ⟳). The Select and Place tool is a new tool available in 3ds Max 2016. Use the Select and Place tool to position an object accurately on the surface of another object.

When you first open 3ds Max, the workspace has many UI elements. Each is designed to help you work with your models, access tools, and edit object parameters.

Viewports

You'll be doing most of your work in the viewports. These windows represent 3D space using a system based on Cartesian coordinates. That is a fancy way of saying "space on the X-, Y-, and Z-axes."

You can visualize X as left-right, Y as in-out (into and out of the screen from the Top viewport), and Z as up-down within the Perspective and Camera viewports. In the orthographic viewports, you visualize Y as up-down and Z as in-out. The coordinates are expressed as a set of three numbers, such as (0, 3, −7). These coordinates represent a point that is at 0 on the X-axis, three units up on the Y-axis, and seven units back on the Z-axis.

Viewport label menus contain commands that let you change what is shown in the viewports. These are shortcut menus for easy access to tools such as overall viewport display, changing what is displayed in a viewport, and viewport shading.

The General Viewport menu (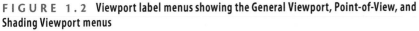), in the upper-left corner of each viewport, provides options for overall viewport display or activation, as shown in Figure 1.2. It also gives you access to the Viewport Configuration dialog box, which gives further access to viewport layout commands.

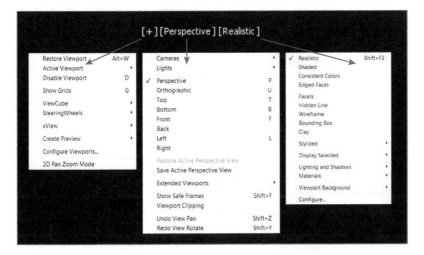

FIGURE 1.2 Viewport label menus showing the General Viewport, Point-of-View, and Shading Viewport menus

The Point-of-View (POV) viewport menu ([Perspective]) contains options that change what is displayed in the viewport. For example, you can choose to dock the graph or Material Editor into the viewport for ease of use during a project.

The Shading label menu ([Realistic]) contains commands for how objects are displayed in the viewports. By default, three of the viewports (Top, Front, and Left) are set to Wireframe, which displays the wire mesh. The Perspective viewport is set to Realistic, which is a shading style that shows realistic texturing, shading, and lighting.

The Perspective viewport displays objects in 3D space using perspective, which shows the distant objects getting smaller in the distance. In actuality, they are the same size, as you can see in the Orthographic viewports. The Perspective viewport gives you the best representation of what your output will be.

To make a viewport active, click in a blank part of the viewport (not on an object). If you do have something selected, it will be deselected when you click in the blank space.

> You can also right-click anywhere in an inactive viewport to activate it without selecting or deselecting anything.
◄

When active, the viewport will have a highlighted border around it. If you right-click in an already active viewport, you will get a pop-up context menu called the quad menu. You can use the quad menu to access some basic commands for a faster workflow. We will cover this topic in the "Quad Menus" section later in this chapter.

ViewCube

The ViewCube® 3D navigation control, shown in Figure 1.3, provides visual feedback of the current orientation of a viewport; it lets you adjust the view orientation and allows you to switch between standard and isometric views.

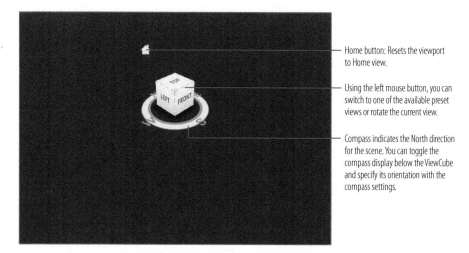

Home button: Resets the viewport to Home view.

Using the left mouse button, you can switch to one of the available preset views or rotate the current view.

Compass indicates the North direction for the scene. You can toggle the compass display below the ViewCube and specify its orientation with the compass settings.

FIGURE 1.3   The ViewCube navigation tool

The ViewCube is displayed by default in the upper-right corner of the active viewport; it is superimposed over the scene in an inactive state to show the orientation of the scene. It does not appear in Camera or Light view. When you position your cursor over the ViewCube, it becomes active. Using the left mouse button, you can switch to one of the available preset views, rotate the current view, or change to the Home view of the model. Right-clicking over the ViewCube opens a context menu with additional options.

Mouse Buttons

Each of the three buttons on your mouse plays a slightly different role when manipulating viewports in the workspace. When used with modifiers such as the Alt key, they are used to navigate your scene, as shown in Figure 1.4.

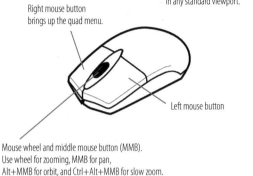

Right mouse button
brings up the quad menu.

Specialized quad menus become available
when you right-click with Shift or Ctrl or Alt
in any standard viewport.

Left mouse button

Mouse wheel and middle mouse button (MMB).
Use wheel for zooming, MMB for pan,
Alt+MMB for orbit, and Ctrl+Alt+MMB for slow zoom.

FIGURE 1.4 Breakdown of the three mouse buttons

Quad Menus

When you click the right mouse button anywhere in an active viewport, except on the Viewport label menus and the ViewCube, a quad menu is displayed at the location of the mouse cursor, as shown in Figure 1.5. The quad menu can display up to four quadrant areas with various commands without you having to travel back and forth between the viewport and rollouts on the command panel (the area of the interface to the right—more on this later in the section "Command Panel").

Some of the selections in the quad menu have a small icon next to them. Clicking this icon opens a dialog box where you can set parameters for the command.

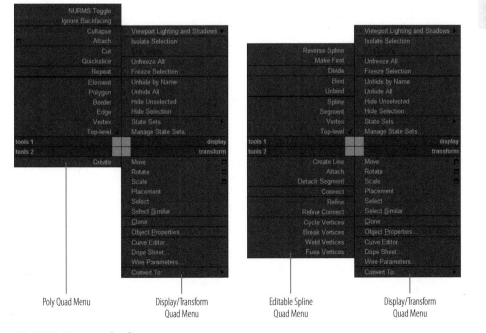

Poly Quad Menu

Display/Transform
Quad Menu

Editable Spline
Quad Menu

Display/Transform
Quad Menu

FIGURE 1.5 Quad menus

When you activate the quad menu (right mouse click), the default quad menu displays generic commands, which are shared among all objects. When you're working in certain modes (polygon or spline editing), quadrant menus contain context-specific commands, such as mesh tools and editing commands. You can also repeat your last quad menu command by clicking the title of the quadrant.

The quad menu's contents depend on what is selected. The menus are set up to display only the commands that are available for the current selection; therefore, selecting different types of objects displays different commands in the quadrants. Consequently, if no object is selected, all of the object-specific commands will be hidden. If all of the commands for one quadrant are hidden, the quadrant will not be displayed.

Cascading menus display submenus in the same manner as a right-click menu. The menu item that contains submenus is highlighted when expanded. The submenus are highlighted when you move the mouse cursor over them.

To close the menu, right-click anywhere on the screen or move the mouse cursor away from the menu and click the left mouse button. The last menu item selected is highlighted when the quadrant is displayed.

Displaying Objects in a Viewport

Viewports can display your scene objects in a few ways. If you click the viewport's name, you can switch that panel to any other viewport angle or point of view. If you click the Shading label menu, a menu appears to allow you to change the display driver. The display driver names differ, depending on the graphics drive mode you selected when you first started the program. This book uses the default display mode Nitrous. Other display modes include:

Wireframe mode   Wireframe mode displays the edges of the object, as shown on the left in Figure 1.6. It is the fastest to use because it requires less computation on your video card.

Realistic mode   The Realistic mode is a shaded view in which the objects in the scene appear solid. It shows realistic textures with shading and lighting, as shown in the middle in Figure 1.6.

Edged Faces mode   In Edged Faces mode, the wireframe edges of objects appear along with the shaded surfaces, as shown on the right in Figure 1.6.

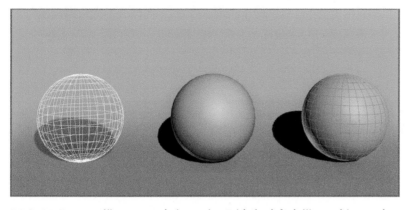

FIGURE 1.6 Viewport rendering options with the default Nitrous driver modes

Each viewport displays a ground plane grid, called the *home grid*. This is the basic 3D-space reference system where the X-axis is red, the Y-axis is green, and the Z-axis is blue. It's defined by three fixed planes on the coordinate axes (X, Y, Z). The center of all three axes is called the *origin*, where the coordinates are (0, 0, 0). The home grid is visible by default, but it can be turned on and off in the right-click General Viewport menu or by pressing the G key.

Selecting Objects in a Viewport

Click an object to select it in a viewport. If the object is displayed in Wireframe mode, its wireframe turns white while it is selected. When the cursor is passed over an object in the scene, a yellow edge highlight appears around the object. When the object is selected, a blue edge highlight appears around the object.

To select multiple objects, hold down the Ctrl key as you click additional objects to add to your selection. If you Alt+click an active object, you will deselect it. You can clear all your active selections by clicking in an empty area of the viewport.

Changing/Maximizing the Viewports

To change the view in any given viewport—for example, to go from a Perspective view to a Front view—click the current viewport's name. From the menu, select the view you want to have in the selected viewport. You can also use keyboard shortcuts. To switch from one view to another, press the appropriate key on the keyboard, as shown in Table 1.2.

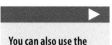

You can also use the Alt+W keyboard shortcut to toggle between the maximized and four-viewport views.

If you want to have a larger view of the active viewport than is provided by the default four-viewport layout, click the Maximize Viewport Toggle icon (⬛) in the lower-right corner of the 3ds Max window.

TABLE 1.2 Viewport shortcuts

Viewport	Keyboard shortcut
Top view	T
Bottom view	B
Front view	F
Left view	L
Camera view	C
Orthographic view	U
Perspective view	P

Viewport Navigation

3ds Max allows you to move around its viewports by using either key/mouse combinations, which are highly preferable, or the viewport controls found in the lower-right corner of the 3ds Max UI. The navigation icons for the Top viewport are shown in Figure 1.7, although it's best to become familiar with the key/mouse combinations.

FIGURE 1.7 Viewport navigation controls are handy, but the key/mouse combinations are much faster to use for navigation in viewports.

Open a new, empty scene in 3ds Max. Experiment with the following controls to get a feel for moving around in 3D space. If you are new to 3D, using these controls may seem odd at first, but it will become easier as you gain experience and should become second nature in no time.

Pan   Panning a viewport slides the view around the screen. Using the middle mouse button (MMB), click in the viewport and drag the mouse pointer to pan the view.

Zoom   Zooming moves your view closer to or farther away from your objects. To zoom, press Ctrl+Alt and MMB+click in your viewport and then drag the mouse up or down to zoom in or out. The zoom will occur around the cursor location. You may also use the scroll wheel to zoom.

Orbit   Orbit will rotate your view around your objects. To orbit, press Alt and MMB+click and drag in the viewport. When no object is selected, the viewport camera will rotate about the center of the viewport; when an object is selected, the viewport camera will orbit around the object.

Transforming Objects Using Gizmos

Using gizmos is a fast and effective way to transform (move, rotate, and/or scale) your objects with interactive feedback. When you select a transform tool such as Move, a gizmo appears on the selected object. Gizmos let you manipulate objects in your viewports interactively to transform them. Coordinate display boxes at the bottom of the screen display coordinate, angular, or percentage information on the position, rotation, and scale of your object as you transform it. The gizmos appear in the viewport on the selected object at their pivot point as soon as you invoke one of the transform tools, as shown in Figure 1.8.

You can select the transform tools by clicking the icons in the main toolbar's Transform toolset ( ) or by invoking shortcut keys: W for Move, E for Rotate, R for Scale.

In a new scene, create a sphere by choosing Create ➤ Standard Primitives ➤ Sphere. In a viewport, click and drag to create the Sphere object. Follow along as we explain the transform tools next.

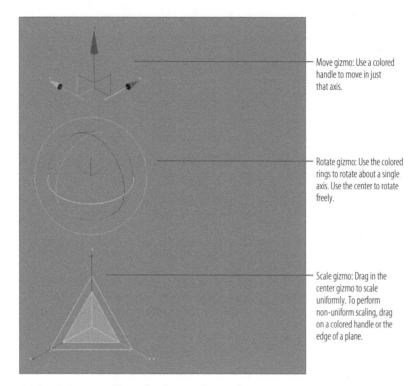

Move gizmo: Use a colored handle to move in just that axis.

Rotate gizmo: Use the colored rings to rotate about a single axis. Use the center to rotate freely.

Scale gizmo: Drag in the center gizmo to scale uniformly. To perform non-uniform scaling, drag on a colored handle or the edge of a plane.

FIGURE 1.8 **Gizmos for the transform tools**

Move   Invoke the Move tool by pressing W (or accessing it through the main toolbar), and your gizmo should look like the top image in Figure 1.8. Dragging the X-, Y-, or Z-axis handle moves an object on a specific axis. You can also click on the plane handle, the box between two axes, to move the object in that two-axis plane.

Rotate   Invoke the Rotate tool by pressing E, and your gizmo will turn into three circles, as shown in the middle image in Figure 1.8. You can click on one of the colored circles to rotate the object on the axis only, or you can click anywhere between the circles to freely rotate the selected object in all three axes. The gray circle is for rotating perpendicularly in the viewport.

Scale   Invoke the Scale tool by pressing the R key, and your gizmo will turn into a triangle, as shown in the bottom image of Figure 1.8. Clicking and dragging anywhere inside the yellow triangle will scale the object uniformly on all three axes. By selecting the red, green, or blue handle for the appropriate axis, you can scale along one axis only. You can also scale an object on a plane between two axes by selecting the side of the yellow triangle between two axes.

Graphite Modeling Tools Set

The ribbon interface is a toolbar containing these tabs: Modeling, Freeform, Selection, Object Paint, and Populate. Each tab comprises a number of panels and tools whose availability depends on the context. The ribbon can be oriented horizontally or vertically. The default for the ribbon is horizontal, docked immediately below the main toolbar, as shown earlier in Figure 1.1. The Modeling tab provides you with a wide range of modeling tools to make building and editing models in 3ds Max fast and easy. All the available tools are organized into separate panels for convenient access. In the following chapters, you will make copious use of the Modeling tab, which is shown in Figure 1.9.

FIGURE 1.9 **The Modeling tab found in the ribbon**

The following panels are found in the Graphite Modeling Tool set:

▶ Polygon Modeling panel

▶ Modify Selection panel

▶ Edit panel

▶ Geometry (All) panel

▶ [Sub-Object] panel

▶ Loops panel

▶ Additional panels

One easy way to customize the ribbon is by using the Minimum/Maximum toggle switch, as shown in Figure 1.10. By clicking on the button, you toggle the minimum/maximum options; when you maximize the ribbon, you are able to view most of the controls. The Minimize drop-down list, which is the small arrow next to the Minimum/Maximum toggle switch, gives access to different ribbon states.

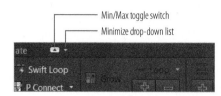

FIGURE 1.10   The Minimum/Maximum toggle for the Graphite Modeling Tools set

Command Panel

Everything you need to create, manipulate, and animate objects can be found in the command panel running vertically on the right side of the UI (Figure 1.1). The command panel is divided into tabs according to function. The function or toolset you need to access will determine which tab you need to click. When you encounter a panel that is longer than your screen, 3ds Max displays a thin vertical scroll bar on the right side. Your cursor also turns into a hand you can use to click and drag the panel up and down.

You will be exposed to more panels as you progress through this book. Table 1.3 is a rundown of the command panel functions and what they do.

TABLE 1.3   Command panel functions

Icon	Name	Function
	Create panel	Create objects, lights, cameras, etc.
	Modify panel	Apply and edit modifiers to objects
	Hierarchy panel	Adjust the hierarchy for objects and adjust their pivot points
	Motion panel	Access animation tools and functions
	Display panel	Access display options for scene objects
	Utilities panel	Access several functions of 3ds Max, such as motion capture utilities and the Asset Browser

Object Parameters and Values

The command panel and all its tabs give you access to an object's parameters. *Parameters* are the values that define a specific attribute of or for an object.

For example, when an object is selected in a viewport, its parameters are shown in the Modify panel, where you can adjust them. When you create an object, that object's creation parameters are shown (and editable) in the Create panel.

Modifier Stack

In the Modify panel, you'll find the modifier stack, as shown in Figure 1.11. This UI element lists all the modifiers that are active on any selected object. Modifiers are actions applied to an object that change it somehow, such as bending or warping. You can stack modifiers on top of each other when creating an object and then go back and edit any of the modifiers in the stack (for the most part) to adjust the object at any point in its creation. You will see this in practice in the following chapters.

— Modifier Stack

FIGURE 1.11   The modifier stack in the Modify panel

Objects and Sub-Objects

An object or mesh in 3ds Max is composed of polygons that define the surface. For example, the facets or small rectangles on a sphere are *polygons*, all connected at common edges at the correct angles and in the proper arrangement to make a sphere. The points that generate a polygon are called *vertices*. The lines that connect the points are called *edges*. Polygons, vertices, and edges are examples of sub-objects and are all editable so that you can fashion any sort of surface or mesh shape you wish.

To edit a sub-object, you have to convert it to an editable poly object, which you will learn how to do in the following chapters.

Time Slider and Track Bar

Running across the bottom of the 3ds Max UI are the time slider and the track bar, as shown earlier in Figure 1.1. The time slider allows you to move through any frame in your scene by *scrubbing* (moving the slider back and forth). You can move through your animation one frame at a time by clicking the previous-frame and next-frame arrows on either side of the time slider.

You can also use the time slider to animate objects by setting keyframes. With an object selected, right-click the time slider to open the Create Key dialog box, which allows you to create transform keyframes for the selected object.

The track bar is directly below the time slider. The track bar is the timeline that displays the timeline format for your scene. More often than not, the track bar is displayed in frames, with the gap between each tick mark representing frames. On the track bar, you can move and edit your animation properties for the selected object. When a keyframe is present, right-click it to open a context menu where you can delete keyframes, edit individual transform values, and filter the track bar display.

The Animation Playback controls in the lower right of the 3ds Max UI (⟨◁ ◁ ▷ ▷ ▷⟩) are similar to the ones you would find on a VCR or DVD player.

File Management

Different kinds of files are saved in categorized folders under the project folder. For example, scene files are saved in a `scenes` folder, and rendered images are saved in a `renderoutput` folder within the project folder. The projects are set up according to the types of files you are working on, so everything is neat and organized from the get-go.

The conventions followed in this book and on the accompanying web page (www.sybex.com/go/3dsmax2016essentials) follow this project-based system so that you can grow accustomed to it and make it a part of your own workflow. It pays to stay organized.

> Designating a specific place on your PC or server for all your project files is important, as is having an established naming convention for the project's files and folder.

Setting a Project

The exercises in this book are organized into specific projects, such as the `Clock` project that you will tackle in the next chapter. The `Clock` project will be on your hard drive, and the folders for your scene files and rendered images will be in that project layout. Once you copy the appropriate projects to your hard drive, you can tell 3ds Max which project to work on by clicking the Application button and choosing Manage ≻ Set Project Folder. Doing so will send the current project to that project folder. For example, when you save your scene, 3ds Max will automatically take you to the scenes folder of the current project.

For example, if you are working on a project about a castle, begin by setting a new project called Castle. Click the Application button and choose Manage ≻ Set Project Folder, as shown in Figure 1.12. In the dialog box that opens, click Make New Folder to create a folder named Castle on your hard drive. 3ds Max will automatically create the project and its folders.

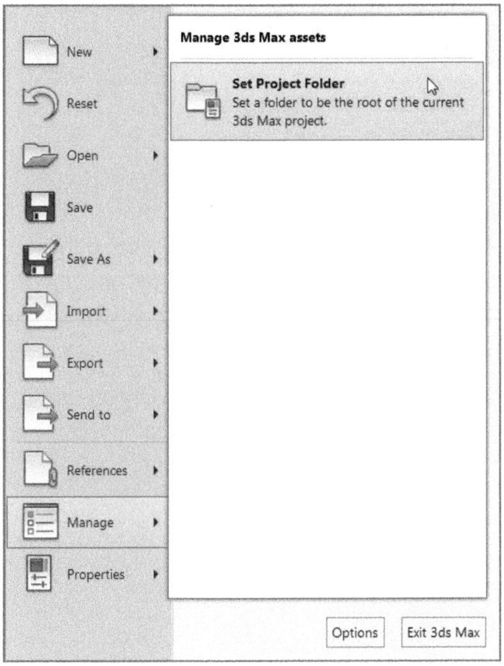

FIGURE 1.12 Choosing Set Project Folder

Once you save a scene, one of your scene filenames should look like this: Castle_GateModel_v05.max. This tells you right away that it's a scene from your Castle project and that it is a model of the gate. The version number tells you that it's the fifth iteration of the model and possibly the most recent version. Following a naming convention will save you oodles of time and aggravation.

Version Up!

After you've spent a significant amount of time working on your scene, you will want to *version up*. This means you save your file using the same name, but you increase the version number by 1. Saving often and using version numbers are useful for keeping track of your progress and protecting yourself from mistakes and from losing your work.

To version up, you can save by clicking the Application button, choosing Save As, and manually changing the version number appended to the end of the file-name. 3ds Max also lets you do this automatically by using an increment feature in the Save As dialog box. Name your scene file and click the Increment button (the + icon) to the right of the filename text. Clicking the Increment button appends the filename with 01, then 02, then 03, and so on as you keep saving your work using Save As and the Increment button.

NOW YOU KNOW

In this chapter, you learned the basic operation of the 3D workspace and user interface, starting with a tour of the UI. Then you saw how to access the Graphite Modeling Tools set and how a scene can be controlled with the command panel. Next, you learned how the time slider and track bar work, and lastly, you saw how to best manage files for a clean workflow using projects.

As you continue with the following chapters, you will gain experience and confidence with the UI, and many of the features that seem daunting to you now will become second nature. Meanwhile, use this chapter as a reference to help you navigate the UI as you progress in your knowledge of the 3ds Max workflow.

CHAPTER 2

Your First 3ds Max Project

In production work, setting down a plan and having clear goals for your project is very important. Without a good idea of where you need to go, you'll end up floundering and losing out on the whole experience. In any project, the beginning of the workflow starts with modeling.

Modeling in 3D programs is like sculpting or carpentry; you create objects out of shapes and forms. Even a complex model is just an amalgam of simpler parts or shapes/volumes. The successful modeler can dissect a form down to its components and translate them into surfaces and meshes. Autodesk® 3ds Max® 2016 modeling tools are incredibly strong for polygonal modeling, so the focus of the modeling in this book is on polygonal modeling. In this chapter, you will learn modeling concepts and how to use 3ds Max modeling toolsets.

In this chapter, you will learn to

▶ **Set up a project workflow**

▶ **Model accurately using reference material**

▶ **Build a simple model**

▶ **Create details using splines**

▶ **Create 3D from 2D using lathing, extruding, and beveling**

Setting Up a Project Workflow

You will begin by modeling a clock body to develop your modeling muscles. This exercise introduces you to primitives and polygons. You will be modeling by editing the polygon component; it's called *editable poly* modeling. Why buy a clock when you can just make one using 3ds Max tools?

Exercise 2.1: Setting Up a Project

Download c02_First Project, c02_First Project.zip, from the book's web page at www.sybex.com/go/3dsmax2016essentials. Place the files on your hard drive. Open the 3ds Max 2016 program and set a 3ds Max project. Choose the c02_First Project folder from your hard drive, flash drive, or network drive and follow these steps:

1. Set your project folder to the c02_First Project you just down-loaded (select the Application button () and choose Manage ➤ Set Project Folder).

2. Navigate to the place on the hard drive where you saved the book projects.

3. Click c02_First Project, and then click OK.

Now when you want to open a scene file, just click the Application button and choose Open, and you will automatically be in the c02_First Project\ scenes folder.

The Secret to Accurate Modeling: Reference Material!

Using reference materials will help you efficiently create your 3D model and achieve a good likeness in your end result. The temptation to just wing it and start building the objects is strong, especially when time is short and you're raring to go. You should always suppress this temptation in deference to a well-thought-out approach to the task. Sketches, photographs, and drawings can all be used as resources for the modeling process. Not only are references useful for giving you a clear direction in which to head, but you can also use references directly in 3ds Max to help you model. Photos, especially those taken from different sides of the intended model, can be added to a scene as background images to help you shape your model.

In a Windows Explorer window, go to the c02_First Project folder on your hard drive; in the sceneassets\images subfolder, you will see some additional reference images of the clock. These sample reference images will give you an idea of what kind of images will be useful for a project like the clock. Of course, if this were your clock, you would have captured tons of pictures already, right?

You're so close to modeling something! You'll want to get some sort of reference for what you're modeling. Study the photo in Figure 2.1 for the model.

FIGURE 2.1 The clock to be modeled

Exercise 2.2: Setting Up the Modeling Reference

For the best in modeling references, bring in photos of your model and use the *crossing boxes* technique, which involves placing the reference images on crossing plane objects or thin boxes in the scene.

To begin the clock body, start with a new 3ds Max file:

1. Open a new 3ds Max file by clicking the Application button ( ) and choosing New. This clears the contents of the current scene without changing any of the system settings.

2. On the Create tab ( ), click the Geometry icon ( ), and in the Object Type drop-down menu, click the Plane button.

3. Make sure the Front viewport is selected by right-clicking it. This will align the plane to that viewport when it is created.

4. In the Command panel ➤ plane primitive parameters, expand the Keyboard Entry rollout.

5. Change the value in the X Position type-in box to 3.0, the Y box to 0.0, and the Z box to 0.0, as shown in Figure 2.2. This will place the plane three units away from the center of the scene along the X-axis.

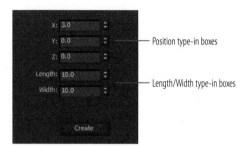

FIGURE 2.2   Position, Length, and Width type-in boxes in the Plane Keyboard Entry rollout

6. Change the Length value to **10** and the Width value to **10**, and then click the Create button (Create). This creates the image plane in the Front viewport, which you will use for the front-view image plane.

7. Change the name of the Plane001 object to **Front_View_Image**.

8. Now right-click the Left viewport to activate it. Back in the Standard Primitives drop-down menu, select the Plane button, if it is not already active from the previous steps. Expand the Keyboard Entry rollout.

9. Change the X axis to 3; leave Y and Z at 0.

10. Change the Length parameter in the Keyboard Entry rollout to 10 and the Width parameter to 10, if they are not already set that way. The parameters will stay set from the previous plane that was created.

11. Click the Create button in the Keyboard Entry rollout. Then go to the Modify panel and change the Length Segs from 4 to 1 and the Width Segs from 4 to 1.

12. Rename the Plane001 object to **Side View Image**.

13. Go to the Viewport Label menus at the top left of the Left viewport. Click the Shading viewport label menu and choose Shaded, as shown in Figure 2.3.

FIGURE 2.3 Shading viewport label menu

14. Do the same for the Front viewport.

15. Open a Windows Explorer window; navigate to the sceneassets\ images folder in the c02_First Project folder that you downloaded to your hard drive. In this folder, you will find the reference JPEG images for each of the image planes you just created in the scene.

16. Select the front-view reference image called Front.jpg, drag it into the Front viewport, and then drop it onto the Front View Image plane. This automatically places the image onto the plane, so the image is viewable in the viewport.

17. Repeat the previous step to place the Side.jpg image onto the Side View Image plane in the Left viewport. Figure 2.4 shows the image planes with the reference images applied.

Use the Zoom Extents All tool on all the viewports by pressing the shortcut Ctrl+Shift+Z, or you can use the viewport navigation tool, Zoom Extents All. You may have to click and hold the icon to access the flyout, and then choose the desired tool.

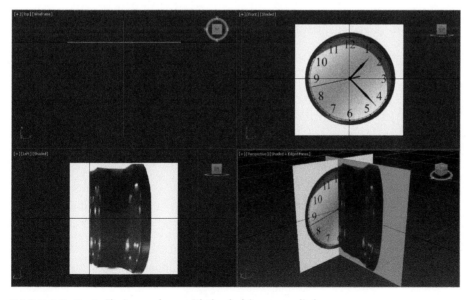

FIGURE 2.4 The image planes with the clock images applied

18. To finish, click the Application button ( ) and choose Save As. Save the file. To check the progress of your work against our example, you can open c02_ex2_ref_end.max.

Certification
Objective

Building a Simple Model

When modeling any object, it is always best to study the object and break it up into smaller, easier-to-model components. To begin modeling the clock body, you will start with a cylinder because the clock body has a cylindrical shape as its base.

Exercise 2.3: Starting with a Primitive

For this procedure, continue with the file from a previous exercise or use the c02_ex3_body_start.max file, which has the image planes set up. Follow these steps:

1. Select the Front viewport, which should still be set to Shaded display mode from the previous steps.

2. If it isn't already set, enable Edged Faces mode in the viewport by using the keyboard shortcut F4.

Edged Faces places the wireframe over the shaded object, making the object easier to see when you're modeling.

3. In the command panel, choose the Create tab, click the Geometry icon, and make sure Standard Primitives is selected.

4. In the Object Type rollout, click Cylinder, and select the Keyboard Entry rollout to expand the parameters.

5. Leave the X, Y, and Z values at 0, but enter **4.2** for Radius and **3.0** for Height, and then click the Create button.

7. Open the Modify panel ( ); this is where you go to edit the parameters of an object.

Alternatively, you could select Cylinder from the Create panel, and in the Front viewport, click and drag to create the cylinder, eyeballing the size from the Front and Left viewports.

8. Set Height Segments to **1** and Sides to **30**; then press Enter on your keyboard to set the new parameter. Leave all the remaining parameters at the default. Rename the Cylinder001 object **Clock_Body**.

9. To turn on See-Through mode, use the keyboard shortcut Alt+X. See-Through mode will ghost out the cylinder and allow you to see through it to the image planes.

Save the file. To check the progress of your work against our example, open
c02_ex3_body_end.max.

Exercise 2.4: Modeling in Sub-Object Mode

To start the process of modeling the clock, you need to access the cylinder's
components. At their core, all 3D objects are made up of three main components: vertices, edges, and polygons. These components are the basis of polygon
modeling. To access the components of any object, you need to convert it to
an *editable poly*, which means a polygon that allows access to the components.
There are many ways to do this; we will be using the Graphite Modeling Tools
set, also called the *ribbon*. For this procedure, use the c02_ex4_body_start.max
file or the file that you saved in the previous section. Follow these steps:

While you're modeling
the clock body, the
Front_View_Image
might get in the way.
It's best to hide it.
Select the image plane,
and then right-click
over the image. The
quad menu will appear;
choose Hide Selection.

1. Select the cylinder; go to the Ribbon ➤ Modeling tab ➤ Polygon
   Modeling and select the Convert to Poly button, as shown in
   Figure 2.5.

FIGURE 2.5 Converting the cylinder to an editable poly

All the editable-poly-
gon sub-object levels
have keyboard short-
cuts to quickly navigate
through the sub-object
levels. Vertex level is 1,
Edge is 2, Border is 3,
Polygon is 4, Element
is 5, and Ctrl+B returns
you to object level.

2. Using the keyboard shortcut F4, turn on Edged Faces in the Front,
   Left, and Perspective viewports if it isn't already enabled. This will
   allow you to see the wireframe while modeling.

3. Select the Polygon icon (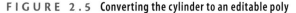) or press 4 on the keyboard to enter the
   Polygon sub-object mode.

4. In the Perspective viewport, orbit around the cylinder so you can see
   the back end.

To orbit, you can use
the keyboard shortcut
Alt+MMB (hold the
Alt key and press the
middle mouse button)
and then drag in the
viewport.

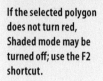

If the selected polygon does not turn red, Shaded mode may be turned off; use the F2 shortcut.

5. Select the back-end polygon. The polygon is shaded red to indicate it is selected, as shown in Figure 2.6. (The Front viewport image plane is hidden in the figure.)

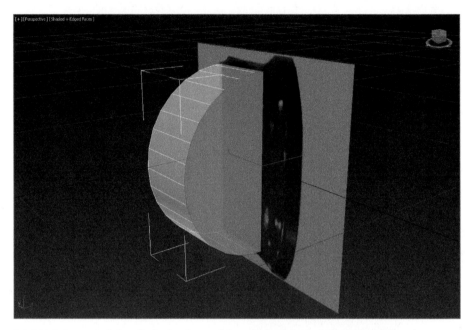

FIGURE 2.6 Select the back polygon of the cylinder; it is shaded red when selected.

6. In the Ribbon ➤ Modeling tab, go to the Polygons panel and select the arrow under the Outline button, and then select Outline Settings. This will open the Outline caddy, which is a dialog box where you input your outline parameters.

7. Change Outline Amount to 0.3 and click the OK button (✓). This will scale the selected polygon larger at one end. Look at the cylinder in the Left viewport. You will see that the end of the cylinder now fits the end of the clock on the image plane.

The Swift Loop tool places new edges that loop around the cylinder, which sub-divides the sides. The subdivisions will allow greater control of the details to be added.

8. In the Ribbon ➤ Modeling tab, go to the Edit panel and select the Swift Loop tool. You will add a new subdivision, or loop, on the cylinder. This will allow you to add more details to the cylinder. To add a loop, just move your cursor over the part of the cylinder, and you will see a preview loop. When the preview is where you want it, just click, and the new loop will be created.

9. View the cylinder in the Left viewport; place the loop at the positions shown in Figure 2.7. With the new loop (or edge loop) in place, you will edit the edge to change the profile of the cylinder to match the clock body.

FIGURE 2.7 Using the Swift Loop tool, place a loop as shown.

When you select Edge mode, the last loop you created will be selected.

◀

For a shortcut for the Loop tool, double-click an edge and the loop will be competed.

◀

10. In the Ribbon ➤ Modeling tab ➤ select Edge mode (keyboard shortcut 2). If the edge is not selected, continue with steps 11 and 12; if it is selected, skip to step 13.

11. Select one of the edges toward the top of the cylinder; only a single edge will be selected, not the entire loop.

12. On the Modify Selection tab of the Ribbon ➤ Modeling tab, select Loop. This will continue the selection around the cylinder.

13. Move your cursor to the main toolbar and select the Select and Uniform Scale tool (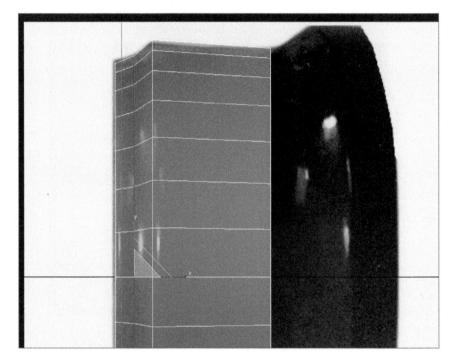). The keyboard shortcut is R.

14. The triangle in the center of the Scale gizmo will turn yellow when active. Scale the edges up until they match the detail in the Left viewport image plane.

15. In the Ribbon ➢ Modeling tab, go to the Edit panel and select the Swift Loop tool. Place a new loop between the front of the clock and the loop you just scaled up.

16. Select the Scale tool and scale the new edge loop down to match the image, as shown in Figure 2.8.

FIGURE 2.8 **Edges are scaled to match the image plane.**

17. Save the file by choosing Save from the Application menu. You will use this file in the next exercise. To check the progress of your work against our example, open c02_ex4_body_end.max.

ORBITING IN THE VIEWPORTS

Orbiting in the viewports is a skill, and the faster you learn the many ways you can do it, the more efficient you will be as a 3D artist. You can orbit using the Orbit tool ( ), which is one of the viewport navigation tools found at the lower right of the interface. Drag the mouse on or around a view rotation *trackball*, which is displayed as a yellow circle with handles placed at the quadrant points. An alternative way to orbit is to use the ViewCube. It is a great way to orbit within the viewports. Simply move your cursor to the ViewCube icon in the upper-right portion of the viewport and click+drag to rotate the current viewport. Another way to orbit is to use the keyboard/mouse shortcut Alt+MMB and drag in the viewport. As the user, you need to decide which method works best for you.

Exercise 2.5: Bringing on the Bevel

Now you will add detail to the back of the clock. On the Clock object, there is a small edge and a depression where the clock face and hands sit. To create this edge in the cylinder, you will use the Bevel tool. Beveling involves first extruding polygons and then scaling the extruded polygons with the Outline tool. The Bevel tool has three parameters:

Bevel Type   Controls how to extrude multiple polygons at once.

Height   Specifies how much extrusion to apply, based on units.

Outline Amount   Scales the outer border of the selected polygons, depending on whether the value is positive or negative.

For the Clock object, the Bevel tool creates many of the details of the body. It allows you to create a rough model that you can refine with further tools. For this procedure, use the c02_ex5_body_start.max file or the file that you saved in the previous section. Follow these steps:

1. If you are starting in a newly opened file, select the clock body first. Select the Polygon icon ( ), or use the keyboard shortcut 4 to enter the Polygon sub-object mode.

2. Select the back face of the cylinder.

3. On the Polygons panel in the ribbon, click the arrow next to the Bevel button. Then select Bevel Settings, as shown in Figure 2.9. This will

open the Bevel caddy, which is a dialog box for inputting your bevel parameters.

FIGURE 2.9 Bevel Settings will bring up the caddy for parameter input.

4. In the Bevel caddy, enter **0.75** in the Height text box, and then press Enter on your keyboard.

5. Enter **0.5** in the Outline text box and press Enter again.

6. Click the Apply and Continue button (). This applies the specified settings without closing the caddy.

7. Now change the Bevel caddy parameters. Enter **1.0** in the Height box, press Enter, enter **0.0** in the Outline box, press Enter again, and then click the OK button.

8. Select the polygon on the front face of the cylinder (this is the smaller end), and enter the Bevel setting again to bring up the caddy.

9. In the Bevel caddy, enter 0.0 in the Height text box, then enter -0.25 in the Outline text box, and then select the Apply and Continue button.

10. Now enter -0.5 in the Outline text box and press OK to complete the front face of the clock.

    Figure 2.10 shows the clock the way it looks with the changes made, the image planes hidden, and See-Through mode turned off. Save your file. To check the progress of your work, open c02_ex5_body_end.max.

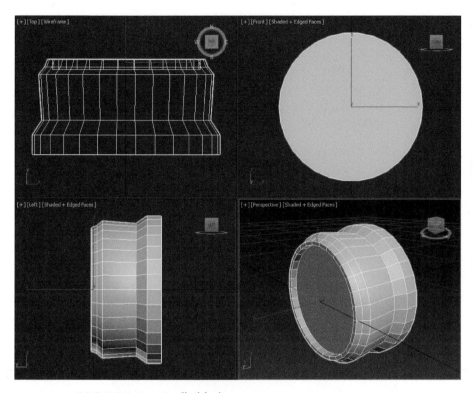

FIGURE 2.10   Clock body progress

ACCESSING MODELING TOOLS

Using the ribbon is a convenient way to access modeling tools, but it isn't the only way. In most software packages, when new tools are added, the older versions of those tools aren't removed. In previous versions of the software, all poly modeling tools were accessed through the Modify panel. Many of the same buttons and functionality can still be found in the Modify panel. You can also right-click an object to access the quad menu. The quad menu allows you to find and activate most commands without having to travel back and forth between the viewport and rollouts on the command panel or main toolbar. In this book, we will be using the Graphite Modeling Tools set (the ribbon) to access the modeling tools.

Exercise 2.6: Chamfering Time

Chamfering refers to the rounding of sharp edges or corners. For the clock, the new details on the sides are too sharp. You will be using the Chamfer tool in Edge mode. For this section, you will turn off See-Through mode and hide the image planes. Use the c02_ex6_body_start.max file or the file that you saved in the previous section, and follow these steps:

1. Select the clock body; then turn off See-Through mode, using the keyboard shortcut Alt+X. To hide the image planes, you will enter Isolate Selection mode. At the bottom of the interface, below the timeline, is an icon of a lightbulb ( ). The keyboard shortcut is Alt+Q.

2. Either click the icon or use the shortcut to hide all but what is selected.

3. In the ribbon, open the Polygon Modeling panel and select Edge mode (keyboard shortcut 2).

4. Select the edge shown in Figure 2.11.

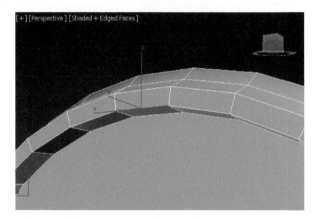

FIGURE 2.11   Select the edge shown in this image.

5. In the Ribbon ➢ Modeling tab ➢ Modify Selection, select Loop. This will select the entire edge loop (or use the shortcut by double-clicking the edge you want to loop).

6. In the main toolbar, click the Select and Move tool (). The keyboard shortcut is W.

7. Zoom out of the viewport, and then use the Y-axis of the Move tool gizmo and move the edges back toward the beveled surface, as shown in Figure 2.12.

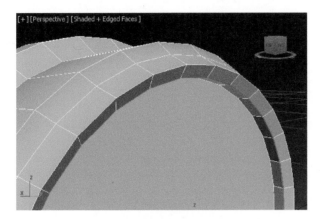

FIGURE 2.12 Move the edges back.

8. Use the keyboard shortcut Alt+X to turn on See-Through mode.

9. To exit Isolate Selection mode, select the lightbulb icon at the bottom of the interface. The image planes will reappear.

10. Looking in the Left viewport, select and loop the middle edge to select the entire edge loop, as shown in Figure 2.13 (the Ribbon ➢ Modeling tab ➢ Modeling ➢ Modify Selection ➢ Loop or double-click on the edge to loop).

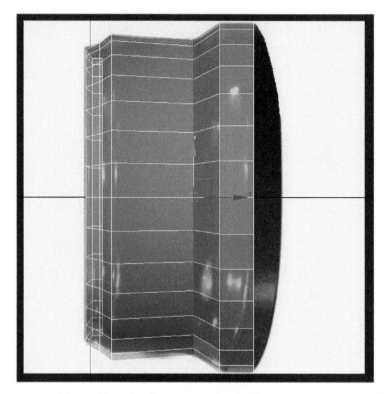

FIGURE 2.13 Select and loop the edge to prepare for chamfer.

11. Go to the Ribbon ➤ Modeling tab ➤ Edges, and click the arrow next to the Chamfer button; then select Chamfer Settings. This will open the Chamfer caddy.

12. To create the smooth curve from the sharp edges, input 0.25 for Edge Chamfer Amount (don't forget to press Enter on keyboard!) and 4 for Connect Edge Segments, and again press Enter.

13. Click OK (⊘). The results are shown in Figure 2.14.

14. On the front face of the clock, select an edge on the lip (where the clock face will be). Then hold the Ctrl key and select three more edges going toward the back of the clock, as shown in Figure 2.15 (which has See-Through mode turned off with shortcut Alt+X).

To achieve the correct smoothness for each curve, the chamfer should be repeated several times on different edges with different Chamfer parameters.

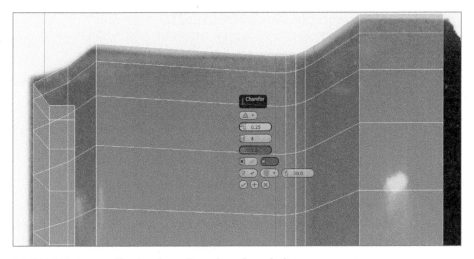

FIGURE 2.14   The chamfer performed on a looped edge

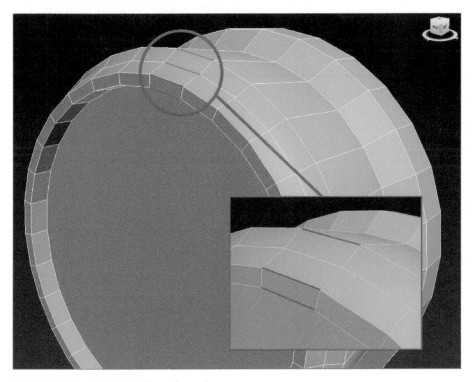

FIGURE 2.15   Select these three edges.

15. Loop the edges (the Ribbon ➤ Modeling tab ➤ Modify Selection ➤ Loop).

16. Go to the Ribbon ➤ Modeling tab ➤ Edges ➤ Chamfer, and click the arrow next to the Chamfer button; then select Chamfer Settings. This will open the Chamfer caddy.

17. To create the smooth curve from the sharp edges, enter **0.065** in the Edge Chamfer Amount text box and press Enter; then enter **3** in the Connect Edge Segments box and press Enter again.

18. Click OK (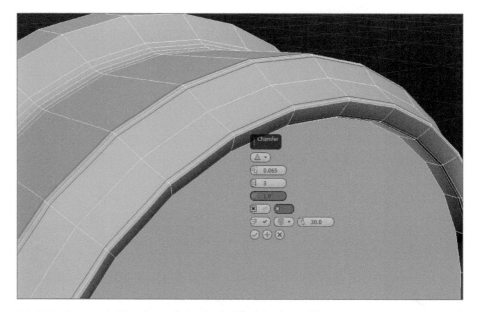). The results are shown in Figure 2.16. The back side of the clock needs some special attention; its detail is a bit more intricate. First, another swift loop needs to be added, and then both edges need to be chamfered. Make sure you are still in Edge mode. If you are not, select Edge or the use the keyboard shortcut 2.

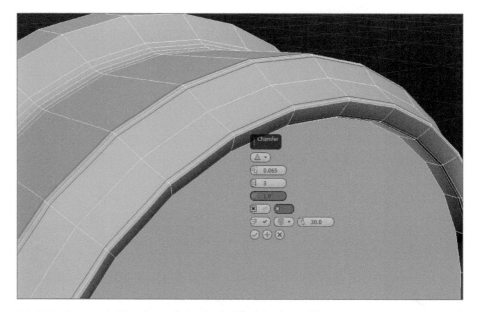

FIGURE 2.16   Chamfer result for the clock body's edge and lip

19. Select the edge shown in Figure 2.17. Then double-click to complete selection on the loop.

20. Select the Ribbon ➤ Modeling tab ➤ Edges panel. Click the arrow next to the Chamfer button, and then select Chamfer Settings; this will open the Chamfer caddy.

When the loop is in place, it will be selected because you are in Edge mode.

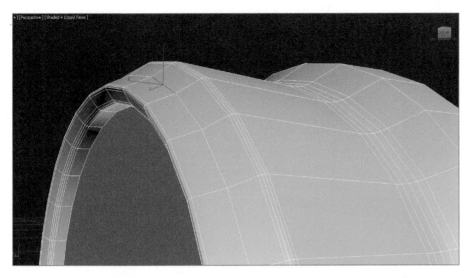

FIGURE 2.17 Select the edge.

21. Enter 0.1 in the Edge Chamfer Amount text box and 3 in the Connect Edge Segments box. Then click OK.

22. Select and loop the edge at the back of the clock, as shown in Figure 2.18 (left side) and then chamfer (Ribbon ➢ Modeling tab ➢ Edges panel ➢ Chamfer ➢ Chamfer Settings).

23. Enter 0.2 in the Edge Chamfer Amount text box and 4 in the Connect Edge Segments box. Then click OK.

FIGURE 2.18 The edge loop is selected (left image), and then the edge is chamfered (right image).

24. Save your file. To check your progress, open c02_ex6_body_end.max.

Certification
Objective

Creating Details Using Splines

Now that the clock body is complete, it's time to move on to some of the clock parts. The parts that will be covered in this section are the handle, the hands, and the bell. To create these objects, you will learn a modeling technique called *spline modeling*. In computer graphics, a *spline* is a group of vertices and connecting segments that form a line or curve. Splines are used to create more complex geometry than can be found in the primitives available in 3ds Max. The first clock part that you will create is the clock handle, shown in Figure 2.19.

F I G U R E   2 . 1 9   **The clock handle**

Exercise 2.7: Building the Handle

To build the clock handle, follow these steps:

1. Open c02_ex7_handle_start.max from the scenes folder of the Clock project on this book's companion web page. This file has a full image of the front of the clock loaded onto an image plane.

2. Start by accessing the Create panel (■), and choose the second icon from the row of icons, Shapes (■), and from there, choose Line. The following actions apply when you use the Line tool:

   ▶ A single click in a viewport creates a point with a linear segment.

   ▶ A click-and-drag maneuver creates a curved segment when you let go of the mouse.

▶ Holding the Shift key will constrain your movement to 90-degree angles; this can be very helpful in creating straight lines.

▶ A right-click exits the Line command.

Creating a line using this method can be difficult; it is easier to start with a simple shape and add more detail later. Figure 2.20 shows a simplified line that represents the clock handle.

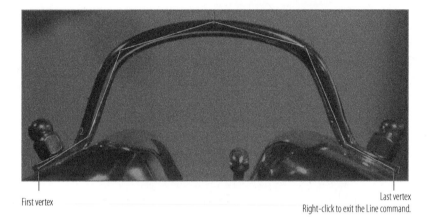

First vertex

Last vertex
Right-click to exit the Line command.

FIGURE 2.20 The intended path for the clock handle

3. In the Front viewport, click to set a vertex and let go (refer to the first vertex in Figure 2.20).

4. Continue to click and move, following the handle around until you reach the seventh vertex; then right-click to exit the Line command. Now that the rough line is finished, it needs to be smoothed out and refined.

5. With the line selected, in the Modify panel's modifier stack, click the plus sign (+) to expand the list of sub-objects.

6. Select Vertex, as shown in Figure 2.21.

FIGURE 2.21 From the three sub-objects of the Line command, select Vertex.

7. In the Front viewport, right-click the middle vertex.

8. In the upper-left quadrant of the quad menu, choose Bezier, as shown in Figure 2.22.

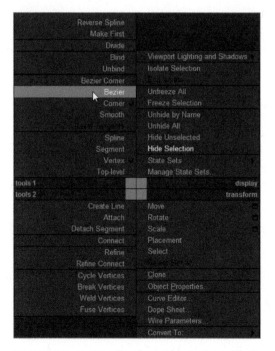

FIGURE 2.22 Use the quad menu to modify the vertex type.

VERTEX TYPES

When working on splines, you may want to change the vertex type:

Smooth   Has a smooth continuous curve without tangent handles to edit.

Corner   Has sharp corners without tangent handles to edit.

Bezier   Has adjustable tangent handles that are locked.

Bezier Corner   Has adjustable tangent handles that are unlocked or broken and can adjust the curve entering and exiting the vertex independently.

9. Choose the Select and Move tool (W), then grab one of the green boxes on either side of the vertex at the end of the tangent handle, and move it until the curve matches the handle in the image plane.

10. Use See-Through mode (Alt+X) to ghost out the handle model; this will allow you to see the clock on the image plane.

11. Adjust the tangent handles to smooth out the remaining vertices on the spline, except the first and last, as shown in Figure 2.23.

There are now tangent handles coming from the vertex; the tangent handles control the amount of curve in the line. Tangents are edited using the Move tool.

◀

◀

Moving the handle up or down moves the segment attached to the handle in the same direction. Moving the handle closer to the vertex creates a tighter curve, and moving it farther away creates a looser curve.

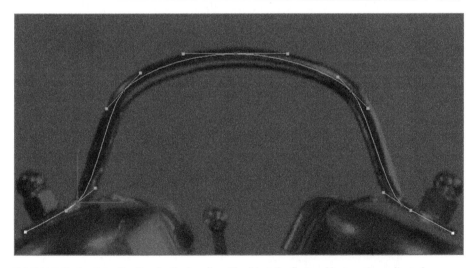

FIGURE 2 . 2 3   The line for the handle with all but the first and last vertices adjusted

12. In the Rendering rollout in the Modify panel, check the boxes Enable In Renderer and Enable In Viewport.

13. Change Thickness to 0.35 and leave the rest at the default values, as shown in Figure 2.24.

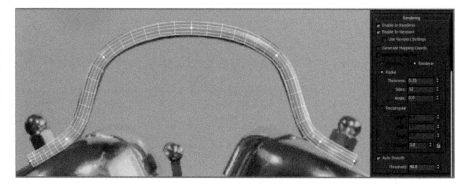

FIGURE 2.24   Rendering enabled on the clock handle line, set to Radial

14. In the Ribbon ➤ Modeling tab, expand the Polygon Modeling panel and choose Convert To Poly. This will keep the radial thickness and allow for component manipulations.

15. Click the Select Object tool ( ) (Q) and switch to Vertex mode. The handle has the correct shape, but the area where the handle is between the bell and the bolt needs to be scaled down.

16. To make this simpler, in the main toolbar, click and hold down the Rectangular Selection Region tool; this will bring up a flyout.

17. Choose the Fence Selection Region, as shown in Figure 2.25. In the main toolbar, to the right of the Scale tool, is the Reference Coordinate System dropdown menu.

FIGURE 2.25   On the Selection Region flyout, choose the Fence Selection Region.

18. Drag a custom selection from the end of the handle line past the seventh row of vertices, as shown in Figure 2.26. To close the selection, click the part of the selection where you started.

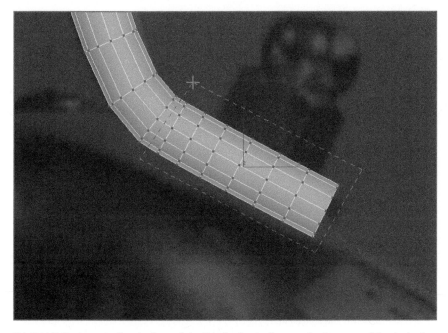

FIGURE 2.26 Use the Fence Selection Region to draw a selection around the desired vertices.

19. Select the Select and Uniform Scale tool (R).

20. Click the arrow and choose Local from the list.

21. Move your cursor over the Y-axis of the Scale gizmo. Scale the vertices down until they match the image.

22. Continue selecting and scaling vertices until they match the image. Use the Select and Move tool if necessary.

23. Exit Vertex mode and then repeat the same process on the left side of the handle, as shown in Figure 2.27. When finished, name the object **Handle**.

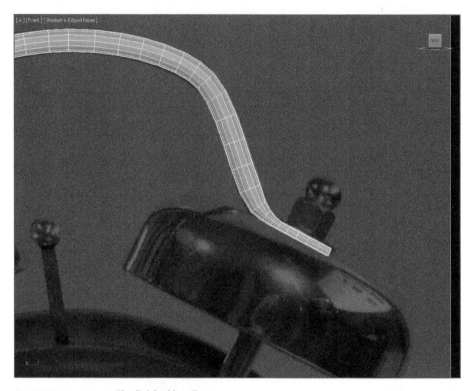

FIGURE 2.27   The finished handle

24. It's time to save the file, but this time choose Save As and name the file **Clock_Handle_End.max**. To check your progress, open c02_ex7_ handle_end.max.

UNDERSTANDING THE 3D COORDINATE SYSTEMS

A 3D environment is defined in terms of 3D Cartesian coordinates. In 3ds Max, the main coordinate space is used to describe the scene as a whole and is known as the coordinate system. To scale the vertices correctly, you need to change the coordinate system. By default, 3ds Max uses the View hybrid coordinate system. In the View coordinate system, all orthographic views use the Screen coordinate system, while perspective views use the World coordinate system. That is all fine and good, but it won't work for vertex selection. To allow proper gizmo orientation for the scale, change the coordinate system to Local, which defines the coordinates of the object or sub-object's local center.

Lathing, Extruding, and Beveling to Create 3D from 2D

Now that the body of the clock and the handle are done, it's time to make the bells. You will use splines and a few surface-creation tools that are new to your workflow. You are going to create a profile of the bell and then rotate the profile around its axis to form a surface. This technique is known as *lathe* (not to be mistaken for *latte*, which is a whole different deal and not covered in this book).

Exercise 2.8: Lathing to Make a Whole

Open c02_ex8_bell_start.max from the scenes folder of the Clock project on the companion web page. You are going to create a cross section of the bell. To build the bell, follow these steps:

1. Select Create ➤ Shapes ➤ Line. Figure 2.28 shows the cross section with the vertices numbered according to their creation order.

FIGURE 2.28 The bell's profile line with the vertices numbered according to their creation order

Before moving forward with the bell profile, go to the Line Parameters on the right of the interface. In the Rendering rollout, uncheck Enable In Viewport and Enable In Renderer. The parameters will retain the value of the previous use.

2. Starting at the bottom-right side of the bell image, click and let go of the mouse. This will create the first vertex as a corner (1).

3. Now move the mouse up where the bell curves and drag out a tangent to create a Bezier vertex (2).

4. Continue the drag until the line's curve follows the bell image.

5. Again, move the mouse to the left and to the middle of the bell, and click to create a corner vertex (3).

6. Right-click to end the Line tool. The profile should match Figure 2.28.

7. On the Modify panel, choose Lathe from the Modifier List, as shown in Figure 2.29.

FIGURE 2.29 Choose the Lathe modifier from the Modifier List.

> When the Lathe modifier is added, the profile gets revolved 360 degrees around the center of the line. The bell doesn't look so good. That is because the center of the lathe is in the wrong place.

8. To reposition the center of the lathe, open the Lathe Parameters roll-out, and in the Align area, click Min. This should change the lathe to look more like a bell, as shown in Figure 2.30.

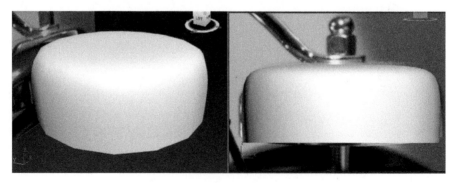

FIGURE 2.30 The bell with the lathe center in the correct place

9. To finish the bell, create a cylinder to represent its base post. Then create another cylinder to represent a bolt above the bell and a sphere for the ball at the top, as shown in Figure 2.31 and Figure 2.32. Switch to a four-viewport view; then use the shortcut Alt+W to create the object through the Top viewport.

FIGURE 2.31 The image of the bell showing the three pieces to be created

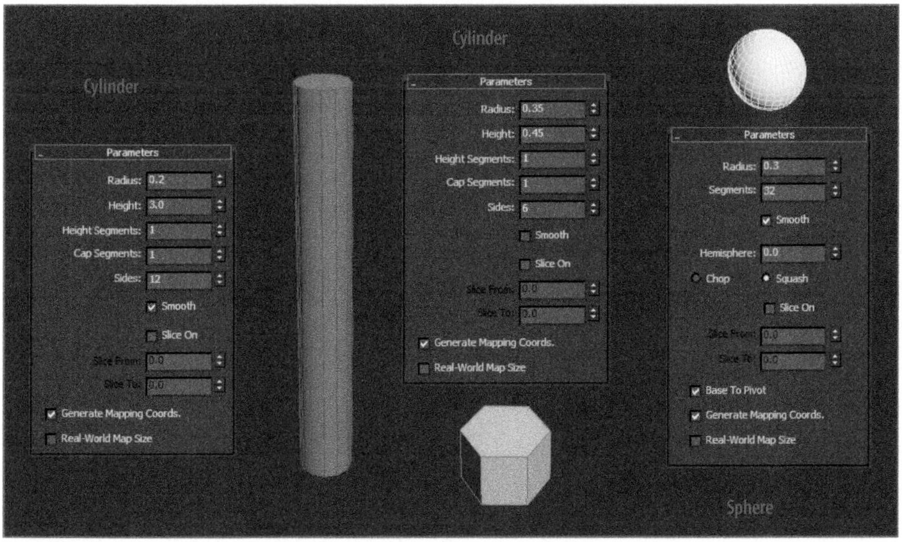

FIGURE 2.32 The parameters for the three objects to be created

10. Using the Move and Rotate tools, position the two cylinders and the sphere to resemble Figure 2.31.

11. Make sure to leave a gap where the handle will go.

12. Select each object and name it appropriately.

13. From the main toolbar, select Group ➤ Group, as shown in Figure 2.33, and then name the group **Bell**.

▶

This will allow you to orient the Bell group object to fit with the other Clock objects. We are moving on, but don't worry; we will get back to the bell later in the chapter.

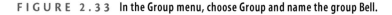

F I G U R E   2 . 3 3   In the Group menu, choose Group and name the group Bell.

14. Save the file as **c02_Bell_End.max** and use it for the next section. To check your progress, open c02_ex8_bell_end.max.

The next step in the process is to make the clock face by creating the hour hand, the minute hand, and the second hand. This could be done by creating an image of a clock face in a graphics program like Photoshop and then applying that image as a surface onto the 3D Clock object. For this exercise, you will create the clock face elements—the numbers and hands—as 3D objects, using another set of modifiers, Extrude and Bevel. The Extrude modifier adds depth to a shape—that's it. It's simple and incredibly useful. The Bevel modifier also adds depth to a shape, and it allows you to add a round bevel to the edges.

Exercise 2.9: Creating the Clock Numbers and Hands

Load c02_ex9_face_start.max from the scenes folder of the Clock project on the companion web page or continue working with the file you have been using. To create the clock numbers, follow these steps:

1. Start in the Create panel ➤ Shapes ➤ Text. Before you create the text shape, set up the text parameters.

2. Select the Typeface down arrow next to the font name in the Parameters rollout.

3. Choose Times New Roman. If you do not have that typeface, just choose whichever font you desire.

4. Change Size to **1.45**.

5. In the Text type-in box, type **12**. All of your parameters should match Figure 2.34.

FIGURE 2.34   Text shape parameters

6. Move the mouse into the viewport over the number 12 on the image of the clock face, and then click.

7. Open the Modify panel, and in the Modifier List, click Bevel.

8. In the Bevel Values rollout, change Level 1: Height to **0.01** and Outline to **0.01**. This will extrude the 12 shape and taper the mesh wider at the top.

9. Check the box next to Level 2 and change Height to **0.01**; leave Outline set to 0.0.

10. Check the box next to Level 3 and change Height to **0.01**; set Outline to **-0.01**.

11. Match all bevel levels to those in Figure 2.35.

FIGURE 2.35 Bevel Values rollout showing all of the shape parameters for the numeral 12

12. In the Parameters rollout in the Surface group, select Curved Sides.

13. Change Segments to **2**, and check the box next to Smooth Across Levels, as shown in Figure 2.36. This will give the 12 its rounded smooth sides.

FIGURE 2.36 Parameters rollout for the Bevel modifier

14. At the top of the Modify panel, change the name to **12**, click the color swatch next to the Name (text field) type-in box, and choose black. Select OK. Figure 2.37 shows the results of the Bevel modifier. Move the number into place over the number in the image plane.

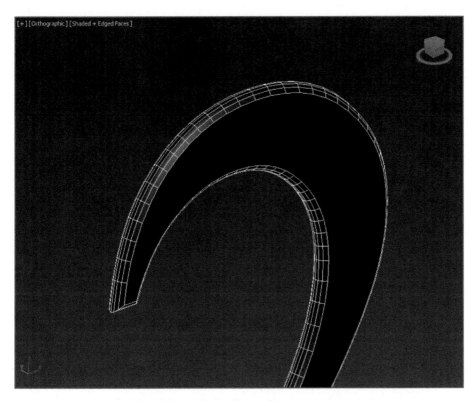

[+] [Orthographic] [Shaded + Edged Faces]

FIGURE 2.37 **Bevel modifier applied to the number**

15. To create the remaining numbers, select Create ➤ Shapes ➤ Text and place the cursor over the number 1.

16. Add the Bevel modifier; the same parameters you used for the number 12 will be repeated. This makes it easy to finish off the rest of the clock numbers. Rename the number and change the color to black.

17. Repeat steps 15 and 16 for each number on the clock face.

18. Select all the numbers by holding Ctrl and clicking each.

19. Choose Group from the Group menu, as you did with the Bell object.

20. Name the group **Numbers**.

◀

Because you set up the parameters for the number 12, the text shape will repeat the same parameters for the number 1.

Follow these steps to create the clock hands:

1. Zoom out and use the image with the clock hands. Select the Create panel ≻ Shapes ≻ Rectangle. Create a rectangle over the minute-hand image.

2. Back in the Create panel, uncheck the box next to Start New Shape. This will allow you to create a second piece that is connected to the rectangle.

3. Select Circle and create a circle over the circle base of the minute hand.

4. Open the Modify panel, and in the modifier stack, in the Selection rollout, select Vertex mode (■).

5. In the Geometry rollout, select Refine and click each side of the rect-angle in the middle, as shown in Figure 2.38.

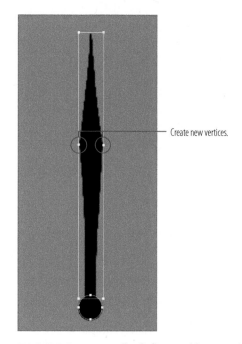

Create new vertices.

FIGURE 2.38 Use Refine to add two vertices to the right and left sides of the rectangle.

6. Select and move the vertices on the top of the rectangle so they come to a point. Move the vertices on the bottom so they match the image of the minute hand in the viewport.

7. Go to the Modify panel, and from the Modifier List, add the Extrude modifier.

In the modifier stack, you will see that the rectangle and circle objects have combined into an editable spline—a 2D object that provides controls for manipulating an object's three sub-object levels: vertex, segment, and spline.

8. Change the Amount to 0.025.

9. Change the Name to **Minute hand** and the color to black.

10. Repeat the same steps (1–9) on the hour hand. The second hand is even easier; just create a rectangle, make sure Start New Shape is still unchecked, and then create another rectangle.

11. Move and rotate each clock hand into the position you see on the clock image, shown in Figure 2.39. Of course, you don't have to position the hands exactly as they are shown in the image.

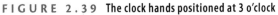
FIGURE 2.39 The clock hands positioned at 3 o'clock

12. When you have finished positioning the hands, save the file as **c02_Face_End.max**. To check the progress of your work, you can open c02_ex09_face_end.max.

Bringing It All Together

Most of the pieces are created for the clock. Now you just have to put it all together. Each piece was created in its own 3ds Max file. To bring them all together, you will use Merge. Merge allows you to bring different 3ds Max files into one scene. You can also just build all the parts of your model in a single 3ds Max file; we will look at that technique in later chapters.

Exercise 2.10: Using Merge

Follow these steps to merge all the parts:

1. To begin, click the Application button and choose Reset. This will clear any data from previous work and reset the 3ds Max settings. Read the dialogs carefully; they might prompt you to save your previous file and to reset.

2. Click the Application button, choose Import, and click Merge, as shown in Figure 2.40.

FIGURE 2.40 Merge is found in the Application menu under Import.

3. Navigate to the scenes folder of the Clock project, and select c02_ex6_body_end.max. Click Open.

4. From the list in the Merge dialog box, choose the Clock_Body object and click OK to close the dialog box. In the new scene, the clock body will appear, located in the same spot as it was in the other 3ds Max file.

5. Because of the way the clock body was built, it will need to be rotated 180 degrees so the front of the clock and the clock hands and numbers are in the correct places.

6. Repeat steps 3-5 to merge in the handle, face and bell.

7. Select the Bell group object, and from the Edit menu, choose Clone. This opens a Clone Options dialog box with clone options that are explained in more detail in the sidebar "The Clone Options Dialog Box."

8. Click OK to close the Clone Options dialog box, choose the Select and Move tool (W), and move the new Bell object to the other side of the clock body using the X-axis of the Move gizmo.

9. Rotate the Bell group so it is positioned correctly on the clock body.

10. The objects will need to be adjusted; use the transform tools and your best judgment. To check your progress, you can open c02_ex10_merge_end.max.

◄

We prefer to use the Shift+transform technique, which uses Shift+Move/Rotate/Scale to create a clone of the object. Hold the Shift key and move the Bell group object to the desired location. When you let go of the mouse, the Clone Options dialog box appears.

THE CLONE OPTIONS DIALOG BOX

Making a *copy* creates a completely separate clone from the original. An *instance* is a copy, but it is still connected to the original. If you edit the original or an instance, all of the instances change (including the original). A *reference* is dependent on the original, and the connection goes only one way. Change the original, and the reference will change; but change the reference, and only it will be affected, depending on its location in the modifier stack. The changes are for modifiers and not for transforms.

Still something missing? Well, this is where we leave you. With 90 percent done, it's time to use the many tools you learned about in this chapter to finish the clock. All you have left to create are the clock feet and the bell hammer. Take a look at Figure 2.41 for an example of the finished clock to this point.

F I G U R E   2 . 4 1   The clock so far

Now You Know

In this chapter, you learned how to set up reference images in your scene for more accurate modeling of an existing object, an alarm clock. You saw how to create a primitive and convert it into an editable poly object to add edge loops and edit its shape. You also created 2D shapes and splines to outline your model's initial shapes, and then you used the Graphite Modeling Tools set to flesh out the alarm clock, learning how to use the Lathe, Extrude, and Bevel tools along the way. Finally, in this chapter, you learned how to combine all the pieces of the alarm clock model into a single scene using the Copy and Merge functions.

CHAPTER 3

Modeling in 3ds Max: Architectural Model Part I

Building models in 3D is as simple as building them out of clay, wood, stone, or metal. Using Autodesk® 3ds Max® 2016 software to model something may not be as tactile as physically building it, but the same concept applies: You have to identify how the model is shaped and figure out how to break it down into manageable parts that you can piece together into the final form.

Instead of using traditional tools to hammer or chisel or weld a shape into form, you will use the vertices of the geometry to shape the computer-generated (CG) model. As you have seen, the 3ds Max polygon toolset is quite robust.

In this chapter, you will explore the many 3ds Max architectural modeling tools by building components such as walls, doors, and windows. These objects are called *Architecture Engineering and Construction (AEC)* tools, and they are parametric to give them an advantage over imported geometry from CAD programs. There are many ways you can build an interior space—simply put, just create a couple of boxes, and you're done—but to really create a refined and realistic interior, you will need to take time to add details.

In this chapter, you will learn to:

▶ **Set up the scene**

▶ **Build the room**

▶ **Add special details to the room**

Setting Up the Scene

When you open the 3ds Max program, a system of measurement is set up to measure geometry in your scene. By default, your file is set to Generic Units, where one unit is defined as 1.000 inch.

You can change the generic units to equal any system of measurement you prefer; you can use US Standard units (feet and inches) or metric units. You should choose your units of measure before you begin creating your scene, not during the modeling process.

Exercise 3.1: Setting Up Units

First, download the c03_ArchModel project folder from the book's web page at www.sybex.com/go/3dsmax2016essentials. Place the files on your hard drive. Open the 3ds Max 2016 program and set a 3ds Max project. Choose the c03_ArchModel folder from your hard drive, flash, or network drive and follow these steps. To start with a new file, go to the Application menu ➤ New.

1. Go to the Customize menu and choose Customization, and then choose Units Setup, as shown in Figure 3.1.

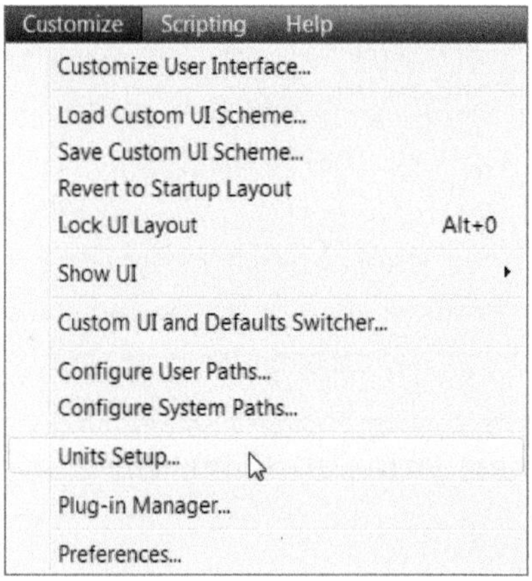

FIGURE 3.1 Accessing the Units Setup options

2. Change the units from the default Generic Units to US Standard.

3. From the US Standard drop-down menu, choose Feet w/Decimal Inches, as shown in Figure 3.2, and click OK.

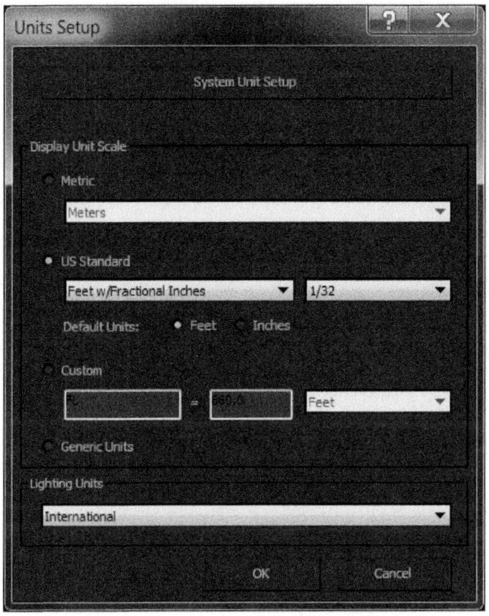

FIGURE 3.2   From the US Standard drop-down menu, choose Feet w/Decimal Inches.

4. Save the file and use it to continue to the next exercise.

Exercise 3.2: Importing a CAD Drawing

Using reference materials will help you efficiently create your 3D model and achieve a good likeness in your end result. The temptation to just wing it and start building the objects is strong, especially when time is short and you're raring to go. You should always suppress this temptation in deference to a well-thought-out approach to the task. Sketches, photographs, and drawings can all be used as resources for the modeling process. Not only are references useful for giving you a clear direction in which to head, but you can also use them directly in the 3ds Max software to help you model. Photos, especially those taken from different sides of the intended model, can be added to a scene as background images to help you shape your model.

For this chapter, you will be using an AutoCAD drawing as the reference and as a template to build the walls, doors, and windows. You will be supplied with a CAD drawing that will make it much easier to follow the reference.

Figure 3.3 shows the room that you will create in this chapter. There are a few changes from the original room. The opening that leads to the hallway is going to become a door. We will add decorative elements, such as a fancy baseboard.

F I G U R E 3 . 3 Images of the room to be created

In the future, if you don't have a drawing using detailed measurements of a room, you can create your own layout or blueprints. Proper measurements and scale are vital when you're creating a convincing interior space.

1. Select the Application button ( ) ➢ Manage ➢ Set Project Folder and choose the c03_ArchModel project folder, downloaded from the book's web page at www.sybex.com/go/3dsmax2016essentials. For this procedure, either continue with the file from the previous exercise or use the c03_ex2_import_start.max file.

2. Again, select the Application button and choose Import ➢ Import. Because you have already set your project to the ArchModel project, you will be taken straight to the import folder for that project.

3. Select the Room.dwg file. This is an AutoCAD drawing file that contains no 3D objects; it contains a drawing using 2D lines. Click Open. The AutoCAD DWG/DXF Import Options dialog box will open, as shown in Figure 3.4.

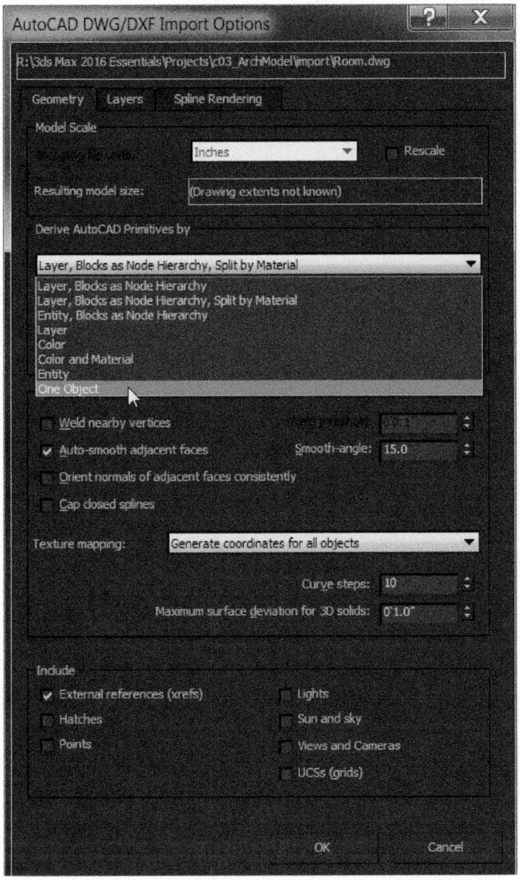

FIGURE 3.4   The AutoCAD DWG/DXF Import Options dialog box

4. In the Derive AutoCAD Primitives By drop-down menu, choose One Object and then click OK. The AutoCAD drawing shown in Figure 3.5 will appear.

The viewport should show a 2D collection of lines making up the layout of a room. The drawing has three basic parts: the walls, the window, and the doors. The figure has some colors associated with those three parts. These colors will not be reflected in the imported drawing.

This is a CAD drawing of the living room and dining room of a typical house, which was created for this book by Nastasia Jorgenson, an interior design student from the Art Institute of California – Los Angeles.

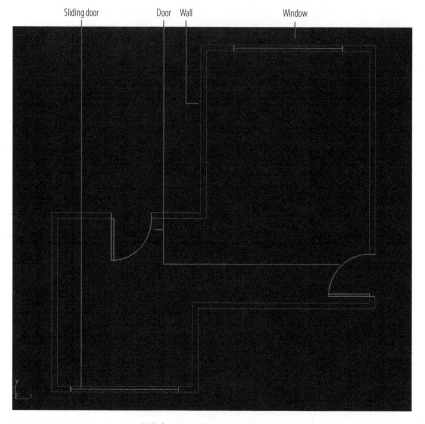

FIGURE 3.5 An AutoCAD drawing showing walls, doors, and a window

5. Select the imported AutoCAD drawing, and then choose the Move tool in the main toolbar. At the bottom of the interface are the Transform Type-In boxes and three type-in boxes labeled X, Y, and Z.

6. Change the X, Y, and Z values in the type-in boxes to X: 0'0.0", Y: 0'0.0", and Z: 0'0.0". This will center the AutoCAD drawing of the floor plan to the center of the environment.

7. In the command panel, go to the Create panel, and in the Name and Color rollout, rename the AutoCAD drawing **Floorplan**.

8. Save the file. To check your work, open c03_ex2_import_end.max.

Building the Room

The Wall objects you will create are a part of the AEC Extended objects and are designed for use in the architectural, engineering, and construction fields.

Exercise 3.3: Creating the Walls

To perform this exercise, you can use your completed file from Exercise 3.2, or you can load c03_ex3_walls_start.max from the scenes folder of the c03_ArchModel project on the book's companion web page at www.sybex.com /go/3dsmax2016essentials.

1. Select and maximize the Top viewport (Alt+W).

2. In the main toolbar, click and hold the Snaps Toggle button; and from the Tool flyout, choose the 2D Snaps button (![2D Snaps button]).

3. Right-click the Snaps Toggle button to bring up the Grid and Snap Settings dialog box.

4. Uncheck Grid Points and check Vertex, as shown in Figure 3.6.

FIGURE 3.6 The Grid and Snap Settings dialog box

5. Close the dialog box. This will make it possible to snap from the vertices in the AutoCAD drawing.

6. Go to the Create panel and from the Geometry drop-down menu, choose AEC Extended and click the Wall button.

7. You should see the wall parameters:

   a. Set Width to 0′5.0″ unless it is already set to this value. This will define the thickness of the wall.

   b. Set Height to 8′0.0″ unless it is already set to this value. This will define the height of the wall.

   c. Change Justification to Left, as shown in Figure 3.7.

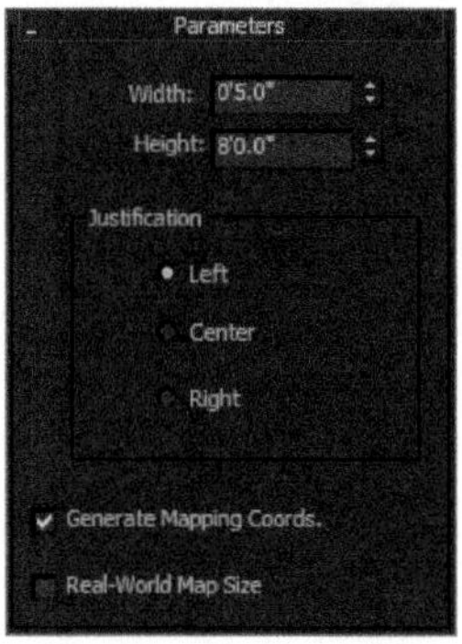

FIGURE 3.7 **The Parameters rollout for the Wall object**

8. In the Top viewport, click and release an outside corner of the room in the AutoCAD drawing; then move in a clockwise direction to a connected corner, and click to set the position of that corner. This will create a wall 0′5.0″ thick and 8′0.0″ tall between the two corners you clicked.

9. Continue around the room, clicking the outside wall corners, making sure you snap to the vertex of the lines at each corner. Disregard the doors and windows in the drawing and put your walls right over them.

10. When you have made it all the way around the room, click the corner where you started.

11. A Weld Point pop-up warning will ask, "Weld Point?" Click Yes and right-click to release the Wall tool.

> If you mistakenly click something, you can press Backspace, which will undo the last click.

12. Press Alt+W to return to the four-viewport layout, and look at the walls in the Perspective viewport. The finished wall is shown in Figure 3.8. The wall color is assigned randomly and may be a different color than the wall in the figure. Either press Esc on your keyboard or right-click the mouse button to exit Create mode.

FIGURE 3.8 The finished walls shown in the Perspective viewport

13. Select the walls, and go to the Modify panel. The Wall object parameters will be in the modifier stack.

14. In the modifier stack, click the black box with the plus sign.

15. To edit the walls—for example, to straighten out a wall or extend a wall to make a space bigger—select the Vertex component in the Modify panel.

16. From the Top viewport, at the corners of the room, you should see small plus signs. The plus signs are the Wall object vertices, allowing the walls to be edited. Select one of the vertices and move it to adjust the wall sections to which it is connected.

The wall has three components: Vertex, Segment, and Profile. You can edit a wall primitive in a way that's similar to how you edit splines.

17. Click the Segment component, and then click a wall in your scene.

18. You can use the Parameters section at the bottom of the rollout to change the settings for the wall, as shown in Figure 3.9. Exit sub-object mode before moving onto the next step.

FIGURE 3.9 **Wall parameters**

19. Save the scene file. To check your work, open c03_ex3_walls_end .max. Now that the walls are laid out, we'll move on to the doors.

Exercise 3.4: Creating the Doors

Door objects are one of the arrays of architectural objects available within the Create ➤ Geometry drop-down menu. The Door object is a type of primitive that allows you to control the look of the door—not just the size, but the frame and glass inserts as well. The door object parameters also let you determine whether the door is open or closed. The types of door are Pivot (which is the most common), BiFold, and Sliding. To perform this exercise, you can use your previous file from the ArchModel project, or you can load c03_ex4_doors_start.max from the scenes folder of the c03_ArchModel project on the book's companion web page at www.sybex.com/go/3dsmax2016essentials.

1. Select the Wall object if it isn't already selected.

2. Turn on See-Through mode using Alt+X. This will make the wall appear slightly transparent with a gray cast, but you will be able to see the AutoCAD drawing underneath.

3. Go to the Create ➤ Geometry and from the drop-down menu, choose Doors. Choose Pivot under Object Type.

4. Make sure the Top viewport is active, and zoom in on the door in the horizontal wall on the left in the AutoCAD drawing.

► You can also adjust the wall primitive by changing the Height or Width value of the wall in the Modify panel.

5. The 2D Snaps Toggle button should still be active. If it's not active, go to the main toolbar, click the 3D Snaps Toggle button, hold it down, and choose 2D Snaps from the flyout. Make sure the snap is set to Vertex.

6. Starting at the left of the door opening on the outside of the wall, click and drag to the right side of the opening in the AutoCAD drawing underneath until it snaps; then release the mouse button. Then move the cursor and click the opposite side of the wall to set the door thickness.

7. Move the cursor toward the top of the viewport to adjust the door height.

8. Click again to set any height. Don't try to get the exact height; you will set the correct height in the next step.

9. Go to the Modify panel and enter the correct value for the Height parameter for the door: 6′8.0″.

FIGURE 3.10   **The Door object parameters**

10. If the door doesn't create the cutout, click the Select and Link tool ( ), and click and drag from the door to the wall, as shown in Figure 3.11. This will make a doorway opening in the wall.

You won't be able to see the adjustment in the Top viewport, but you can look in another viewport as you drag to set the height.

When door primitives are created using snaps, you can insert a door in a Wall object, automatically linking the two and creating a cutout for the door. This doesn't always work; many factors can affect the outcome. If the door fails to create the cutout, you can move on to step 10. If it does create the cutout, skip step 10.

FIGURE 3.11 Use the Select and Link tool to create an opening in the wall for the door. This is necessary only if autolinking doesn't work.

11. In the Top viewport, zoom into the sliding door in the AutoCAD drawing.

12. In the Create panel, choose Sliding under Object Type.

13. Start by clicking and dragging from the right outside of the door to the left outside of the door, making sure to snap to the vertices where the door lines meet the wall lines. This will establish the width of the sliding door. Release the mouse button.

14. Move your cursor to the inside of the door and click when your cursor snaps to the vertex.

15. Click and drag the cursor to set any height, and click to finish.

16. Don't worry if you can't get the height correct; just type 6′8.0″ in the Height type-in field, as you did for the previous door.

17. Switch to the Perspective viewport and check to see if the sliding door looks correct.

18. The automatic linking should create a cutout for the door. If it does not, use the Select and Link tool and click and drag from the door to the wall to create the opening in the wall. The finished sliding door is shown in Figure 3.12.

19. Add the remaining door by repeating steps 3 to 10.

20. This is a good time to save your file. To check your work, open c03_ ex4_doors_end.max. You will create the window in the room in the next exercise.

> The best way to test whether the door was created correctly is to open it. Select the door, go to the Modify panel, and adjust the Open parameter. When Door and Window objects are created, the most common problem is that the Depth and Width get swapped.

> Because of the Snaps Toggle tool, the width and depth of the door will already be correct.

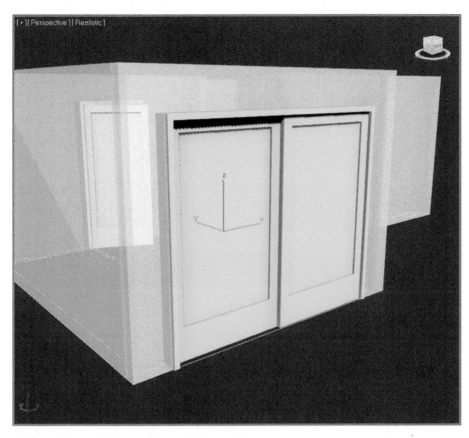

FIGURE 3.12   The sliding door in the wall

Exercise 3.5: Creating the Window

AEC Window objects work in a way that is similar to the way the Wall and Door objects work. There are six window types: Awning, Fixed, Projected, Casement, Pivoted, and Sliding. You will be using the Fixed window for this section. You can continue with your file from the previous exercise, or you can load c03_ex5_windows_start.max from the scenes folder of the ArchModel project on the companion web page to continue.

1. Go to the Create panel, and from the drop-down menu, choose Windows. Choose Fixed under Object Type.

2. 2D Snaps should still be active from the previous exercise, but if they are not active, refer to step 5 in the previous exercise.

3. Create the Window object as you did the Door objects: Use the snaps to click/drag from left to right, following the drawing; then move the mouse to create the depth and then the height.

4. In the Modify panel, go to the Fixed Window parameters and change Height to 6′0.0″. If the automatic linking failed to work, move on to the next step. If it does create the cutout, repeat the same process as in step 18 of the previous exercise.

6. Press S on your keyboard to turn off Snaps.

7. Switch to a Perspective viewport so you can see the newly created window; then select and move the window up so it is centered on the wall, as shown in Figure 3.13.

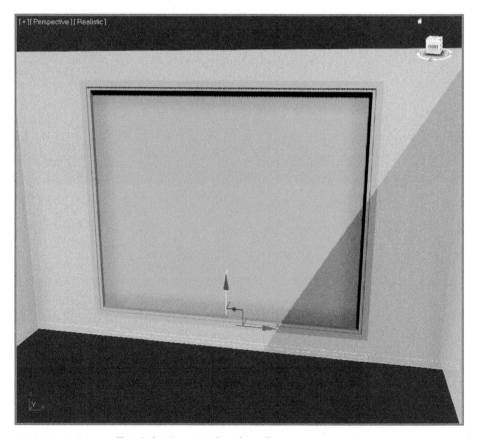

FIGURE 3.13   **The window is centered on the wall.**

8. Save the file for use in the next section. To check the finished file, open c03_ex5_window_end.max. The model to this point is shown in Figure 3.14.

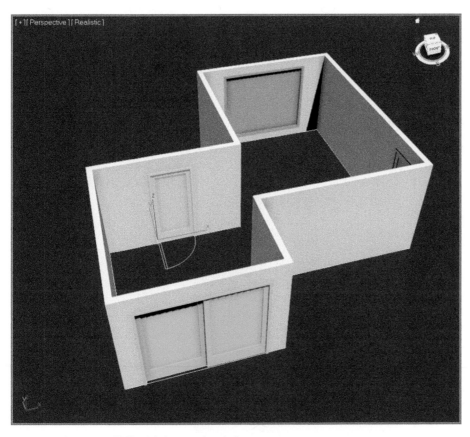

FIGURE 3.14 Walls with doors and a window

Exercise 3.6: Adding a Floor and a Ceiling

You can continue with your file from the previous exercise, or you can load c03_ex6_floors_start.max from the scenes folder of the ArchModel project on the companion web page. What's a room without a floor and ceiling? Not any room we want to walk into. To create the floor and ceiling for your room, you will use the Line tool to create a shape:

1. Go to the Create panel and click the Shapes button ( ); then click the Line tool.

2. Press S on your keyboard to turn on the Snaps Toggle tool, if it isn't already turned on. Right-click the Snaps Toggle tool to bring up the Grip and Snap Setting dialog box, and verify that Grid Points is unchecked and Vertex is checked.

> The Snaps Toggle tool should still be set to the 2D Snaps Toggle option. Keep it that way. This will ensure that the line stays at the ground plane of the scene.
>
> ◀

3. In the Top viewport, click the outside corner of the room, then click the other corners around the room in a clockwise direction, and then click again on the corner where you started.

4. The Spline dialog box will appear. Select Yes to "Close Spline?" This closes the line to form a closed shape.

5. Choose the Select Object tool (Q), and select the line you just created, if it is not already selected. It may be difficult to select the line because it is under the wall; to help identify it, you can use the Scene Explorer panel, which you will find running along the right of the interface, as shown in Figure 3.15.

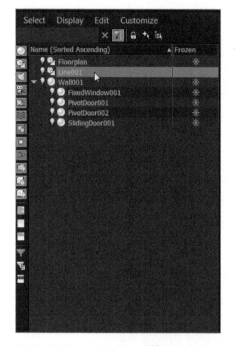

FIGURE 3.15   For a difficult selection, you can use the Scene Explorer panel.

6. Go to the Modify panel (), and from the Modifier List drop-down menu, choose Extrude, as shown in Figure 3.16.

FIGURE 3.16 From the Modifier List drop-down menu, choose Extrude.

7. Now look at the Extrude parameters, and change the Amount value to 0'0.1". You need to give just a little thickness to the floor.

8. Switch to the Front viewport, and move the new Floor object down so the top of the floor lines up with the bottom of the walls. Turn off the Snaps Toggle tool (S).

9. Rename the new object **Floor**. To create the ceiling, you are going to make a clone of the floor.

10. In the Perspective viewport, select the floor. While holding the Shift key, move the Floor object in the Z-axis up to the top of the Wall object.

11. Let go of the mouse button; a Clone Options dialog box will appear, as shown in Figure 3.17.

◀

Holding Shift while moving, rotating, or scaling will activate the clone feature.

FIGURE 3.17 The Clone Options dialog box

12. Choose Copy from the Object section, rename the object **Ceiling**, and click OK.

13. Center your cursor over the Ceiling object and right-click.

14. From the quad menu, choose Hide Selection.

15. When you are ready to have the ceiling back in your scene, you can right-click anywhere in your scene and select Unhide All.

16. Save the file. To check your progress, open c03_ex6_floors_end.max.

For now, you don't need to have the Ceiling object visible; you will be using it in a later chapter. You can hide the Ceiling object for now.

You can also choose Unhide by Name to bring up a dialog box from which you can choose a specific item from a list to unhide.

Adding Special Details to the Room

In architectural terminology, a *baseboard* is a board covering the area where the wall meets the floor. Baseboards are used to cover the gap between the wall and the floor, as well as add a sense of style to a room. An example of the baseboard we will be creating is shown in Figure 3.18.

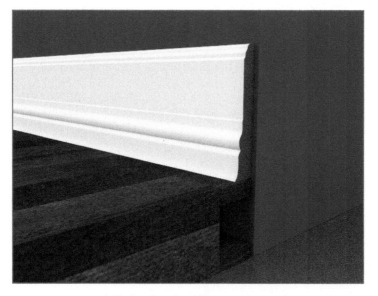

FIGURE 3.18   The baseboard molding

The room (shown in Figure 3.3) has a baseboard but not a very nice one, so creating a more stylish one would be a great way to add some pizzazz to the room. Feel free to modify the baseboard to meet your skill level with the Line tool.

Exercise 3.7: Creating Baseboard Moldings

You can use your file from the previous exercise, or you can load c03_ex7_details_start.max from the scenes folder of the ArchModel project on the book's companion web page. To begin creating the baseboard, you will use a spline that has already been created: the floor:

1. In the Perspective viewport, select the Floor object.

2. Right-click to select and then maximize the Top viewport (Alt+W), and in the Edit menu, choose Clone.

3. In the Clone Options dialog box, choose Copy and change the name to **Baseboard Path**. Click OK.

4. In the Modify panel, remove the Extrude modifier by right-clicking over the modifier in the modifier stack and choosing Delete when the context menu appears, as shown in Figure 3.19.

FIGURE 3.19 Deleting the Extrude modifier in the modifier stack

5. In the modifier stack, click the plus sign in the black box to expand the Line entry to display the sub-objects of the line. Select Spline mode.

6. Select the sub-object spline of the baseboard line, as shown in Figure 3.20. It will turn red when selected. You may not be able to see it because the walls are on top of the shape.

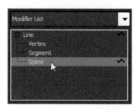

FIGURE 3.20 In the modifier stack, select Spline mode.

7. In the Geometry rollout, scroll down to Outline.

8. In the Outline type-in box, which is to the right of the Outline button, change the amount to -0′6.0″, as shown in Figure 3.21.

> ▶
>
> Outline clones the spline and offsets as specified by the amount in the Outline type-in box.

FIGURE 3.21 To offset the spline, change the Outline amount to -0′6.0″.

9. Select the original spline and delete it. Click Line to exit Spline mode. Because you are using the newly created spline for the baseboards, you don't need the original line. Now you'll create the shape of the molding, shown in Figure 3.22.

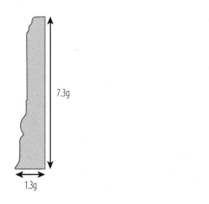

FIGURE 3.22 Profile of the baseboard molding

10. Switch from the Top viewport to the Front viewport.

11. Click the Application button, and choose Import ≻ Merge. From the scenes folder of the `ArchModel` project folder, choose the `Baseboard Image Plane.max` file. Click Open.

12. Select the Baseboard Image Plane object. Click OK in the Merge dialog box.

13. Change the viewport shading to Realistic. Enter Isolate Selection mode ( ) (F3) by selecting the icon at the bottom of the interface below the timeline. This will hide everything in the scene except the image plane.

14. Choose Create ≻ Shapes ≻ Line, and at the top-right corner of the baseboard, click and release the left mouse button. This will create a corner point.

15. Move the mouse to the left, where the baseboard begins to curve down, and click and drag to create a *Bezier vertex*. This is a vertex type that has handles, which allow for greater control over the curve in the line segments.

16. Drag until the curve is following the curve of the baseboard.

17. Continue around the baseboard cross section until you are back at the first vertex you created. Click the first vertex and select Yes from the dialog box to close the spline.

18. Rename the shape **Baseboard Shape**. If the line needs to be edited, go to the Modify panel and select Vertex mode. In Vertex mode, you can edit the path to match the image on the image plane.

19. Exit Isolate Selection mode and then select the baseboard path. Go to the Modify panel, and from the Modifier List, choose Sweep.

20. In the Section Type rollout, choose Use Custom Section, and in the Custom Section Types area, select Pick.

21. In the Front viewport, switch to Wireframe mode (F3), and pick the baseboard shape to create the baseboard, as shown in Figure 3.23. Some parameters need to be adjusted.

You can use the keyboard shortcut (F) to switch from the Top viewport to the Front viewport.

If you don't want to create your own baseboard shape, you can merge with one that is already created. Refer to step 11 and select the `Baseboard Path.max` file.

The Sweep modifier extrudes a cross section along a path, creating a 3D version of the baseboard cross section.

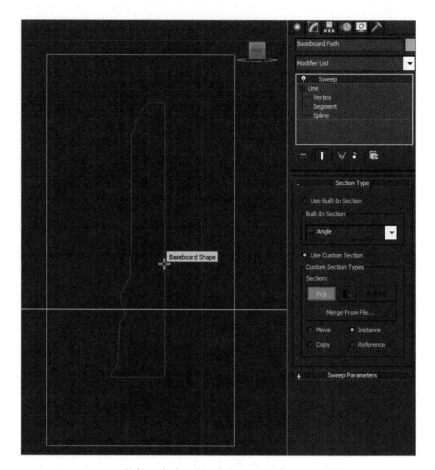

FIGURE 3.23 Picking the baseboard shape in the Sweep modifier

22. In the Sweep Parameters rollout, check the box next to Mirror On XZ Plane. This will flip the baseboard shape so it is facing toward the room. The baseboard molding should run along the floor except at the door openings. Right now, the molding is going straight through the door opening, as shown in Figure 3.24. This isn't difficult to fix; just edit the path.

FIGURE 3.24 The baseboard molding is going through the door opening.

23. Switch to a Perspective viewport (Alt+W) to exit Maximize Viewport and then Ctrl+click the Floorplan and Baseboard Path objects to select them both.

24. Enter Isolate Selection mode (Alt+Q), and then select just the baseboard.

25. Zoom in on the door on the right of the Top viewport.

26. Go to the Modify panel, and in the modifier stack, choose Vertex mode.

27. Go to the Geometry rollout and click the Refine button.

28. Move to the baseboard spline and click directly on the spline on both sides of the door to add new vertices. Right-click to exit Refine.

29. Switch to Segment mode; select the segment between the two new vertices and delete it, as shown in Figure 3.25.

The Refine button allows you to add vertices without affecting the spline curve.

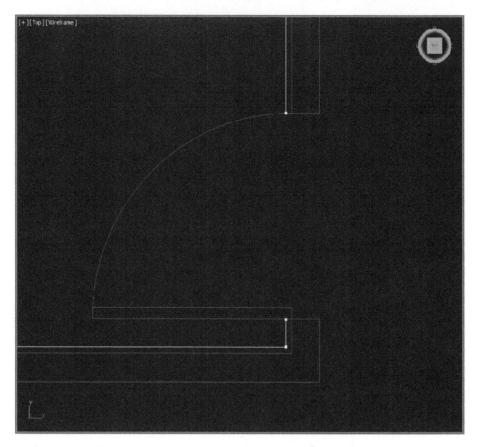

FIGURE 3.25 Use Refine to add the new vertices on either side of the door; then delete the segment.

30. Repeat the same process for the remaining pivot door and sliding door.

31. When you finish, select the Line entry to exit sub-object mode, and then select Sweep to exit. Exit Isolate Selection mode. The finished results of the Sweep modifier are shown in Figure 3.26.

32. Save the file. You can check your work by opening c03_ex7_details_end.max.

FIGURE 3.26 The baseboard with proper gaps at the doors

The next thing that needs to be done is to create *crown molding,* which is a decorative type of trim that is typically used to line the area where the ceiling meets the wall. You can do this using the same techniques learned in the previous exercise. You can import either the image plane or the finished crown molding path from the scenes folder of the ArchModel project. Figure 3.27 shows the finished room with crown molding.

FIGURE 3.27 The finished room with crown molding

Now You Know

In this chapter, you learned how to use some of the 3ds Max architectural modeling tools. Starting with an imported AutoCAD drawing and using it to build up the walls, you then added doors and windows. The walls, doors, and windows are part of the AEC (Architectural, Engineering, and Construction) primitives and make modeling architectural spaces very simple. You then used the 2D spline tools to create the floors and moldings. By adding the Sweep modifier to the spline, you transformed the baseboard moldings into beautiful details that are special additions to the room.

CHAPTER 4

Modeling in 3ds Max: Architectural Model Part II

In this chapter, you will continue working within the interior design subject from the previous chapter by modeling and adding some furniture—specifically, a couch and chair.

In this chapter, you will learn to

▶ **Model a couch**

▶ **Model a lounge chair**

Modeling the Couch

When you start a modeling project, make sure you have plenty of measurements, like those in the photo of the couch that will be modeled in this chapter, shown in Figure 4.1. Always remember to reference images for your modeling project. Modeling this couch is a straightforward process. If you break it down into separate components, it is just 16 different-sized boxes. The boxes are soft and cushy; they have various details, but nonetheless, they are still just boxes, with the exception of the chaise lounge at the end of the couch, which is the only piece that isn't a typical box shape.

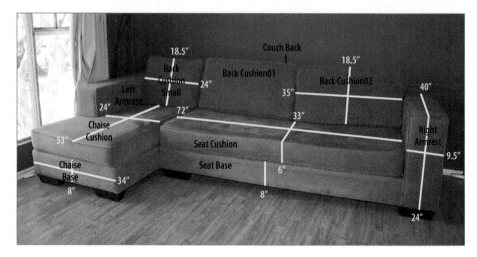

FIGURE 4.1 Couch with measurements

Exercise 4.1: Blocking Out the Couch Model

Certification
Objective

Blocking out the model means creating a simpler version of the model starting with whatever primitives fit the bill—in this case, boxes. Using the measurements shown in Figure 4.1, you will create a series of boxes and then orient them to mimic the couch. The first piece you'll create is the bottom (the part between the seat cushions and the feet). It is 8-inches high by 72-inches wide by 33-inches deep. In the previous chapter, you used standard units of measurement (feet and inches), but for this chapter, you will use the default generic units. If your units are still set to feet and inches, refer to Exercise 3.1, "Setting Up Units," in the previous chapter (Chapter 3, "Modeling in 3ds Max: Architectural Model Part I") to review how to change the setting to Generic Units.

1. Start by setting a new project. Select Application menu ➢ Manage ➢ Set Project Folder, and navigate to c04_ArchModel folder from your hard drive. Then start a new file and select the Perspective viewport. Then go to the command panel, and choose from the Create panel, then from the Standard Primitives drop-down menu, select Geometry, and click Box.

2. In the Keyboard Entry rollout, enter 33 for Length, **72** for Width, and 8 for Height, but don't change the XYZ type-in boxes.

3. Select the Create button. Creating the box in the Perspective view-port will orient the box correctly.

4. Rename the box **Seat Base.**

5. Create the cushion above this box: Select the box with the Move tool, and then hold the Shift key and move the box up in the Z-axis to create a new box so that it is on top of the old box. This is a quick method you can use to clone an object. The Clone Options dialog box will appear, as shown in Figure 4.2.

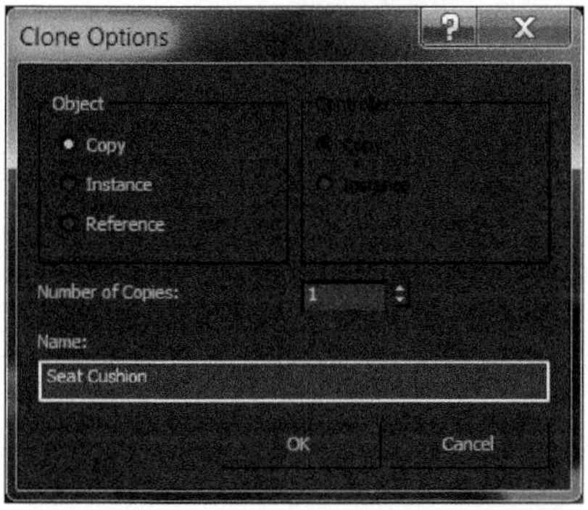

FIGURE 4.2 The Clone Options dialog box

6. In the Clone Options dialog, select Copy. Change the name from Box to **Seat Cushion** and click OK.

7. Go to the Modify panel and change the Height of the new cushion box to **6.0.**

8. As in step 2, create another box, but change the parameters to 40 for Length, **9.5** for Width, and 24 for Height. Rename the box **Right Armrest.**

9. Move the box so it sits on the right side of the two stacked boxes.

10. Create a clone for the left side of the couch using the same Shift+Move technique you used in steps 5 and 6. Move the box to the left side of the couch. Rename the new box **Left Armrest.**

11. Now for the back piece: the part that the back cushions rest against. You don't see it in the picture in Figure 4.1, but it is there. Create a

box with Length set to **6**, Width set to **96**, and Height set to **27**. Move it behind the seat-cushion boxes to form the backrest, as shown in Figure 4.3 (left).

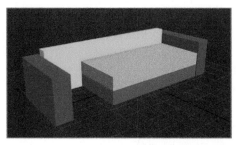

FIGURE 4.3 The first few pieces to start the couch (left); the blocked-out couch (right)

12. Create another box with the following measurements: Length = **8**, Width = **36**, and Height = **18.5**. Click the Create button to create a box for the back pillows.

13. Move the box so that it is sitting on top of the seat cushions and against the right armrest.

14. Make a clone of this box and move it to the left, so it is next to the other pillow.

15. Make one more clone, and move it to the left so it sits on top of the chaise seat cushions. This box is too wide. With the box selected, go to the Modify panel and change Width to **24.0**.

Save the file. To check your work, you can open c04_ex1_block_end.max from the scenes folder of the c04_ArchModel project files from the companion web page at www.sybex.com/go/3dsmax2016essentials.

Exercise 4.2: Using NURMS to Add Softness

Non-Uniform Rational Mesh Smooth (NURMS) is a subdivision surface technique that allows you to take a low-poly model and smooth the surface into a high-poly model. This isn't a lighting trick; you are actually changing the geometry of the model. When you apply NURMS to your model, you will see a control cage in the shape of the low-poly model; this is the mesh you actually model.

Subdivision increases the poly count of your model; every level of subdivision increases the number of polygons by a factor of four. At a subdivision level (or iteration) of 1, one polygon in the control cage will become four polygons in the subdivided model. At an iteration level of 2, that one polygon becomes 16 polygons, and so on. When you're working on a model with NURMS, it is best to work with a lower iteration level and then render with a higher level of iterations.

Polygons are flat between the vertices, but when NURMS is turned on, a flat polygon starts to curve and smooth out as it subdivides. When you use NURMS smoothing, the more distance there is between the edges on a mesh, the smoother the result will be. When you want sharp corners, just place the edges close together. When turning on NURMS, those close edges will retain their sharpness better. If you want a smoother, more rounded surface, then place the edges farther apart.

The best way to model with smooth surfaces is to use quad polygons in a grid formation; two edges will cross each vertex—and because each edge flows from vertex to vertex uninterrupted, the edges will continue and the 3D form will be smoothed predictably. If you have a vertex with no more than four edges coming out of it, the splines will end and the mesh may not smooth the way you expect.

All of the couch cushions will receive the same treatment, so let's go over the next technique using one of the armrests of the couch and the chaise lounge section. After you're finished with that, you can practice the techniques on the remaining couch boxes yourself. Continue with the file from the previous exercise or open the `c04_ex2_NURMS_start.max` file from the `scenes` folder of the `c04_ArchModel` project folder. When this file opens, an Isolate Selection warning will appear. The file has only the Right Armrest showing; the remaining objects are hidden. Continue by following these steps:

1. Select the Right Armrest object. Click the Isolate Selection Toggle button (⬛). This turns off the view of the other objects in the scene to allow you to focus on this one piece.

2. In the Ribbon ➤ Modeling tab, select Polygon Modeling ➤ Convert to Poly.

3. In the Edit panel, click Use NURMS (⬛). You will see a box that looks as if the air was let out of it, as shown in Figure 4.4.

◄

Be cautious: Poly counts rise very quickly, and an iteration count that's needlessly high can slow you down.

◄

If you want to fully understand how edges flow and end across a 3D surface as a result of subdivision leads, spend some time studying topology, which is key to creating good 3D models that subdivide well when animated.

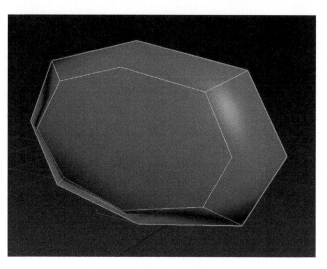

F I G U R E   4 . 4 **Armrest object with NURMS applied**

4. Back in the modeling ribbon, in the Edit panel, select the Use NURMS button again to turn it off.

5. In the Edit tab, click the Swift Loop tool ( ) and hover your cursor over the box to reveal a loop of edges on the box.

6. Place one of the loops by clicking where you want the edges to be added on the box, and then place the other three loops, as shown in Figure 4.5. Right-click with your mouse to release the Swift Loop tool.

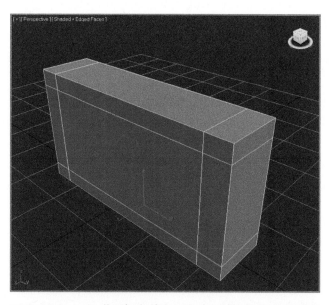

F I G U R E   4 . 5 **Use the Swift Loop tool to add edge loops to the box.**

7. Turn on Use NURMS again to see the difference after using the Swift Loop tool. Then turn Use NURMS off again to prepare for the next section.

8. Save the file. To check your work, open c04_ex2_NURMS_end.max from the scenes folder of the c04_ArchModel project.

If you refer to the picture in Figure 4.1, you can see that the couch arm is even more squared off than the current mesh. In the next section, you will learn how to add more detail.

If you refer to the picture of the couch from Figure 4.1, you'll see that the arm is much more structured and closer to the shape of a box.

Exercise 4.3: Building Detail on the Couch Model

The next step in the process of creating the couch is to add the *piping*, which is the round decorative trim along the seams of the pillows, as shown in Figure 4.6. Continue with the file from the previous exercise or open the c04_ex3_detail_start.max file from the scenes folder of the c04_ArchModel project.

Certification Objective

F I G U R E   4 . 6   Decorative piping runs along the seams of the couch.

1. Start by selecting the Armrest object. In the Edit tab, turn off Use NURMS, if it isn't already off. Then in the Modeling tab, enter Edge mode. Ctrl+click to select the edges on the box that are identified in Figure 4.7.

Select these edges on both sides of the box.

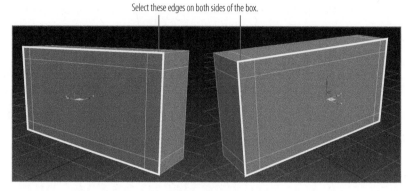

FIGURE 4.7   Select the highlighted edges.

2. Go to the Edges panel, and open the Chamfer Settings caddy. Change the Edge Chamfer Amount to 0.15, press Enter on your keyboard, and then click the OK button.

3. Switch to Polygon mode and select the new polygons that were created with the chamfer.

4. In the Modeling tab, go to the Polygons panel and open the Extrude caddy.

5. Change the extrusion type to Local Normal, as shown in Figure 4.8.

FIGURE 4.8   Set the extrusion type to Local Normal.

6. Set the Height to -0.2, press Enter, and then click the Apply and Continue button (⊕). This will keep the caddy open and allow you to perform another extrusion.

7. Change the Height to 0.3, press Enter, and then click the OK button (✓) in the caddy.

8. Go to the Edit panel and select Use NURMS. The Use NURMS tab appears in the modeling ribbon (sometimes a floating window will appear instead).

9. Turn up the Iterations to 2. The finished product looks pretty good, as shown in Figure 4.9. Now it is time to perform the same piping detail on the seat and back cushions of the couch.

The couch looks pretty good; but if you look closely, you can see that it is still very choppy around the corners. The NURMS iterations need to be turned up.

FIGURE 4.9 The finished couch armrest

10. Exit Isolate Selection mode and exit Polygon mode by selecting the Polygon button in the Polygon Modeling tab.

11. The seat cushion, three back cushions, and the left armrest need to have piping just like the right armrests, so repeat steps 1 through 10 for the cushions.

12. The seat base and couch back don't have any piping, so smooth those using NURMS and the Swift Loop tool to add more edges where needed.

13. Select vertices and polygons and move them around to give the surfaces a more random and organic or "lived-in" appearance.

14. Save the file. To check your work, open c04_ex3_detail_end.max from the scenes folder of the c04_ArchModel project.

Now is your chance to practice adding detail to the remaining pieces on the couch. We finished everything but the chaise lounge part of the couch using NURMS with an Iterations level of 2. In the Name and Color rollout, we changed the color so the finished pieces would be a consistent color. This is not required to continue with the exercise.

Certification Objective

Exercise 4.4: Creating the Chaise Lounge

The chaise lounge isn't that much different from the rest of the couch. It just has a wing section that comes out from the side, as shown in Figure 4.11. Continue with the file from the previous exercise or open the c04_ex4_chaise_start.max file from the scenes folder of the c04_ArchModel project. Begin by creating the rough chaise cushion:

1. Start by choosing Create ➢ Geometry ➢ Standard Primitives and create a box. Set the Parameters to Length = **53.0**, Width = **24.0**, and Height = **8.0**. It should be positioned between the left armrest and the seat cushion. Rename the box **Chaise Base**.

2. Convert the box to a polygon (Ribbon ➢ Modeling tab ➢ Polygon Modeling ➢ Convert to Polygon).

3. Add a new edge, as shown in Figure 4.10. Use the Swift Loop tool and then right-click to release it.

4. Enter Polygon mode, and select the polygon on the outside edge of the box.

5. In the Ribbon ➢ Modeling tab ➢ Polygons panel ➢ Extrude ➢ Extrude Settings, enter **10.0** as the Height and click OK. Figure 4.11 shows the extruded wing of the chaise. Exit Polygon mode.

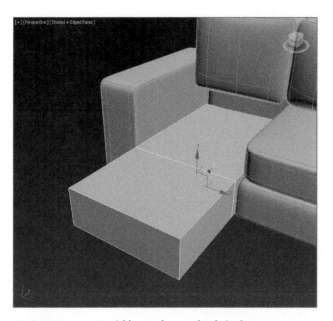

F I G U R E 4 . 1 0 Add a new loop to the chaise box.

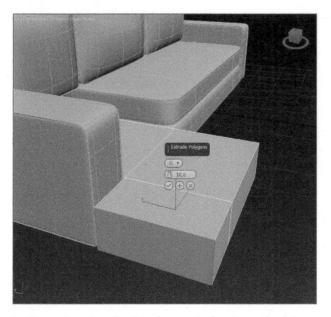

F I G U R E 4 . 1 1 Use Extrude to create the wing on the chaise.

6. Clone the base using the Shift+Move technique, and move the clone upward until it is sitting on top of the base. Release the mouse button. In the Clone dialog, choose Copy and rename the clone **Chaise Cushion.**

7. The new cushion is too tall; in the main toolbar, select the Scale tool. Scale down the cushion in the Z-axis to 75 percent.

8. Now that you have completed the chaise lounge section of the couch, you just have to add the finishing touches. Enter Isolate Selection mode.

9. Add new edges using the Swift Loop tool, matching Figure 4.12.

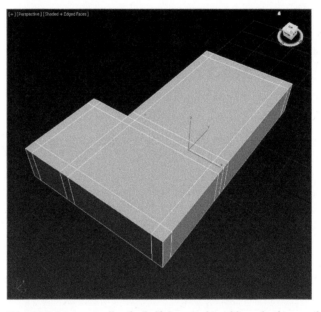

FIGURE 4.12 Use the Swift Loop tool to add an edge loop on the chaise cushion box.

10. Enter Edge mode, and select the outside edges of the chaise cushion on the top and bottom. Use the Ctrl+click selection method to make multiple selections at once.

11. Go to the Edges panel and open the Chamfer Settings caddy. Change the Edge Chamfer Amount to **0.15**, press Enter, and then click OK.

12. Switch to Polygon mode and select the polygons that were created with the chamfer.

13. In the Ribbon ➤ Modeling tab, go to the Polygons panel and open the Extrude caddy.

14. Change the Extrusion type to Local Normal.

15. Set the Height to **-0.2**, press Enter, and then click the Apply and Continue button. This will keep the caddy open and allow you to perform another extrusion.

16. Change the Height to **0.3**, press Enter, and then click OK in the caddy.

17. Go to the Edit panel and select Use NURMS. The Use NURMS tab appears in the modeling ribbon (sometimes a floating window will appear instead). Change the Iterations in Use NURMS to 2. Exit Isolate Selection mode.

Repeat the same steps for the chaise base, except the base has no piping. Save your file. To check your work, open c04_ex4_chaise_end.max from the scenes folder of the c04_ArchModel project.

Exercise 4.5: Modeling the Couch Feet

The final pieces you need to create for the couch are the feet. The feet are all the same, so you just need to create one foot, copy it, and put the copies in place under the couch. Look at the feet in Figure 4.13 and note that they are a box shape that is thinner on the bottom. Continue with the project from the previous exercise or open the c04_ex5_feet_start.max file from the scenes folder of the c04_ArchModel project.

Certification
Objective

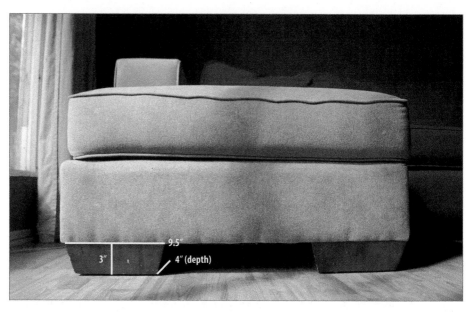

FIGURE 4.13   The couch feet with measurements

A *modifier* changes the geometric structure of a model, and a Taper modifier will move the vertices near the top or bottom closer together or farther apart. Using a Taper modifier is an easy way to make simple changes to your model.

▶

▶

When the Taper modifier is applied, nothing will happen to your model until you change the Taper parameters.

1. Go to the command panel's Create panel, select Geometry and click Box.

2. In the Perspective viewport, create a box that will be the first foot.

3. Go to the command panel's Modify panel, and enter 4.0 for the Length, 9.5 for Width, and 3.0 for Height.

4. In the Modify panel, click the Modifier List to expand it and choose Taper.

5. Change the Amount to 0.15, as shown in Figure 4.14. Press Enter on your keyboard to set the amount.

FIGURE 4.14   The Taper parameters

6. Now move the couch foot into place under one of the corners of the couch. Use the clone operation (hold down the Shift key while you move the foot) to make duplicates of the foot, and place them around the bottom of the couch at the remaining corners.

7. Take the time to select each couch foot box and rename it; use a simple naming convention such as CouchFoot01, 02, 03, and so on.

8. Save the file. To check your work, open c04_ex5_feet_end.max from the scenes folder of the c04_ArchModel project.

Now that the couch is finished, as shown in Figure 4.15, it should resemble the original couch but perhaps without the lived-in look and feel the real couch has. You can create some of that look by moving vertices and polygons so that it does not appear quite so perfect.

FIGURE 4.15 The final couch

Modeling the Lounge Chair

To model the chair, you'll be taking a different approach. You'll use a spline technique that the software is particularly good at. If you are used to Maya CV curves, the Bezier will seem a bit awkward, but if you are used to Photoshop's Pen tool, then the 3ds Max Line tool's way of making lines should be pretty easy.

It isn't just the way you create the lines that makes using them so nice; it's also the tools you use to turn those lines into 3D object.

Figure 4.16 shows the chair that will be modeled in this section. Click the Application button and choose Reset from the list that appears. This will set your interface and file back to a startup state.

FIGURE 4.16   The chair for the spline-modeling exercise

Exercise 4.6: Creating Image Planes

This exercise begins with creating planes and applying reference images to them. Open c04_ex6_image_start.max. The image with measurements is shown in Figure 4.17.

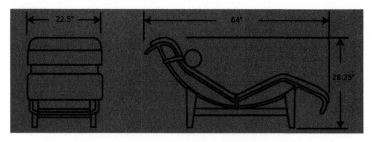

FIGURE 4.17   The lounge chair with measurements

1. In the new scene, go to the Left viewport and create a plane.

2. In the Parameters rollout of the command panel, set the Length to 28.25 and Width to 64.

3. Rename this box **Lounger_Side**.

4. With the plane still selected, go to the Modify tab, and in the Parameters rollout, set Length Segs and Width Segs to 1.

5. Select the Move tool (W) in the main toolbar. In the Transform Type-In areas at the bottom of the user interface, input 0.0 for X, 0.0 for Y, and 0.0 for Z to place the image at the center of the scene, known as the origin point.

6. Repeat steps 1 through 4 with the active Front viewport. The plane parameters are 28.25 for Length and 22.5 for Width.

7. Move the plane to these coordinates using the Transform Type-In area: X = -11.0, Y = 32, Z = 0.

8. Rename the plane **Lounger_Front**.

9. Save the file. To check your work, open the c04_ex6_image_end.max file from the scenes folder of the c04_ArchModel project.

> The units are in generic units (inches), which is the 3ds Max default.

Exercise 4.7: Adding the Images

While adding the material to the image planes, it's critical to ensure that the features of the chair that appear in both reference images (the front and the side) are at the same height. For instance, the top of the chair should be at the same height in both the front and side views to make the modeling process easier. Continue with the file from the previous exercise or open the c04_ex7_image_start.max file from the scenes folder of the c04_ArchModel project folder.

1. Make sure the Front and Left viewports are set to Shaded.

2. Open Windows Explorer and navigate to the c04_ArchModel \sceneassets\images folder on your hard drive from the c04_ArchModel project you downloaded from the book's web page.

3. Drag Lounger_Side.tif from the Explorer window to the image plane in the Left viewport.

4. Drag Lounger_Front.tif onto the image plane in the Front viewport.

5. Save the file. To check your work, open the c04_ex7_image_end.max file from the scenes folder of the c04_ArchModel project folder.

The image planes should have the two images mapped on them, as shown in Figure 4.18.

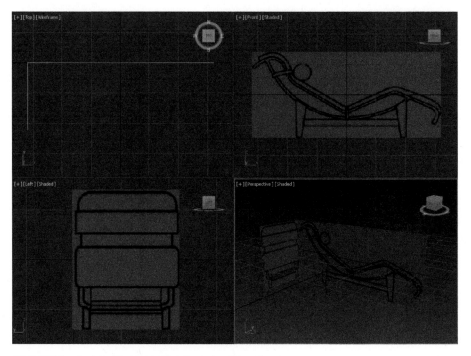

FIGURE 4.18   Mapped image planes in viewports

Exercise 4.8: Building the Splines for the Chair Frame

Now it's time to create the splines for the lounge chair. Continue with your own couch file or load c04_ex8_spline_start.max from the scenes folder of the c04_ArchModel project from the book's web page. The colors added to the images that we used on the planes are to help you build the splines for the lounge chair. To begin, you will build a spline using the green line as a reference.

1. Select the Left viewport and then maximize the viewport (Alt+W).

2. Go to the command panel and enter Create ➣ Shapes (📷), and then select the Line tool. You will use the Line tool to create a spline that follows the side view of the chair. Refer to Figure 4.19; it shows where the vertices should go (corresponding to the numbers in parentheses in the following steps).

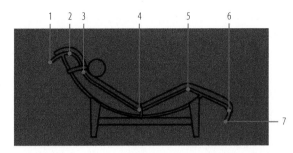

FIGURE 4.19 Create vertex points by following the numbers.

3. Starting at the left of the yellow line in Figure 4.19, click and release the mouse button to create a corner vertex (1).

4. Move your mouse up and to the right; click and release for a corner vertex (2).

5. Move to the right; click and release for a corner vertex (3).

6. Continue right; click and release for a corner vertex (4).

7. Continue right; click and release for a corner vertex (5).

8. Continue right; click and release for a corner vertex (6).

9. Click and release to create another corner vertex (7), and then right-click to release the Line tool.

10. In the Modify panel ➤ Modifier Stack, select the plus sign (+) next to Line and enter Vertex mode.

11. Select vertex 2 shown in Figure 4.19. In the Geometry rollout, click the Fillet button and drag the vertex until the curve matches the curve in Figure 4.20, an approximate amount of 0.8.

> Fillet will split the vertex into two separate vertices and curve the segment in between them.

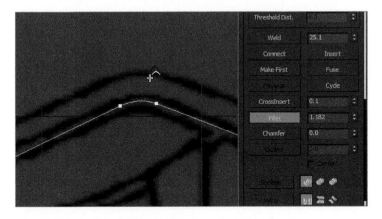

FIGURE 4.20 Fillet the vertex to create a smooth curve.

12. Repeat the process on vertices 3, 4, 5, and 6. The completed spline is shown in Figure 4.21. Use whatever Fillet value is appropriate for the part of the lounge chair you are working on.

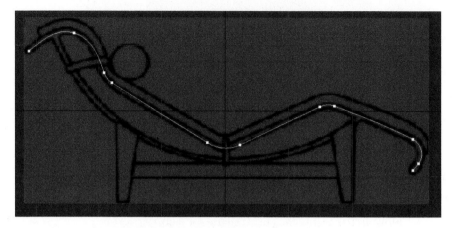

FIGURE 4.21 The competed spline for the side of the lounge

13. When you've finished, exit Vertex mode.

14. Switch to the Move tool (W) and select the spline.

15. In the Left viewport, Shift+Move and align the spline to the frame of the chair on the left side, as shown in Figure 4.22.

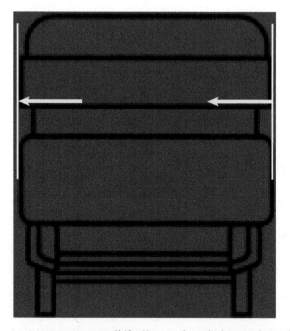

FIGURE 4.22 Shift+Move to clone the lounge chair spline.

16. When the Clone Options dialog box pops up, select Copy and then click OK. Now these two splines need to be attached to form a single spline. This will allow you to create the bridge piece that runs along the two ends of the frame. Let's get the image planes out of the way.

17. Select both image planes and right-click to bring up the quad menu. Choose Hide Selection from the display menu.

18. With either spline selected, go to the Geometry rollout, click the Attach button, and then click the other spline, as shown in Figure 4.23.

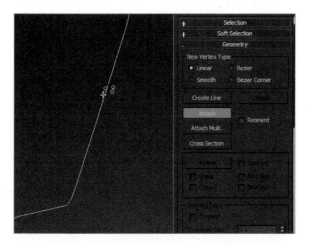

FIGURE 4.23 Attach both sides of the chair frame.

19. Enter Vertex mode. In the Geometry rollout, click the Connect button (below the Weld button).

20. Rotate the Perspective viewport so you can see both splines.

21. Click and drag from the vertex on the bottom end of the spline to the vertex on the other side, as shown in Figure 4.24. Do the same for the top end of the spline frame.

FIGURE 4.24 Use Connect to create a segment between the two separate splines.

22. Right-click to exit from Connect.

23. Select the four vertices at the ends of the frame, and in the Geometry rollout, click the Fillet button and move to one of the selected vertices. Drag the vertex until the curve looks appropriate, an amount of about 1.8.

24. With the spline selected, go to the Rendering rollout and check the boxes for Enable In Viewport and Enable In Renderer.

25. Select Radial and change Thickness to 0.8.

26. Click the Render Production button (■) in the main toolbar to see the results of the spline rendering, shown in Figure 4.25.

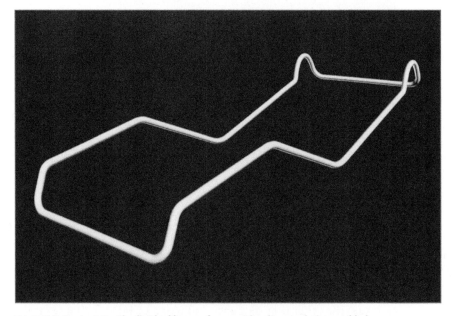

FIGURE 4.25   The finished lounge frame with spline rendering enabled

SPLINE RENDERING

When you're modeling using splines, you can use a very cool function to create a shape along a path. The splines you just created are the paths. In the parameters of the editable spline, there is a rollout called Rendering. The controls let you turn on and off the "renderability" of the spline and specify its thickness. Once you enable the function, the mesh can be seen in the viewport and will show as a solid 3D object when rendered. The default 3D mesh that is enabled is a radial mesh, which would make a pipe of sorts, but there is also a rectangular mesh, and both shapes have parameters that can be edited.

You can create the remaining parts of the frame, the arc shape, using the same technique. Continue with your chair file or load c04_ex8_spline_end.max from the scenes folder of the c04_ArchModel project from the book's web page. This file has the completed seat/back frame, as shown in Figure 4.26.

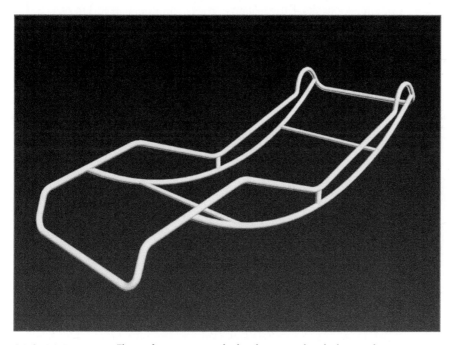

FIGURE 4.26   The arc frames are attached and connected at the base and top.

Exercise 4.9: Building the Chair Cushion

For the lounge chair cushion, you can't use the same spline technique you used on the frame. To create it, you have to return to the technique you used for the couch: Create a simple box representation and then use NURMS to soften it. Continue with your own lounge chair file or load c04_ex9_cushion_start.max from the scenes folder of the c04_ArchModel project from the book's web page.

1. Go to the command panel, select Create ➤ Geometry, and click Box.

2. In the Perspective viewport, create a box, and then in the Modify panel, change the Length to **64.0**, Width to **22.0**, and Height to **3.0**. Change Length Segs to **4**. Move the box so it is over the lounge chair frame.

3. In the Ribbon ➤ Modeling tab, select Polygon Modeling ➤ Convert To Poly.

4. In the Ribbon ➤ Modeling tab, choose Edit ➤ Swift Loop, and add two edge loops close to the ends. These will help you rough out the shape of the lounge cushion. Right-click in a selected viewport to exit Swift Loop.

5. Switch to Vertex mode (1); select and move the vertices where the segments are and line them up to follow the chair frame, as shown in Figure 4.27.

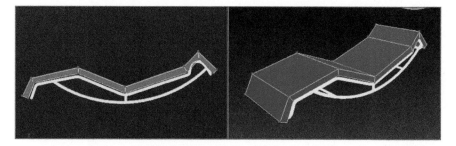

FIGURE 4.27 Arrange the vertices on the box so they follow the lounge chair frame.

6. Use Swift Loop again, and place edge loops along the left and right edges as well as along the sides. This will keep the outer edges from curving in too much to keep the box shape.

7. Go to the Ribbon ➢ Modeling tab ➢ Edit ➢ Use NURMS. In the Use NURMS panel, set Iterations to 2, as shown in Figure 4.28. NURMS has smoothed out the model and molded the lounge-chair cushion to the frame, but it still needs some work.

8. Use Swift Loop to add edge loops, as shown in Figure 4.28. This will help to mold the cushion to the frame.

◄

Turn off Use NURMS if you need to see the model more clearly.

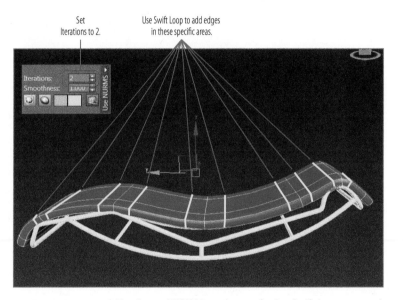

FIGURE 4.28 Turning up NURMS iterations and using Swift Loop to smooth out the model

9. Save your file. To check your work, open c04_ex9_cushion_end.max from the scenes folder of the c04_ArchModel project from the book's web page.

To finish the cushion, continue adjusting the edges/vertices to create the perfect shape. Also, look at the original reference image in Figure 4.16. There are straps that connect the cushion to the frame. Using the same spline techniques, create the straps to add realism to the overall look. Use the Line tool to create an oval shape that surrounds the frame, and in the Rendering rollout, choose Rectangular, as shown in Figure 4.29.

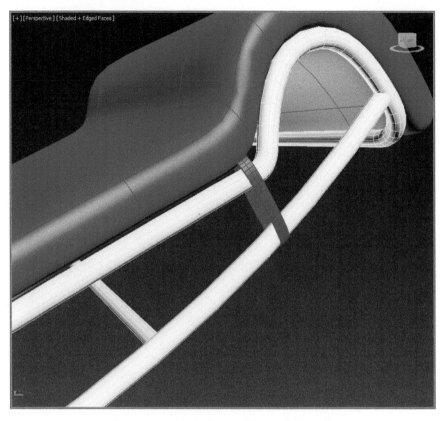

FIGURE 4.29 Create straps using splines and the Rendering rollout.

Exercise 4.10: Creating the Chair's Base

Certification
Objective

The base is made up of the objects on which the frame of the lounge chair sits. There are nine different objects: the four legs, four blocks that sit between the legs, and a block that connects the legs together, as shown in Figure 4.30.

FIGURE 4.30 **The lounge base**

Follow these steps to create the lounge base:

1. Continue with your chair file or load c04_ex10_base_start.max from the scenes folder of the c04_ArchModel project on the companion web page.

2. Start by unhiding the side image plane. Maximize the Left viewport and zoom in so you can see one of the base legs.

3. Create a box that is the general size of the front base leg. The parameters are as follows: Length = 13.2, Width = 4.0, Height = 0.35, Length Segs = 1, Width Segs = 1, and Height Segs = 1.

4. Activate See-Through mode (Alt+X) so you can see the image plane through the box primitive, and move the box so it is aligned with the lounge chair frame, as shown in Figure 4.31.

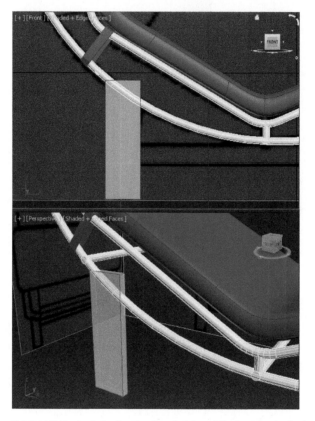

FIGURE 4.31 Create a box the size of the base leg in the image plane.

5. Choose the Ribbon ➤ Modeling tab ➤ Polygon Modeling ➤ Convert to Poly, and enter Vertex mode.

6. In the Left viewport, move the vertices so they line up with the yellow box in the image plane, as shown in Figure 4.32.

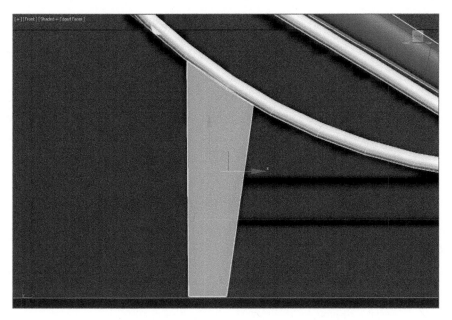

FIGURE 4.32   Move the vertices so they line up with the image plane.

7. Choose the Ribbon ➢ Modeling tab ➢ Edit ➢ Swift Loop, and add a loop at the bottom. This will set things up so you can add the foot. Right-click to exit Swift Loop.

8. Switch to a Perspective viewport, and then rotate the viewport so you can see an angled view.

9. Enter Polygon mode, and select the polygons between the new edge loop and the bottom of the Leg object. Exit See-Through mode (Alt+X).

10. Choose the Ribbon ➢ Modeling tab ➢ Polygons ➢ Extrude ➢ Extrude Settings. In the caddy, change the Extrusion type to Local Normal and change the Height to **1.6**. Press Enter to set the input; then click the OK button in the caddy, as shown in Figure 4.33.

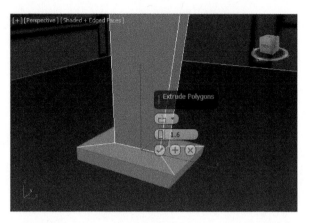

FIGURE 4.33   Use Extrude to begin creating the foot.

11. Choose the Ribbon ➤ Modeling tab ➤ Edit ➤ Swift Loop, and add edge loops, as shown in Figure 4.34, with Edged Faces turned on for better visibility.

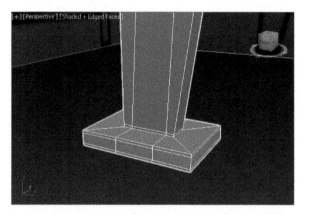

FIGURE 4.34   Add edge loops using Swift Loop in designated areas.

12. Choose the Ribbon ➤ Modeling tab ➤ Edit and turn on Use NURMS.

13. This looks very good, but you'll need to move the vertices and/or edges to refine the shape of the object to match the leg shown in Figure 4.30.

14. When the leg is finished, copy it three times and position the copies so they are aligned with the frame (use Figure 4.16 as a reference for the position of the legs).

15. Create the remaining pieces using the same techniques you used to create the leg.

16. Save the file. To check your work, open `c04_ex10_base_end.max` from the `scenes` folder of the `c04_ArchModel` project on the companion web page.

The final result is shown with the appropriate colors applied in Figure 4.35.

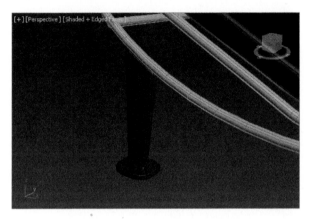

FIGURE 4.35   The final base shown with frame and cushion

Bringing It All Together

Now that the furniture is built, it's time to furnish the room you built in Chapter 3. You can do this by merging the 3ds Max furniture files into the room file. Merge allows you to load objects from one 3ds Max file into your current file. You can use the file that you completed in Chapter 3, or you can open the `c03_room_final.max` file from the `c03_ArchModel` project folder. Then follow these steps:

1. In the `c03_room_final.max` project file, click the Application button ( ) and select Import ➤ Merge.

2. When the Merge File dialog box opens, navigate to the `c04_ArchModel` project folder, select the `c04_Couch_Final.max` file or use your own file, and click Open. The Merge dialog box will open, and you will see a list of objects available to merge from that file.

▶

Merged objects come into a scene already selected. They always merge into a scene at the same X-, Y-, Z-coordinates as in their original file.

3. Select the All button and click OK. If you use your own files, the names may be different from those in the figure. The Merge dialog is shown in Figure 4.36.

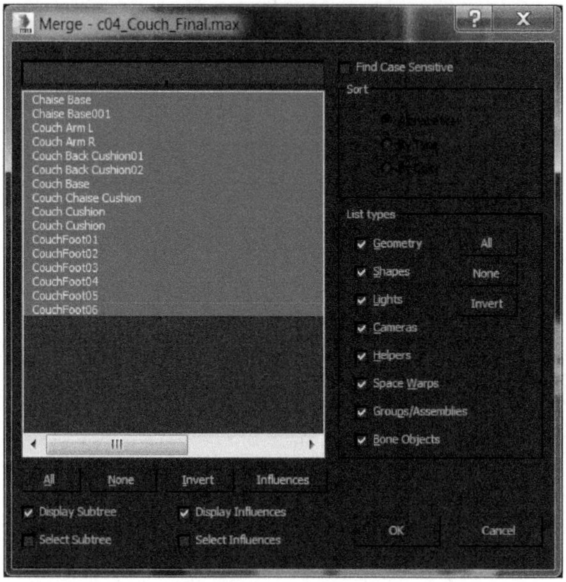

FIGURE 4.36 The Merge dialog box

4. Click the Zoom Extends All Selected button located at the lower-right corner of the interface; it is a flyout, which means there are more buttons under Zoom Extends All. This will zoom in on the already selected Couch objects.

5. Go to the Group menu and select Group. Name the group **Couch** and click OK.

▶

Groups can also be *nested*, meaning you can have a group within a group.

6. Position the couch in the room.

7. Refer to figure 4.1 from the beginning of the chapter for placement of couch in the room. Check the Front and Left viewports to make sure the couch is level with the floor.

8. Repeat steps 1 through 7 to merge in and place the spline chair using the file c04_LoungeChair_Final.max.

GROUPING

Grouping lets you combine objects into a group. A group uses something like an invisible carrying case, called a *dummy object*, to hold your objects. Select the group and move it around, and the objects will move along with it. A group has its own pivot point. You can transform and modify a group as if it were a single object. If you want to modify an individual object in the group, do the following:

1. Select the group, and then go to the Group menu and choose Open. A pink bracket will appear. The objects can be individually selected.

2. Select and modify an individual object inside the group, as needed.

3. When you have finished and want to close the group with one object selected, choose Group ➢ Close.

4. When you want to dissolve a group, just select the group, and in the Group menu, choose Ungroup.

These two pieces of furniture look great, but they don't fill up the room. To help furnish your newly built room, you can merge some prebuilt items into the space. Repeat steps 1 through 7 for the extra furniture pieces, which can be found in the Chapter 04 Extra Furniture folder in the scenes folder of the c04_ArchModel project. The room will look better after you merge the objects. The next phase for you may be to create some of your own objects to populate the room.

NOW YOU KNOW

In this chapter, you learned how to make further use of the various modeling tools to build a couch and chair. You started by blocking out the couch and then added NURMS to create smoothness before moving on to detailing and finishing the couch model. Then, using reference images, you created splines with the Line tool to draw out the shape of a chair before moving on to the cushions and the frame. From there, we looked at how groups work to bring objects together.

CHAPTER 5

Introduction to Animation

Animation is the process of changing the values of an object over time by setting keyframes and controlling those values. *Keyframing* is the process—borrowed from traditional animation—of setting positions and values at particular frames of the animation. The computer interpolates between these keyframes to fill in the other frames to complete a smooth animation.

Animation puts your scene into action and adds life to your characters. It is change over time. Anything in a scene that needs to change from one second to another will need to be animated to do so.

Everyone has their own reflexive sense of how things move. This knowledge is gleaned through years of perception and observation. Therefore, your audience can be more critical of a CG scene's motion than its lighting, coloring, or anything else. You know when something doesn't look right. So will your audience.

It's thrilling to see your hard work on a scene come to life with animation. On the flip side, it can be extremely aggravating to see your creation working improperly. Making mistakes is how you learn things, and your frustrations will ease over time. The results of your first several attempts at animating a scene will not look like Pixar films, but that should not dissuade you from working on more animations and scenes. You will get better with more practice.

The best way to learn how to animate is to jump right in and start animating. By doing so, you'll get a good look at the Autodesk® 3ds Max® 2016 software animation tools so you can start editing animation and developing your timing skills.

In this chapter, you will learn to

▶ **Animate the ball**

▶ **Read animation curves**

▶ **Refine the animation**

Animating the Ball

Certification
Objective

A classic exercise for all animators is to create a bouncing ball. It is a straight-forward exercise, but there is much you can do with a bouncing ball to show character. Animating a bouncing ball is a good exercise in physics as well as cartoon movement. You'll first create a rubber ball, and then you'll add cartoonish movement to accentuate some principles of the animation. Aspiring animators can use this exercise for years and always find something new to learn about bouncing a ball.

Exercise 5.1: Setting Keyframes

In preparation, download the c05_IntroAnimation project from the companion web page at www.sybex.com/go/3dsmax2016essentials to your hard drive. Set your current project by clicking the Application button, choosing Manage ➤ Set Project Folder, and navigating to the c05_IntroAnimation project that you downloaded.

Open the c05_ex1_ball_start.max scene file from the scenes folder of the c05_IntroAnimation project folder you downloaded. If you receive a Gamma & LUT Settings Mismatch warning, click OK.

Start with the *gross animation,* or the overall movements. This is also called *blocking.* First, move the ball up and down to begin its choreography.

Follow these steps to animate the ball:

1. Select the ball, and then go to the Hierarchy panel ().

2. Choose Pivot, and under the Adjust Pivot rollout, click the Affect Pivot Only button.

3. Zoom in on the ball in the Front viewport, and with the Move tool, drag on the Y-axis of the pivot to move to the bottom of the ball.

4. Click the Affect Pivot Only button again to deactivate.

5. Move the time slider to frame 10. The time slider is at the bottom of the screen below the viewports, as shown in Figure 5.1.

FIGURE 5.1   The time slider is used to change your position in time, counted in frames.

An animation is made up of a series of images. When viewed together in quick succession, these images simulate continuous motion. Each image is called a *frame*.

6. Click the Auto Key button below the time slider. The Auto Key button, the border of the currently selected viewport, and the time slider all turn red, as shown in Figure 5.2. This means that any movement in the objects in your scene will be recorded as animation.

FIGURE 5.2   The Auto Key button records your animations.

7. Using the Camera viewport, select the ball and move it down along the Z-axis to the ground plane, so it is 0 units in the Z-axis Transform Type-In box at the bottom of the interface. You can also just enter the value in the Z-axis Transform Type-In box and press Enter. This will work the same as using the Move tool to transform.

8. Save the file. To check your work, open the c05_ex1_ball_end.max file from the scenes folder of the c05_IntroAnimation project folder from the companion web page at www.sybex.com/go/3dsmax2016essentials.

SCRUBBING THE TIME SLIDER

You can click and drag the horizontal time slider to change the frame in your animation on the fly; this is called *scrubbing*. The slider bar displays the current frame/end frame. By default, your 3ds Max window shows a start frame of 0 and an end frame of 100. When you move the time slider, the movement is reflected in the viewports.

This exercise has created two keyframes, one at frame 0 for the original position of the ball and one at frame 10 for the position to which you just moved the ball.

Exercise 5.2: Copying Keyframes

Now you want to move the ball up to the same position in the air as it was at frame 0. Instead of trying to estimate where that was, you can just copy the keyframe at frame 0 to frame 20.

You can see the keyframes you created in the timeline; they appear as red boxes. Red keys represent Position keyframes, green keys represent Rotation, and blue keys represent Scale. When a keyframe in the timeline is selected, it turns white. Now let's copy a keyframe:

1. Continue with the project from the previous exercise, or open the `c05_ex2_ball_start.max` scene file from the `scenes` folder of the `c05_IntroAnimation` project folder you downloaded. If you start with the file from the `scenes` folder, you will need to turn on the Auto Key button.

2. Select the keyframe at frame 0; it should turn white when it is selected.

3. Hold down the Shift key (this is a shortcut for the Clone tool), and click and drag the selected keyframe to copy it to frame 20. This will create a keyframe with the same animation parameters as the keyframe at frame 0, as shown in Figure 5.3.

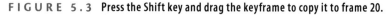

FIGURE 5.3   Press the Shift key and drag the keyframe to copy it to frame 20.

4. Click and drag the time slider to scrub through the keyframes. You should see the ball start in the up position and then move down and then back up.

5. Turn off Auto Key.

6. Save the file. To check your work, open c05_ex2_ball_end.max from the scenes folder of the c05_IntroAnimation project folder.

Exercise 5.3: Using the Track View - Curve Editor

Certification
Objective

Right now, the ball is going down and then back up. To continue the animation for the length of the timeline, you could continue to copy and paste keyframes as you did earlier—but that would be very time-consuming. A better way is to loop, or *cycle,* through the keyframes you already have. An *animation cycle* is a segment of animation that is repeatable in a loop. The end state of the animation matches up to the beginning state, so there is no hiccup at the loop point.

In 3ds Max, you use the Parameter Curve Out-of-Range Types feature to cycle animation. This is a fancy way to create loops and cycles with your animations and specify how your object will behave outside the range of the keys you have created. This brings us to Track View, which is an animator's best friend. You will learn the underlying concepts of the Curve Editor as well as its basic interface throughout this exercise.

Track View is a function of two animation editors, the Curve Editor and the Dope Sheet. The Curve Editor allows you to work with animation depicted as curves on a graph that sets the value of a parameter against time. The Dope Sheet displays keyframes over time on a horizontal graph, without any curves. This graphical display simplifies the process of adjusting animation timing because you can see all the keys at once in a spreadsheet-like format. The Dope Sheet is similar to traditional animation exposure sheets, or X-sheets.

You will use the Track View - Curve Editor (or Curve Editor for short) to loop your animation in the following steps:

1. Continue with the project from the previous exercise, or open the c05_ex3_ball_start.max scene file from the scenes folder of the c05_IntroAnimation project folder you downloaded.

2. With the ball selected, in the menu bar, choose Graph Editors ➤ Track View - Curve Editor. In Figure 5.4, the Curve Editor displays the animation curves of the ball so far.

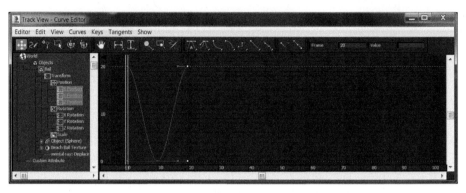

▶

Navigation inside the Track View - Curve Editor is pretty much the same as navigation in a viewport; the same keyboard/mouse combinations work for panning and zooming.

FIGURE 5.4   The Curve Editor shows the animation curves of the ball.

3. A menu bar runs across the top of the Curve Editor. In the Edit menu, choose Controller ➤ Out Of Range Types, as shown in Figure 5.5. Doing so opens the Param Curve Out-of-Range Types dialog box, shown in Figure 5.6.

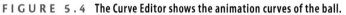

FIGURE 5.5   Selecting Out Of Range Types

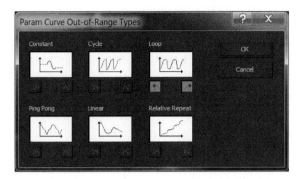

FIGURE 5.6   Choosing to loop your animation

4. Select Loop in this dialog box by clicking its thumbnail. The two little boxes with arrows beneath it will highlight, as shown in Figure 5.6. Click OK. Once you set the curve to Loop, the Curve Editor displays your animation, as shown in Figure 5.7. The out-of-range animation is shown as a dashed line.

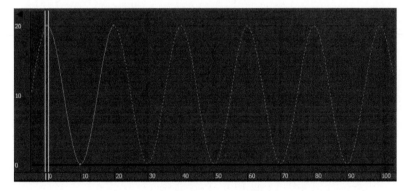

FIGURE 5.7   The Curve Editor now shows the looped animation curve.

5. Scrub your animation in a viewport, and see how the ball bounces up and down throughout the timeline range.

6. Save the file. To check your work, open `c05_ex3_ball_end.max` from the `scenes` folder of the `c05_IntroAnimation` project folder.

Reading Animation Curves

Certification
Objective

As you can see, the Curve Editor gives you control over the animation in a graph setting. The Curve Editor's graph is a representation of an object's parameters, such as Position (values shown vertically) over time (time shown horizontally). Curves allow you to visualize the interpolation of the motion. Once you are used to reading animation curves, you can judge an object's direction, speed, acceleration, and timing at a mere glance.

Here is a quick primer on how to read a curve in the Curve Editor.

In Figure 5.8, an object's Z Position parameter is being animated. At the beginning, the curve quickly begins to move positively (that is, to the right) on the Z-axis. The object shoots up and comes to an *ease-in*, where it decelerates to a stop, reaching its top height. The ease-in stop is signified by the curving beginning to flatten out at around frame 95.

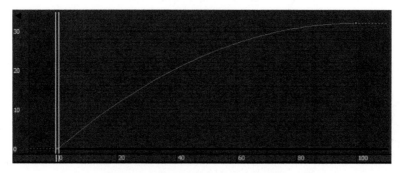

F I G U R E   5 . 8   **The object quickly accelerates to an ease-in stop.**

In Figure 5.9, the object slowly accelerates in an *ease-out* in the positive Z direction until it hits frame 100, where it suddenly stops.

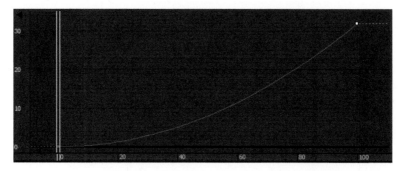

F I G U R E   5 . 9   **The object eases out to acceleration and suddenly stops at its fastest velocity.**

In Figure 5.10, the object eases out and travels to an ease-in where it decelerates, starting at around frame 69, to where it slowly stops, at frame 100.

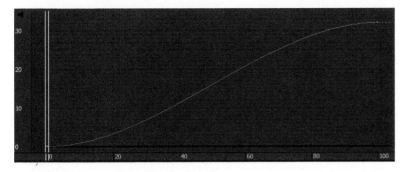

FIGURE 5.10 **Ease-out and ease-in**

Finally, in Figure 5.11, to showcase another tangent type, step interpolation holds its position from frame 0 to frame 20 and then makes the object jump from its Z position in frame 20 to its new position in frame 21.

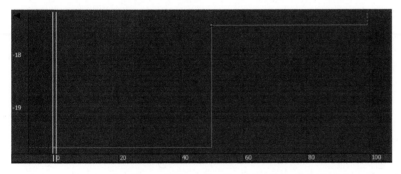

FIGURE 5.11 **Step interpolation makes the object "jump" suddenly from one value to the next.**

Figure 5.12 shows the Curve Editor, with its major aspects called out for your information.

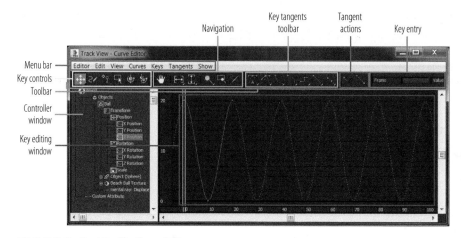

FIGURE 5.12 The Curve Editor

Refining the Animation

Certification
Objective

Try playing your animation as it stands now. In the bottom right of the interface, you will see an animation player with the sideways triangle to signify Play Animation. Select the Camera01 viewport and click the Play Animation button. The framework of the movement is getting there. Notice how the speed of the ball is moving in a consistent way. If this were a real ball, it would be dealing with gravity; the ball would speed up as it got closer to the ground, and there would be "hang time" when the ball was in the air on its way up as gravity took over to pull it back down.

This means you have to edit the movement that happens between the keyframes. This is done by adjusting *how* the keyframes shape the curve itself, using tangents. When you select a keyframe, a handle will appear in the user interface (UI), as shown in Figure 5.13.

This handle adjusts the tangency of the keyframe to change the curvature of the animation curve, which in turn changes the animation. There are various types of tangents, depending on how you want to edit the motion. By default, the Auto tangent is applied to all new keyframes. This is not what you want for the ball, although it is a perfect default tangent type to have.

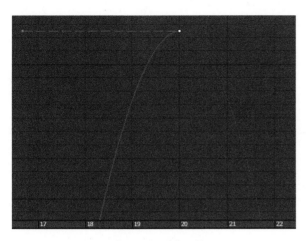

FIGURE 5.13 The keyframe handle

ANIMATION CONTROLLERS

Anything you animate is handled by a controller. Controllers store animation and interpolate between values. There are three default controllers:

Position: Position XYZ

Rotation: Euler XYZ

Scale: Bezier Scale

Exercise 5.4: Editing Animation Curves

In this exercise, you'll edit some tangents to better suit your animation. The intent is to speed up the curve as it hits the floor and slow it down as it crests its apex. Instead of opening the Curve Editor through the menu bar, this time you are going to use the shortcut:

Certification Objective

1. Continue with the project from the previous exercise, or open the c05_ex4_ball_start.max scene file from the scenes folder of the c05_IntroAnimation project folder you downloaded.

2. Close the large Curve Editor dialog box, unless it is already closed.

3. At the bottom-left corner of the interface, click the Open Mini Curve Editor button shown in Figure 5.14.

The Mini Curve Editor is the same as the one you launch through the main menu. A few tools are not included in the Mini Curve Editor toolbar, but you can find them in the menu bar.

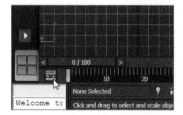

FIGURE 5.14   **Click the Open Mini Curve Editor button.**

If you need to zoom or pan in the Curve Editor's Key Editing window, you can use the same shortcuts you would use to navigate in the viewports.

4. With the ball selected, scroll down the Controller window on the left of the Mini Curve Editor by dragging the Pan tool (the hand cursor) to find the Ball object's position tracks.

5. Click the Z Position track. This will bring to the Key Editing window only the curves that you want to edit. The Z Position curve is blue, as is almost everything relating to the Z-axis. The little gray boxes on the curves are keyframes.

6. Select the keyframe at frame 10. The key will turn white when selected. You will change this key's tangency to make the ball fall faster as it hits and bounces off the ground.

7. In the Mini Curve Editor toolbar, change the tangent type for the selected keyframe from the Auto default to Fast by clicking the Set Tangents to Fast icon (■).When you do this, you will see the animation curve change shape, as shown in Figure 5.15.

You may need to scrub the time slider, which in the Curve Editor appears as double yellow vertical lines, out of the way if you are on frame 10.

FIGURE 5.15   **The effect of the new tangent type**

8. Select the Camera01 viewport and play the animation. You can easily correlate how the animation works with the curve's shape when you watch the time slider travel through the Mini Curve Editor as the animation plays.

9. Save the file. To check your work, open `c05_ex4_ball_end.max` from the `scenes` folder of the `c05_IntroAnimation` project folder.

FINESSING THE ANIMATIONS

Although the animation has improved, the ball has a distinct lack of weight. It still seems too simple and without any character. In situations such as this, animators can go wild and try several different things as they see fit. Here is where creativity helps hone your animation skills, whether you are new to animation or have been doing it for 50 years.

Animation shows change over time. Good animation conveys the *intent,* the motivation for that change between the frames.

Exercise 5.5: Squash and Stretch

The concept of *squash and stretch* has been an animation staple for as long as there has been animation. It is a way to convey the weight of an object by deforming it to react (usually in an exaggerated way) to gravity, impact, and motion.

You can give your ball a lot of flair by adding squash and stretch to give the object some personality. Follow these steps:

1. Continue with the project from the previous exercise, or open the `c05_ex5_ball_start.max` scene file from the `scenes` folder of the `c05_IntroAnimation` project folder you downloaded.

2. Press the N key to activate Auto Key.

3. Open the Mini Curve Editor if it isn't already open, and drag the yellow double-line track-bar time slider to frame 10.

4. Click and hold the Select and Scale tool to access the flyout.

5. Choose the Select and Squash tool ().

6. Select the ball if it isn't already selected, and center the cursor over the Z-axis of the Scale Transform gizmo in the Camera01 viewport.

7. Click and drag down to squash about 20 percent. Doing so will scale down on the Z-axis and scale up on the X- and Y-axes to compensate and maintain a constant volume, as shown in Figure 5.16.

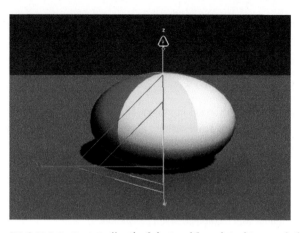

FIGURE 5.16 Use the Select and Squash tool to squash the ball on impact.

8. Move to frame 0, and click and drag up to stretch the ball up about 20 percent, so that the ball's scale in Z is about 120. When you scrub through the animation, you will see that the ball is stretched at frame 0; then the ball squashes and stays squashed for the rest of the time. You'll fix that in the next step.

9. In the Mini Curve Editor, scroll in the Controller window until you find the Scale track for the ball.

10. Highlight it to see the keyframes and animation curves.

11. Click and hold the Move Keys tool in the Mini Curve Editor toolbar to roll out and access the Move Keys Horizontal tool (▓▓).

12. Click and drag a selection marquee around the two keyframes at frame 0 in the Scale track to select them.

13. Hold the Shift key and then click and drag the keyframes at frame 0 to frame 20.

14. In the Mini Curve Editor's menu bar, choose Edit ➢ Controller ➢ Out Of Range Types. Choose Loop, and then click OK.

15. Play the animation. The curves are shown in Figure 5.17.

16. Save the file. To check your work, open `c05_ex5_ball_end.max` from the `scenes` folder of the `c05_IntroAnimation` project folder.

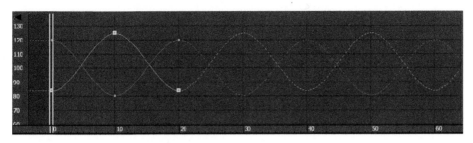

F I G U R E 5 . 1 7 **The final curves**

Exercise 5.6: Setting the Timing

Well, you squashed and stretched the ball, but it still doesn't look right. That is because the ball should not squash before it hits the ground. It needs to return to 100 percent scale and stay there for a few frames. Immediately before the ball hits the ground, it can squash into the ground plane to heighten the sense of impact. The following steps are easier to perform in the regular Curve Editor than in the Mini Curve Editor.

1. Continue with the project from the previous exercise, or open the c05_ex6_ball_start.max scene file from the scenes folder of the c05_IntroAnimation project folder you downloaded.

2. Move the time slider to frame 8; turn on Auto Key if it is not still active.

3. Select the ball and open the Curve Editor; in the Controller window, select the ball's Scale track so that only the scale curves appear in the Key Editing window.

4. In the Curve Editor's toolbar, click the Add Keys icon ( ). Your cursor will change to an arrow with a white circle at its lower right.

5. Click directly on the Scale curve to add a keyframe on all the Scale curves at frame 8. Because scales X and Y are the same value, you will see only two curves instead of three.

6. The keys are white when selected. In the Key Entry toolbar, you will find two text type-in boxes. The box on the left is the frame number, and the box on the right is the selected key's (or keys') value. Because more than one key with a different value is selected, there is no number in that type-in box.

7. Enter **100** (for 100 percent scale) in the right type-in box, for the scale in X, Y, and Z for the ball at frame 8, as shown in Figure 5.18.

FIGURE 5.18   Enter a value of 100.

8. Move the time slider to frame 12, and do the same thing in the Curve Editor. These settings are bracketing the squash so that it squashes only a couple frames before and a couple frames after the ball hits the ground.

9. Select the Auto Key button to turn it off.

10. Save the file. To check your work, open c05_ex6_ball_end.max from the scenes folder of the c05_IntroAnimation project folder.

Once you play back the animation, the ball will begin to look a lot more like a nice cartoonish one, with a little character. Experiment by changing some of the scale amounts to have the ball squash a little more or less, or stretch it more or less to see how that affects the animation. See if it adds a different personality to the ball. If you can master a bouncing ball and evoke all sorts of emotions from your audience, you will be a great animator indeed.

Exercise 5.7: Moving the Ball Forward

Now that you have worked out the bounce, it's time to add movement to the ball so that it moves across the screen as it bounces. Layering animation in this fashion, where you settle on one movement before moving on to another, is common. That's not to say you won't need to go back and forth and make adjustments through the whole process, but it's generally nicer to work out one layer of the animation before adding another. The following steps will show you how:

1. Continue with the project from the previous exercise, or open the c05_ex7_ball_start.max scene file from the scenes folder of the c05_IntroAnimation project folder you downloaded.

2. Press the N key to activate Auto Key again. Move the time slider to frame 0.

3. With the Select and Move tool, select the ball and then move the ball in the Camera01 viewport to the left so it is still within the camera's view. That's about –30 units on the X-axis.

4. Move the time slider to frame 100.

5. Move the ball to the right about 60 units so that the ball's X Position value is about 30. Don't play the animation yet; it isn't going to look right.

6. In the Menu bar ≻ Graph Editors, open Track View - Curve Editor. Scroll down in the Controller window, and select the X Position track for the ball, as shown in Figure 5.19. There is no keyframe at frame 100; this is because of the loop that you set on the ball earlier, which will be addressed in the following steps.

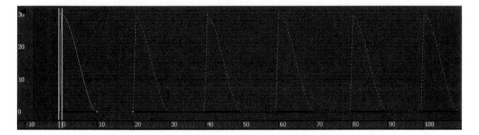

FIGURE 5.19 The X Position track of the ball does not look right.

7. Select the keyframes on the X Position track at frame 10 and frame 20 by dragging a selection box around them, and delete them by pressing the Delete key on your keyboard.

8. In the Param Curve Out-of-Range Types dialog (Edit ≻ Controller ≻ Out Of Range Types), select Constant. This removes the loop from the X Position track but won't affect the Z Position track for the ball's bounce.

9. Repeat step 5. The ball should still be in the same position; just move the ball again to the right so that its X Position value is about 30. This is to create a key at frame 100.

10. Play the animation. You can use the / (slash) button as a shortcut to play the animation. Watch the horizontal movement. The ball is slow at the beginning, speeds up in the middle, and then slows again at the end. It eases out and eases in. This is caused by the default tangent, which automatically adds an ease as the object goes in and out of the keyframes.

When you created the keyframes for the up-and-down movement of the ball (which was along the Z-axis), 3ds Max automatically created keyframes for the X and Y Position tracks, both with essentially no value. To fix this, keep following these steps.

11. In the Curve Editor, select both keys for the X Position curve and click the Set Tangents to Linear icon (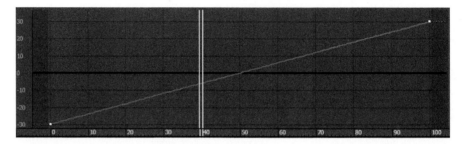) to create a straight line of movement so there is no speed change in the ball's movement from left to right. Figure 5.20 shows the proper curve.

12. Save the file. To check your work, open c05_ex7_ball_end.max from the scenes folder of the c05_IntroAnimation project folder.

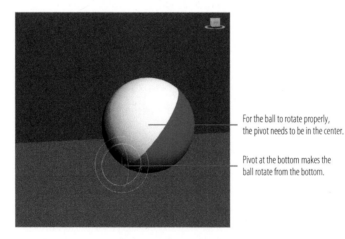

FIGURE 5.20 The X Position curve for the ball's movement now has no ease-out or ease-in.

You need to add some rotation, but there are several problems with this. One, you moved the pivot point to the bottom of the ball in the first step of the exercise. You did that so the squashing would work correctly—that is, it would be at the point of contact with the ground. If you were to rotate the ball with the pivot at the bottom, it would look like Figure 5.21.

For the ball to rotate properly, the pivot needs to be in the center.

Pivot at the bottom makes the ball rotate from the bottom.

FIGURE 5.21 The ball will not rotate properly, because the pivot is at the bottom.

Exercise 5.8: Using the XForm Modifier

You need a pivot point at the center of the ball, but you can't just move the existing pivot from the bottom to the middle—it would throw off all the squash and stretch animation. Unfortunately, the Ball object can have only one pivot point. To solve the issue, you are going to use a modifier called *XForm*. The XForm modifier will send down from the stack a gizmo and center for the ball. The center of the XForm modifier can be used in the same way a pivot point is used.

Certification
Objective

1. Continue with the project from the previous exercise, or open the c05_ex8_ball_start.max scene file from the scenes folder of the c05_IntroAnimation project folder you downloaded.

2. Select the ball, and then from the menu bar, select Modifiers ➤ Parametric Deformers ➤ XForm. XForm will be added to the ball in the modifier stack, and an orange bounding box will appear over the ball in the viewport. XForm has no parameters, but it does have sub-objects.

◀

The modifier can also be selected from the Modifier List in the command panel's Modify tab.

3. Expand the modifier stack by clicking the black box with the plus sign next to XForm, and then click Center. In the next step, you will use the Align tool to move the XForm's center to the center of the ball.

4. Click the Align tool (⬛), and then click the ball.

5. In the resulting dialog box, make sure the check boxes for X, Y, and Z Position are checked, which means those axes are active.

6. Now click Center under Target Object, and then click OK, as shown in Figure 5.22. The XForm's center will move.

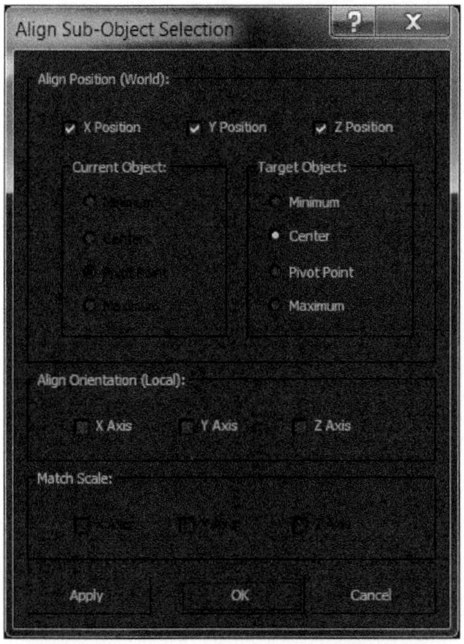

FIGURE 5.22 Align Sub-Object Selection dialog box

7. Save the file. To check your work, open c05_ex8_ball_end.max from the scenes folder of the c05_IntroAnimation project folder.

To reiterate, this *isn't* a pivot point. This is the *center point* on the XForm modifier. If you go to the modifier stack and click Sphere, the pivot point will still be at the bottom.

The XForm modifier allows the ball to rotate without its squashing and stretching getting in the way of the rotation. When the rotation animation for the ball's roll is separated into the modifier, the animation on the ball object is preserved.

Exercise 5.9: Animating the XForm Modifier

To add the ball's roll to the XForm modifier, follow these steps:

1. Continue with the project from the previous exercise, or open the c05_ex9_ball_start.max scene file from the scenes folder of the c05_IntroAnimation project folder you downloaded.

2. Turn on Auto Key and choose the Select and Rotate tool.

3. Select the ball, and then in the modifier stack, select the Gizmo sub-object of XForm. This is a very important step because it tells the modifier to use the XForm's center instead of using the pivot point of the ball.

4. Move the time slider to frame 100. Then in the Camera01 viewport select and drag the green circular gizmo handle to rotate exactly 360 degrees. To help with the rotate use the Angle Snap Toggle (🔼) which is found in the main toolbar.

5. Click the XForm modifier to deactivate the sub-object mode.

6. Play the animation.

7. Save the file. To check your work, open c05_ex9_ball_end.max from the scenes folder of the c05_IntroAnimation project folder.

THE BALL DOESN'T ROTATE 360 DEGREES!

If you rotate the ball in the third step 360 degrees but the ball does not animate, 3ds Max could be interpreting 360 degrees to be 0 degrees in the Curve Editor, thereby creating a flat curve. If this is the case, you can try rotating the ball 359 degrees instead to force the animation to work. You could also manually change the value in the Curve Editor for the keyframe at frame 100 to a value of 360.

Exercise 5.10: Correcting the Rotation

The ball's animation is almost perfect. The rotation still has a slight problem; it has ease at the beginning and at the end. Fixing this issue requires you to go back into the Curve Editor as follows:

Certification Objective

1. Continue with the project from the previous exercise, or open the c05_ex10_ball_start.max scene file from the scenes folder of the c05_IntroAnimation project folder you downloaded.

2. Select the Ball object, and then open the Curve Editor (mini or regular) and scroll down in the Controller window until you see the Ball tracks. Below the ball's transform track is a new track called Modified Object.

3. Expand the track by clicking the plus sign in the circle next to the name.

4. Also expand the XForm track, and then go to the Gizmo track and select the Y Rotation track. You will see the curve in the Key Editing window.

5. Select the keyframe at frame 0; it has a value of 0 and the keyframe at frame 100 has a value of 360.

6. Change the tangents to Linear, as shown in Figure 5.23.

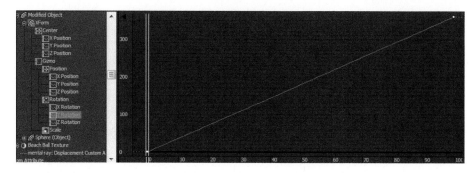

FIGURE 5.23 The Gizmo track's Y-axis rotation is selected in the Controller window and Linear tangents are set.

7. Close the Curve Editor and play the animation.

8. Save the file. To check your work, open c05_ex10_ball_end.max from the scenes folder of the c05_IntroAnimation project folder.

9. Play the c05_BallRender.avi movie file located in the renderoutput folder of the c05_IntroAnimation project to see a render of the animation.

Now You Know

In this chapter, you began your adventure into animation by learning how to set and manipulate keyframes by animating a ball. Using the Track View - Curve Editor, we looked into how to read and edit animation curves to help you refine motion on the animated ball. This chapter also showed you the animation principle of squash and stretch to give weight to an animated object. Finally, you finished the animation using the XForm modifier as a tool to add an additional pivot point with which to animate.

CHAPTER 6

Animation Principles

This chapter is a continuation of the animation work you began in Chapter 5, "Introduction to Animation." It introduces you to some new animation fundamentals. We will look at using some animation principles by completing a knife-throwing project.

In this chapter, you will learn to

➤ **Create anticipation and momentum to make knife throwing appear realistic**

Anticipation and Momentum in Knife Throwing

This exercise will give you more experience with Autodesk® 3ds Max® 2016 software animation techniques. You will edit more in the Curve Editor and be introduced to some animation principles and concepts, including anticipation, momentum, and secondary movement. First, download the project files for this chapter from this book's companion web page (www .sybex.com/go/3dsmax2016essentials). Set your project folder by choosing Application ➤ Manage ➤ Set Project Folder and selecting the c06_Animation Principles project that you downloaded.

Exercise 6.1: Blocking Out the Animation

To begin this exercise, open the c06_ex1_blocking_start.max file in the c06_Animation Principles project folder. When you open the file, you might see a Gamma & LUT Settings Mismatch Error dialog box; click OK, and then follow these steps.

1. Move the time slider to frame 30 and activate the Auto Key button.

2. Move and rotate the knife to the TARGET object, as shown in Figure 6.1.

FIGURE 6.1   Move the knife to the target at frame 30.

3. Move the time slider to frame 15, where the knife is halfway between its start and the target. In the Camera001 viewport, move the knife slightly up on the Z-axis, as shown in Figure 6.2, so that the knife moves with a slight arc.

FIGURE 6.2   Move the knife up slightly at frame 15.

4. Click the Time Configuration icon at the bottom of the UI next to the navigation controls. Figure 6.3 shows the Animation section in the Time Configuration dialog box.

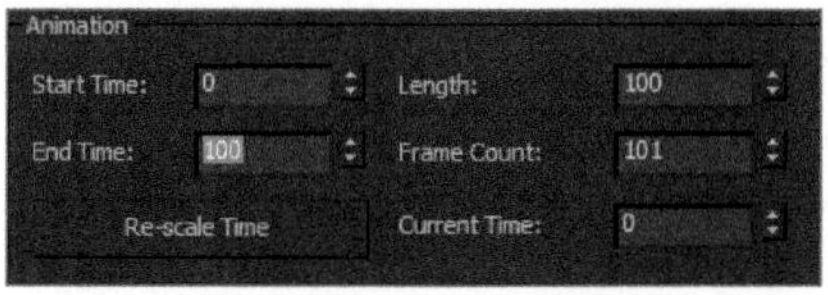

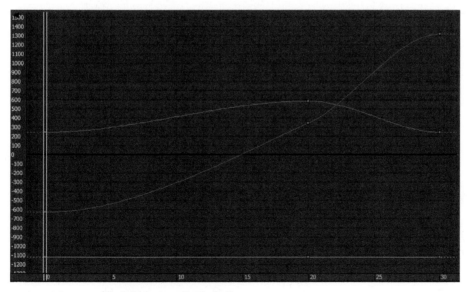

FIGURE 6.3 Change the frame range in the Time Configuration dialog box.

5. In the Animation section, change End Time to 30 and click OK. The time slider will reflect this change immediately.

6. Play your animation, and you should see the knife move with a slight ease-out and ease-in toward the target, with a slight arc up in the middle. You are going to move the keyframes from frame 0 to frame 10 so there is a pause before the knife moves toward the target.

7. Open the Curve Editor and scroll down in the Controller window until you see the THROW KNIFE X, Y, and Z Position tracks.

8. Hold the Ctrl key and select all three tracks to display their curves (if they are not already selected), as shown in Figure 6.4.

FIGURE 6.4 The initial curves for the knife

9. Drag a selection marquee around the three keyframes at frame 0.

10. In the Key Controls toolbar, select and hold the Move Keys tool (⊕) to access the flyout icons, and select the Move Keys Horizontal tool in the flyout (↔). Use this tool to move the keyframes to frame 10.

11. This will compact the curve, so you need to move the keyframes at frame 15 to the new middle, frame 20.

12. Now you can turn off the Auto Key button (N). The finished curve is shown in Figure 6.5.

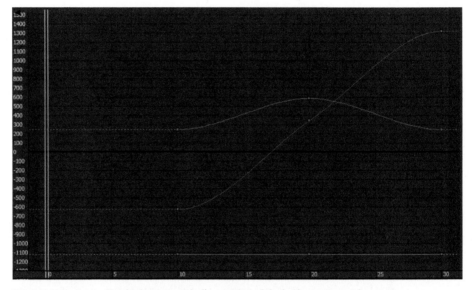

FIGURE 6.5 Finished curves with the position of the knife starting at frame 10

That's it for the gross animation (or *blocking*) of the shot. Save the file. To check your work, open the c06_ex1_blocking_end.max file in the c06_ Animation Principles project folder.

Exercise 6.2: Working with Trajectories

When it comes to animation, it is very helpful to be able to see an object's *trajectory* (the path the object is taking over time). To begin this exercise, open the c06_ex2_trajectories_start.max file in the c06_Animation Principles project folder then follow these steps:

1. Select the THROW KNIFE object.

2. In the command panel, click the Motion icon (◎).

3. Click Trajectories, as shown in Figure 6.6. The viewports will display a red curve to show you the path of the knife's motion as it arcs toward the target, as shown in Figure 6.7.

FIGURE 6.6 Turning on Trajectories for the knife

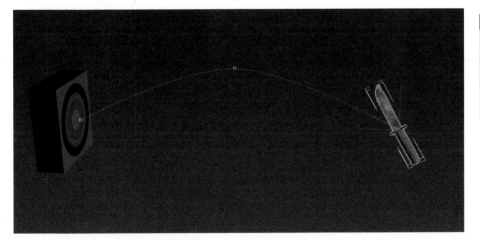

FIGURE 6.7 The curve shows the trajectory for the knife's motion.

The large, hollow, square points on the trajectory curve represent the keyframes set on the knife so far.

4. Select the Sub-Object button at the top of the Motion panel. Your only sub-object choice is Keys in the pull-down menu to the right of the button.

5. Select the middle keyframe and move it up or down to suit your tastes.

6. Once you settle on a nice arc for the path of the knife, turn off Trajectories mode by clicking the Parameters button in the Motion panel.

As you can imagine, the Trajectories option can be useful in many situations. It not only gives you a view of your object's path; it also allows you to edit that path easily and in a visual context, which can be very important. Save the file. To check your work, open the `c06_ex2_trajectories_end.max` file in the `c06_Animation Principles` project folder.

Exercise 6.3: Adding Rotation

Throwing knives in real life is usually a bad idea, but you can throw something else at a target (the inanimate kind) to see how to animate your knife. You'll find that the object will rotate once or twice before it hits its target. To begin this exercise, open the `c06_ex3_rotation_start.max` file in the `c06_Animation Principles` project folder. To add rotation to your knife, follow these steps:

1. Select the knife and then press N to activate Auto Key (if it isn't already active). Move to frame 30, and press E for the Select and Rotate tool.

2. In the Camera001 viewport, rotate on the Y-axis about 443 degrees.

3. With the knife selected, open the Curve Editor.

4. Scroll down to locate the X, Y, and Z Rotation tracks and select the X Rotation track.

5. Select the keys at frame 0, and then use the Move Keys Horizontal tool to move the keyframes to frame 10. Figure 6.8 shows the Curve Editor graph for the rotation on the knife.

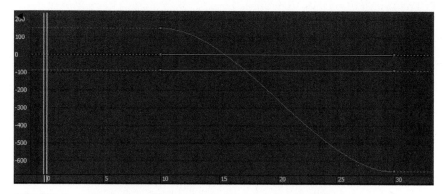

FIGURE 6.8   The Curve Editor graph for the rotation on the knife

6. Press N to deactivate Auto Key.

7. Play the animation, and you will see the knife's position and rotation ease in and out. Stop the animation (/ is the shortcut key).

8. Go back to the Curve Editor; change Move Keys Horizontal back to Move Keys.

9. Select the X Position track; then select both keyframes and change them to Linear by selecting the Set Tangents to Linear button ( ).

10. Now select the Z Position track; you'll need to finesse this one a bit more than you did the X Position track. You are going to use the handles on the tangents that appear when you select a key. These handles can be adjusted.

11. Select the keyframe at frame 10; then center your cursor over the end on the tangent handle and drag using the Move Keys tool. Pull it up so it is even with the curve. Then repeat the same tangent handle edit as above with the keyframe at frame 30. Figure 6.9 illustrates how you want the Z Position animation curve to look. This will give the trajectory a nice arc and a good rate of travel. Now it is time to edit the Rotation keys.

> The rotations or movement would not ease in or out with a real knife. Its speed would be roughly consistent throughout the animation.

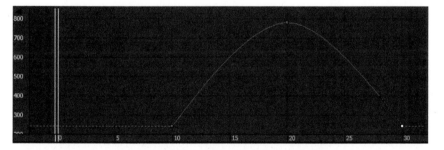

FIGURE 6.9 Adjust the curve for the knife's arc through the air.

12. The first thing you can do is add a bit of drama to the knife to make the action more exciting. To this end, you can see that the rotation of the knife is too slow.

13. Choose the X Rotation track and select its key at frame 30.

If the total value of the rotation is more than 360 degrees, it will increase the speed of the rotation. This will add one full revolution to the animation and some more excitement to the action.

14. In the Key Entry type-in box, change the value to about -660.

15. Adjust the tangent handles to resemble the curve shown in Figure 6.10. The knife will speed up just a bit as it leaves the first rotation keyframe. The speed will be slower as it goes into the last keyframe.

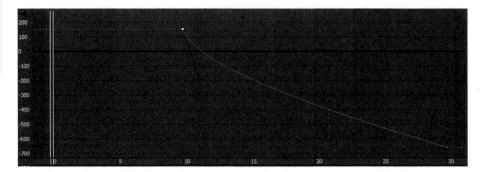

FIGURE 6.10 Match your curve to this one.

With just a little bit of fast rotation as the knife leaves frame 10, you give the animation more spice. The knife should now have a slightly weightier look than before, when it rotated with an ease-in and ease-out. To check your work, open the c06_ex3_rotation_end.max file in the c06_Animation Principles project folder.

Exercise 6.4: Adding Anticipation

Now let's animate the knife to create *anticipation,* as if an invisible hand is holding the knife pulled back just before throwing it to get more strength in the throw. This anticipation, although it's a small detail, adds a level of nuance to the animation that enhances the total effect. To begin this exercise, open the c06_ex4_anticipation_start.max file in the c06_Animation Principles project folder. Follow these steps:

1. Move the time slider to frame 0.

2. Select the knife, go to the Curve Editor, scroll in the Controller window, and then select the X Rotation track for the knife.

3. In the Curve Editor toolbar, click the Add Keys icon ( ), bring your cursor to frame 0 of the curve, and click to create a keyframe.

Doing so creates a key at frame 0 with the same parameters as the next key, as shown in Figure 6.11.

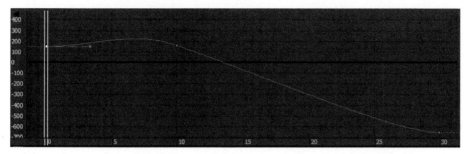

FIGURE 6.11 Add a key to the beginning to create anticipation for the knife throw.

4. Select the Move Keys tool, and select the keyframe at frame 10.

5. In the Key Entry type-in box, change the value of the key at frame 10 to 240. If you play back the animation, it will look weird. The knife will cock back really fast and spin a bit. This is due to the big hump between frames 0 and 10.

6. Keep the tangent at frame 0 set to the default, but change the tangent on the key at frame 10 to Linear ( ). Play the animation. You'll have a slight bit of anticipation, but the spice will be lost, and the knife will look less active and too mechanical.

7. To regain the weight you had in the knife, press Ctrl+Z to undo your change to the tangency on frame 10 and set it back to what you had. You may have to undo more than once.

8. Now, select the Move Keys Vertical tool ( ), which is under the Move Keys tool. Select the keyframe at frame 10, and then select the In tangent handle. This is the tangent handle on the left of the key.

9. Press Shift and drag the tangent handle down to create a curve that is similar to the one shown in Figure 6.12.

10. Play back the animation. It should look much better now.

To check your work, open the c06_ex4_anticipation_end.max file in the c06_Animation Principles project folder.

By pressing Shift as you dragged the tangent handle, you broke the continuity between the In and Out handles so that only the In handle was affected.

◀

◀

It's common to try something and rely on Undo—even several times—to get back to the starting point. You can also save multiple versions of your file to revert to an earlier one.

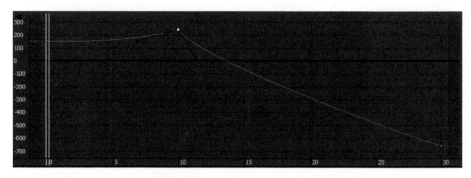

FIGURE 6.12 To create believable anticipation for the knife throw, set your curve to resemble this one.

Exercise 6.5: Following Through

The knife needs more weight. A great way to show that in animation is by adding follow-through so the knife sinks into the target a bit. To begin this exercise, open the c06_ex5_followthrough_start.max file in the c06_Animation Principles project folder.

To add follow-through to your animation, follow these steps:

1. Click the Time Configuration icon and change End Time to 45 to add 15 frames to your frame range.

2. Click OK. Doing so will not affect the animation; it will merely append 15 frames to the current frame range.

3. Select the knife and go to frame 30, where it completes its hit on the target.

4. In the Curve Editor, select the X Position track of the knife.

5. Add a keyframe with the Add Keys tool at frame 35. Select the Move Keys tool, and then select the keyframe at frame 35.

6. Note the value of the key in the type-in boxes at the top right of the Curve Editor (*not* the type-in boxes at the bottom of the main UI). You will want to set the value for the key at frame 35 to about **1290** to sink it farther into the target.

7. With these relative values, scrub the animation between frames 30 and 35. You should see the knife's slight move into the target. The end of your curve should look like the curve in Figure 6.13. You still

need to add a little bit of follow-through to the rotation of the knife to make it sink into the target better.

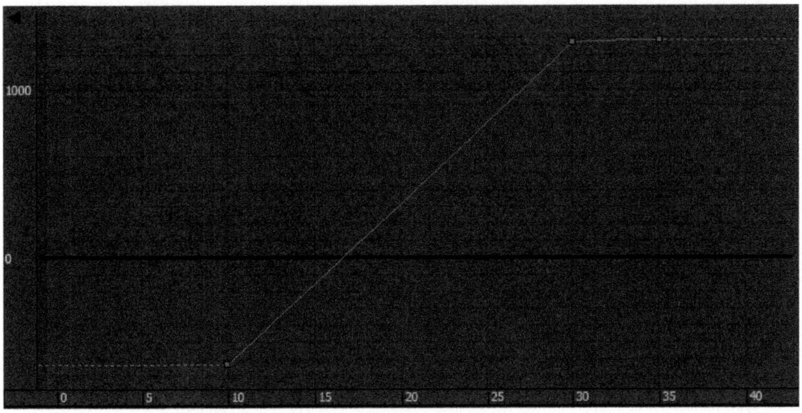

FIGURE 6.13 **Your animation should end like this.**

8. In the Curve Editor, select the X Rotation track to display its curve.

9. Add a key to the curve at frame 35. The value of the key at frame 30 should already be about -660.

10. Set the value of the keyframe at frame 35 to about **-655**. Keep the tangent set at Auto.

11. If your values are different than what is asked for in this exercise, adjust according to what works best in your scene.

Be careful about how much the knife sinks into the target. Although it is important to show the weight of the knife, it is also important to show the weight of the target; you do not want the target to look insubstantial. To check your work, open the c06_ex5_followthrough_end.max file in the c06_ Animation Principles project folder.

Exercise 6.6: Transferring Momentum to the Target

To make the momentum work even better for the knife animation, you will have to push back the target as the knife hits it. The trouble is, if you animate the target moving back, the knife will stay in place, floating in the air. You have to animate the knife *with* the target.

Parent and Child Objects

To animate the knife and target together, the knife has to be linked to the target so that when the target is animated to push back upon impact, the knife will follow precisely because it is stuck in the target. Doing this won't mess up the existing animation of the knife, because the knife will be the child in the hierarchy and will retain its own animation separate from the target. To begin this exercise, open the c06_ex6_momentum_start.max file in the c06_Animation Principles project folder. Then follow these steps:

1. Go to the frame when the knife impacts.

2. On the far left of the main toolbar, choose the Select and Link tool ().

3. Select the knife and drag it to the target, as shown in Figure 6.14 (left image). Nothing should change until you animate the TARGET object.

4. Move the time slider to frame 34 and press the N key to activate the Auto Key tool.

5. With the Select and Rotate tool, select the TARGET object and rotate it back about 5 degrees, as shown in Figure 6.14 (right image).

FIGURE 6.14   Link the knife to the target (left), and then rotate the target in the X-axis (right).

6. Go to the Curve Editor, scroll to find the Y Rotation track for the Target object, select the keyframe at frame 0, and move it to frame 30.

The pivot of the target has already been placed properly, at the bottom back edge.

7. Hold the Shift key, and click and drag the keyframe (which will make a copy of it) to frame 37.

8. Change the tangent for the key at frame 30 to Fast. Leave the other key tangents as they are now.

9. Add a little wobble to the target to make the animation even more interesting. This can be done easily in the Curve Editor. Use Add Keys to add keys at frames 40 and 44.

10. Using the Move Keys Vertical tool, give the key at frame 40 a value of about 1.7. Your curve should resemble the one in Figure 6.15.

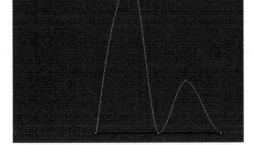

FIGURE 6.15   The target animation curve

11. Finally, add a little slide to the target. Using the Select and Move tool, move the time slider to frame 37, and move the target just a bit along the X-axis.

12. Go to the Curve Editor, scroll to the X position of the TARGET object, select the keyframe at frame 0, and move it to frame 30 so the move starts when the knife hits the target.

13. Change the tangent for frame 30 to Fast, and leave the other tangent at Auto. Deactivate Auto Key.

Done! Play your animation. Experiment and change some of the final timings and values of the target's reaction to the impact to see different weights of the knife and target and how the weight looks to the viewer. To check your work, open the c06_ex6_momentum_end.max file in the c06_Animation Principles project folder.

You can see a sample render of the scene in the c06_knife_animation.avi file in the renderoutput folder of the c06_Animation Principles project.

Now You Know

In this chapter, you learned some new animation fundamentals: anticipation and momentum. Anticipation is used to show the knife preparing for action and makes the action appear more realistic. By adding rotation to the beginning of the animation, it is as if an invisible hand is holding the knife and pulling it back just before throwing. This gives the throw more strength. Momentum describes how heavy the knife is while moving through space, so it pushes the target as the knife hits.

CHAPTER 7

Character Modeling Part I

In games, characters are cleverly designed and created to achieve the best look with the least amount of mesh detail to keep the polygon count low. Drawing on this knowledge, the film industry has taken many game-modeling techniques and modified them for film, creating low-poly efficient models and then adding detail (or polygons) when needed. With that in mind, this chapter and the next introduce you to character modeling, using the Editable Poly toolset to create a cute alien suitable for character animation. The alien character used in this book was designed by Andrew Montemayor, a graduate of the Art Institute of California - Los Angeles, who specializes in storyboarding, character design, and background design.

   This chapter begins with the basic form of the character.

In this chapter, you will learn to

▶ **Set up the scene**

▶ **Block out the alien body**

▶ **Refine the alien body**

Setting Up the Scene

You can import and use sketches of the character's front and side as background images as you create the character using the Autodesk® 3ds Max® 2016 software toolset. You can use additional sketches of your character from several points of view as quick references to help you reach your goal.

HIGH- AND LOW-POLY MODELING

High-polygon-count models are used when a model's level of detail needs to be impeccable, such as when the model is used in close-ups. High-polygon models are also used to generate displacement and normal maps to use on lower-resolution models. This technique is used to add needed detail without the issues that come with high-resolution models.

Low-polygon-count modeling, also called *low-poly modeling,* refers to a style of modeling that sacrifices some detail in favor of efficient geometry and places a very low load on the system on which it is being created or rendered. The number of triangles needed to consider something low-poly is based on the rendering platform and increases as the technology improves.

Exercise 7.1: Creating the Image Planes

You'll begin this exercise by creating crossed boxes and applying reference images to them. Set your project to the c07_CharacterModel project you downloaded from the book's web page at www.sybex.com/go/3dsmax2016essentials.

1. In a new scene, select the Front viewport.

2. In the Create panel ➤ Geometry, select Plane. Expand the Keyboard Entry rollout and set Y to 30. This will move the bottom of the plane in line with the ground plane within the front view. Set the Length to 60 and Width to 42. Click the Create button.

3. Rename the plane **Image Plane Front**.

4. With the plane still selected, choose the Modify tab, and in the Parameters rollout, set Length Segs and Width Segs to **1**.

5. Click in a blank space in the user interface (UI), and then press Ctrl+Shift+Z on your keyboard to initiate the shortcut for Zoom Extents All.

6. In the main toolbar, turn on Angle Snap Toggle ( ) or press A on your keyboard. Doing so will snap your rotation to every 5 degrees.

7. Select the Select and Rotate tool (E) and select the Image Plane Front object. Hold down the Shift key on the keyboard and, in the Front

The 3ds Max default system of measurement is generic units. One generic unit equals one inch.

viewport, rotate the image plane by dragging along the Y-axis 90 degrees.

8. Using the Shift key and a Transform tool activates the Clone Options dialog box, shown in Figure 7.1.

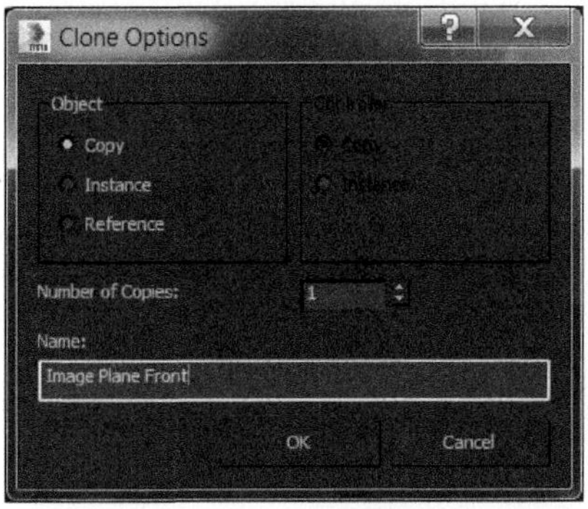

FIGURE 7.1 The Clone Options dialog box

9. In the Clone Options dialog box, under Object, select Copy; name the copy **Image Plane Side** and click OK.

This is a good time to save your file. To check your work, open the `c07_ex1_setup_end.max` file in the `c07_CharacterModel` project folder.

Exercise 7.2: Adding the Images to the Planes

At this point, you add the reference materials onto the planes to provide a reference inside the scene itself while you model the character. Therefore, it's critical to ensure that the features of the character that appear in both reference images (the front and the side) are at the same height. For instance, the top of the head and the shoulders should be at the same height in both the front and side views to make the modeling process easier. Either continue the exercise using your previously saved file or open `c07_ex2_image_start.max`.

1. Change the shading in the Front and Left viewports to Shaded if it isn't already set to Shaded. Turn off the grid in both viewports by selecting the viewport and using the keyboard shortcut G.

2. Open a Windows Explorer window and navigate to the `c07_CharacterModel/sceneassets/images` folder on your hard drive.

When you apply the image to the plane, it is important to keep it proportional, maintaining its width and length with no stretching or squeezing of the images.

3. Drag Alien_Front.jpg from the Explorer window to the Image Plane Front object in the Front viewport.

4. Drag Alien_Side.jpg onto the Image Plane Side object in the Left viewport.

5. Change the Perspective viewport to Shaded and turn on Edged Faces; you can use the keyboard shortcut F4. The image planes should have the two images mapped on them, as shown in Figure 7.2.

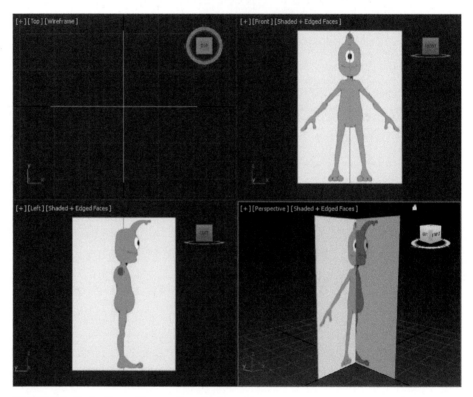

FIGURE 7.2   **Mapped image planes in viewports**

To check your work, open the c07_ex2_image_end.max file in the c07_CharacterModel project folder.

Blocking Out the Alien Model

When you're starting to create a model, a good practice is to block out the basic form of the character and focus on the size and crucial shapes of the major elements, and then add detail for the finer features. The following exercises describe the steps required to block out the alien's major features.

Exercise 7.3: Forming the Torso

The basic structure for the torso begins with a simple box primitive. After converting the box into an editable poly, you will use the Symmetry modifier on the object so that any manipulations performed on one side are also performed on the other. You will begin forming the basic shape of the torso by moving the editable poly's vertices and extruding its polygons in the following steps. Continue with the previous exercise's scene file, or open the c07_ex3_torso_start.max scene file in the scenes folder of the c07_CharacterModel project folder downloaded from this book's web page. Then follow these steps:

Certification
Objective

1. In the Perspective viewport, select the Shading viewport label menu, choose Shaded, and then press F4. This will turn on Edged Faces; do this if it isn't already set that way.

2. Start by creating a box primitive in the Perspective viewport with these parameters: Length: 9, Width: 10, Height: 19, Length Segs: 3, Width Segs: 2, and Height Segs: 4, as shown in Figure 7.3.

The box primitive is a starting point for the detail needed to create the body form.

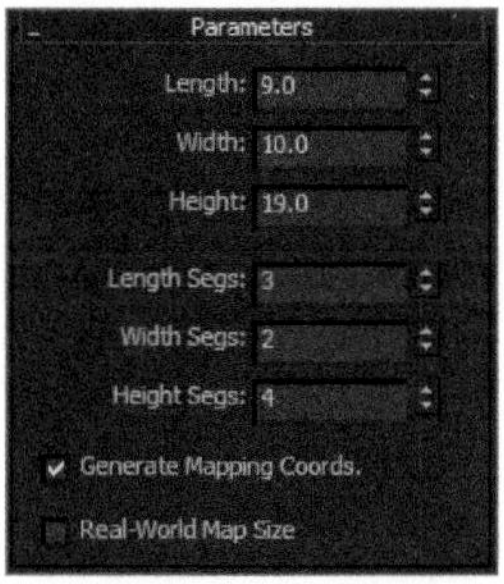

FIGURE 7.3 Box parameters

3. Press Alt+X to make the box see-through.

4. Change the box's name to **Alien Body.**

5. Position the box at X: 0, Y: 0.0, Z: 22.0, so it is aligned with the Alien's torso, as shown in Figure 7.4.

6. In the Ribbon ➤ Modeling tab ➤ Polygon Modeling panel, click Convert to Poly.

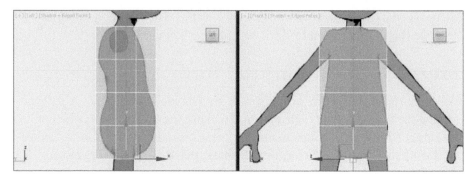

FIGURE 7.4 Box position from the front and side views

7. In the Polygon Modeling panel, enter the Vertex sub-object level.

8. In the Left viewport, select and move the vertices to match the outline of the character on the image plane, as shown in Figure 7.5. Use a selection box to select the vertices from the Left viewport. This will ensure that you are selecting both the back vertex and the vertex that can be seen in the viewport.

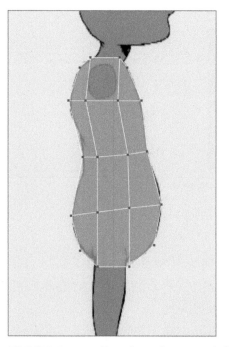

FIGURE 7.5 Move the vertices to match the alien's image in the Left viewport.

9. In the Polygon Modeling panel, select Polygon to enter the polygon sub-object level.

10. In the Front viewport, drag a selection marquee around the right half of the box and delete it. The reason for doing this is to cut your work in half. You will build half of the body and then copy it to the other side.

11. In the Polygon Modeling panel, select Vertex to enter the vertex sub-object level.

12. Move the vertices to match the outline of the character from the Front view, as shown in Figure 7.6.

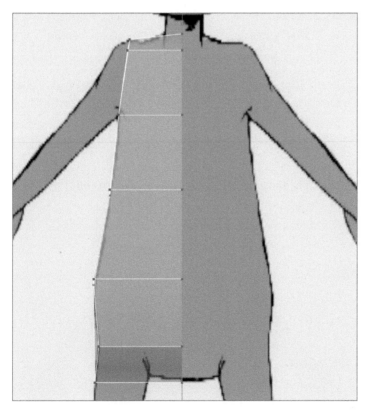

FIGURE 7.6 Move the vertices to match the alien's image in the Front viewport.

13. From the Front viewport, select the vertices (use your cursor, not the selection window) on the front outside edge, and move them closer to the center, as shown in Figure 7.7. Click the Vertex button again to exit Vertex mode.

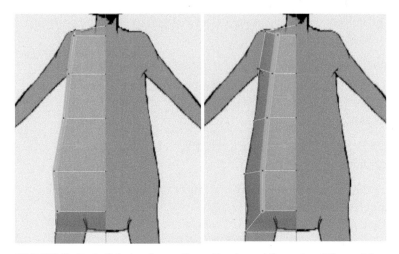

FIGURE 7.7   Select and move the vertices toward the center of the model.

14. In the Ribbon ➤ Modeling tab ➤ Edit ➤ Swift Loop, place a new loop on the inside, as shown in Figure 7.8. You will use this loop when you build the alien's leg.

In this section, you are just building the torso and setting things up for the following exercises. Save the file. To check your work against the example, open the c07_ex3_torso_end.max file in the c07_CharacterModel project folder.

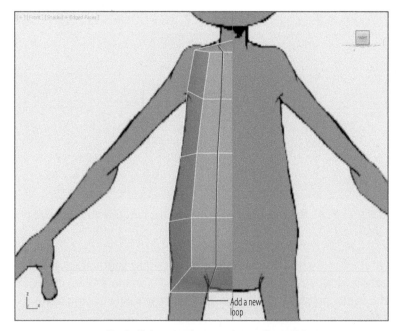

FIGURE 7.8   Use Swift Loop to place an edge on the model.

Exercise 7.4: Creating Symmetry

So far, you've modeled only one half of the torso; you will use a modifier to copy the half torso and mirror it to create the rest of the torso. Continue with the previous exercise's scene file, or open the c07_ex4_symmetry_start.max scene file in the scenes folder of the c07_CharacterModel project downloaded from this book's web page.

Certification Objective

1. Select the alien torso, and in the Modify panel, choose Symmetry from the Modifier List. When the modifier is applied, the model will disappear; this is because of the default parameters in the modifier.

2. In the Parameters rollout, check the Flip box in the Mirror Axis area, as shown in Figure 7.9.

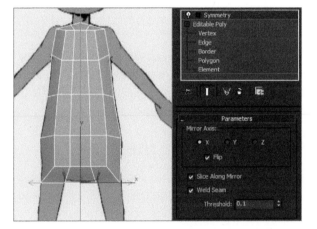

FIGURE 7.9 The Symmetry modifier creates a full torso.

3. Go to the Modify panel, and in the modifier stack, select Editable Poly.

4. In the Ribbon ➤ Modeling tab ➤ Edit, select Use NURMS. This will show the model with smoothing; but because the Symmetry modifier is still active, the end result is not shown, so you see only half of the model smoothed.

5. From the Modifier Stack toolbar, select the Show End Result On/Off Toggle button (![icon]) to show the effect of the entire stack. Now the whole model is visible, as shown in Figure 7.10.

> Any edits you make to the original half of the mesh from the Symmetry modifier in the stack will also occur on the other half when the Symmetry modifier is applied to the mesh.

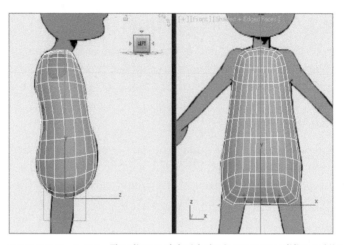

FIGURE 7.10 The alien model with the Symmetry modifier and Use NURMS applied

The model with Use NURMS applied reveals some problems. In the next exercises, you will begin blocking out the arms and refining the torso. Save the file. To check your work, open the c07_ex4_symmetry_end.max file in the c07_ CharacterModel project folder.

Exercise 7.5: Blocking Out the Arms

The arms for the alien are skinny and slightly longer than a human's arms, but other than that, they are similar, with hands, wrists, elbows, and so on. Thus, the alien arms will have three sections: upper arm, lower arm, and hand. Continue with the previous exercise's scene file, or open the c07_ex5_arm_ start.max scene file in the scenes folder of the c07_CharacterModel project folder.

1. Select the model, and start by removing the Symmetry modifier by right-clicking the modifier and choosing Delete from the menu. Then from the Ribbon ➤ Modeling tab ➤ Edit, turn off Use NURMS.

2. Move the Image Plane Front object back along the Y-axis to 20.0.

3. Select the model, and on the Ribbon ➤ Modeling tab ➤ Polygon Modeling panel, enter Polygon mode.

4. From the Left viewport, select the polygon where the armhole is if it isn't already selected, as shown in Figure 7.11.

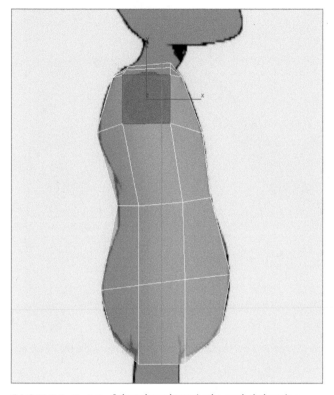

FIGURE 7.11   Select the polygon in the armhole location.

5. Switch to the Front viewport, and in the Ribbon ➤ Modeling tab ➤ Polygons panel, choose Bevel ➤ Bevel Settings. Use the default settings, which are Bevel Height: 10.0 and Bevel Outline: -1.0, as shown in Figure 7.12. Click OK.

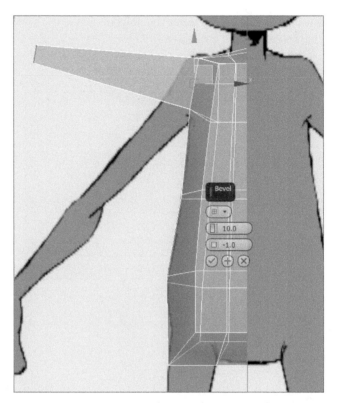

FIGURE 7.12 Position the arm polygons to match the image plane.

6. Use the Move tool to position the new extruded arm to line up with the front-view image.

7. Select the Rotate tool, and rotate the selected polygon 65 degrees on the Z-axis, as shown in Figure 7.13.

8. The polygon at the end of the arm should still be selected, so select the Ribbon ➤ Modeling tab ➤ Polygons panel ➤ Bevel ➤ Bevel Settings. Change the settings on this first bevel to Bevel Height: **1.0** and Bevel Outline: **0.5**. Click Apply and Continue. Then set the second bevel to Bevel Height: **6.5** and Bevel Outline: **-0.5**, as shown in Figure 7.14. Click OK.

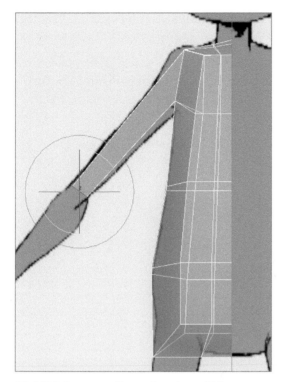

FIGURE 7.13 Rotate the polygon 65 degrees.

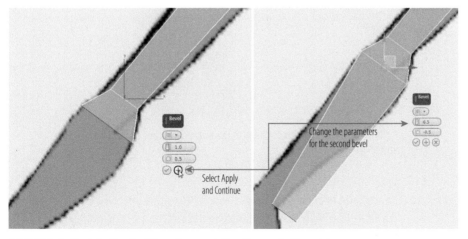

FIGURE 7.14 Bevel settings for completing the arm to the wrist

9. Use the Move tool to line up the arm with the front-view image at the wrist.

10. In the Ribbon ➤ Modeling tab ➤ Edit, select Use NURMS; now the problems with arms are more evident, as shown in Figure 7.15. Turn off Use NURMS, because it is easier to fix these issues on the rough model.

11. Enter Vertex mode; select the vertex at the armpit, and move it down to line up more accurately with the image plane, as shown in Figure 7.15.

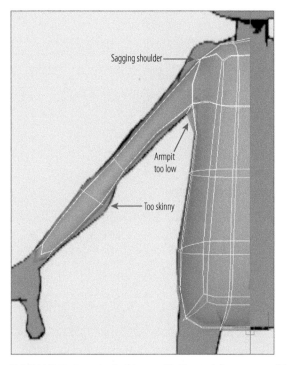

FIGURE 7.15 Problems with the model are more evident with Use NURMS active.

12. Repeat the process on the vertices at the shoulder and lower arm. Turn on Use NURMS again and adjust further. Some parts of the model will not look correct even with the changes. More subdivisions need to be added.

13. Select the Ribbon ➤ Modeling tab ➤ Edit ➤ Swift Loop, and add a loop below where the shoulder begins and another a little bit below that. You should still be in Vertex mode, so move the vertices again to better match the image plane, as shown in Figure 7.16. Do all this with Use NURMS turned on. When you have finished, turn off Use NURMS.

The orange cage surrounding the model is the Use NURMS cage, which shows the model before the subdivisions have been added. Turn on Use NURMS to see the cage.

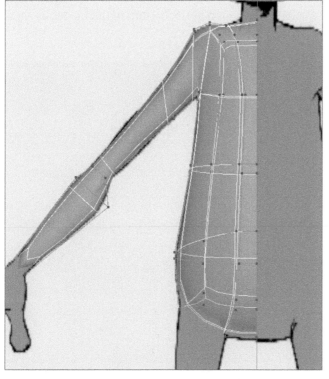

FIGURE 7.16 Use Swift Loop to add edges to fix problems with the model.

Now you are starting to see some shape in the torso and arm. Save the file. To check your work, open the c07_ex5_arm_end.max file in the c07_CharacterModel project folder.

Exercise 7.6: Blocking Out the Leg

The legs for the alien are exactly like a human's legs with three sections: upper thigh, knee, and calf. For the leg modeling, you will use a different technique

Certification
Objective

than you used for the arm. The method has no official name, so for this chapter, it will be called the Shift+Move Extrude method. This method is similar to using the Extrude or Bevel tools and works only with Border and open-ended Edges modes. For this chapter, you will use the Border mode. Continue with the previous exercise's scene file, or open the `c07_ex6_leg_start.max` scene file in the `scenes` folder of the `c07_CharacterModel` project folder.

1. In the Perspective viewport, select the model. Enter Polygon mode and select the polygon at the bottom of the model, as shown in Figure 7.17.

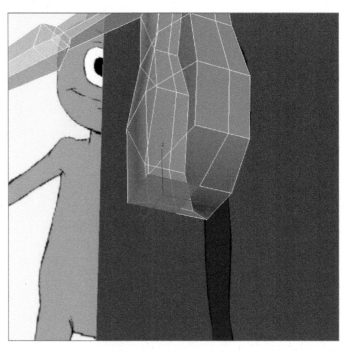

FIGURE 7.17 Select the polygon at the bottom of the alien model to begin blocking out the leg.

Border mode utilizes the edges surrounding a hole in a model. Border mode has all the traditional modeling tools like Extrude and Bevel.

2. Delete the polygon.

3. Enter Border mode ( ).

4. Select the border of the deleted polygon.

5. Press W on the keyboard to access the Move tool.

6. While looking through the Front viewport, hold down the Shift key on the keyboard and move the border down until it sits at the center of the alien's thigh.

7. Switch to the Scale tool (R), and scale the border down so it matches the width of the thigh in the image plane, as shown in Figure 7.18.

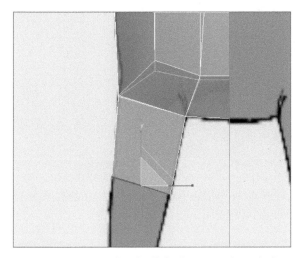

FIGURE 7.18   Use the Shift+Move Extrude method to extrude the thigh and use Scale to change the width of thigh.

8. Switch to the Left viewport, and adjust the model to match the image plane.

9. Repeat the Shift+Move Extrude method to extrude down to just above the knee.

10. Use the Scale and Move tools to adjust the position and size of that section of the leg to match the Front and Left viewports, as shown in Figure 7.19.

11. Use the Shift+Move method again and extrude the leg a small amount in the middle of the knee area, and then repeat to extrude just below the knee.

12. Use the Scale and Move tools to adjust the position and size of that section of the leg to match the Front and Left viewports.

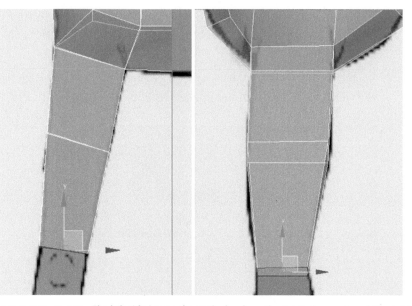

FIGURE 7.19   The left side image shows the leg from the Front viewport, and the right side image shows the leg from the Left viewport.

Notice how Use NURMS is working at the bottom of the leg, but at the end of the arm, it is not. This is because of the deleted polygon. Use NURMS ignores areas where the geometry is deleted.

▶

13. Repeat the Shift+Move method and extrude to the center of the calf; repeat to extrude to above the ankle.

14. Switch to Vertex mode, and move vertices to further adjust the model to match the image planes from the front and left views, as shown in Figure 7.20. Exit Vertex mode by clicking the Vertex button in the Ribbon ➢ Modeling tab ➢ Polygon Modeling.

15. Go to the Ribbon ➢ Modeling tab ➢ Edit ➢ Use NURMS.

16. In the Modify panel ➢ Modifier List, choose the Symmetry modifier. Check the Flip box to see the whole model.

17. Press Alt+X to exit See-Through mode.

18. At the bottom of the interface, select the Isolate Selection Toggle button (💡).

19. Exit Edged Faces mode by selecting a viewport and pressing F4 on the keyboard. Repeat this in all viewports.

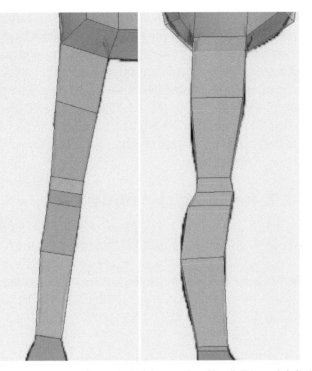

FIGURE 7.20 Front view of the completed leg (left image); left view of the completed leg (right image)

20. Enter Polygon mode, select the polygon at the end of the arm, and delete it. This will create the same look as at the bottom of the leg. The completed model is shown in Figure 7.21.

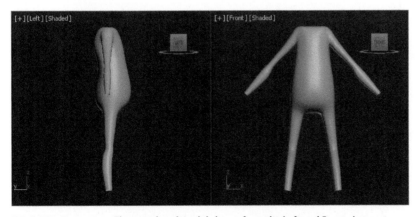

FIGURE 7.21 The completed model shown from the Left and Front viewports

The completed model looks pretty good. The body itself isn't all that exciting. The alien has a soft and blobby body—too much junk food and not enough exercise. There are a few details that need to be refined. The area where the arm and chest meet is too squared off; this transition needs to be smoothed out. The chest needs some simple breast detail. The knees need more definition. The alien has no backside; it looks just like the front. So adding some shoulder blades and some backside definition will help, like a butt crack—sorry to have to be blunt! Save the file. To check your work, open the c07_ex6_leg_end.max file in the c07_CharacterModel project folder.

Exercise 7.7: Refining the Body

Certification Objective Some of the areas to refine are the knees, groin, chest, shoulders (front and back), and backside, as shown in Figure 7.22. Continue with the previous exercise's scene file, or open the c07_ex7_body_start.max scene file in the scenes folder of the c07_CharacterModel project folder. This file has the alien model isolated. The Symmetry modifier has been removed, and Use NURMS is turned off. If you are using your own file, exit Isolate mode, remove the Symmetry modifier, and turn off Use NURMS.

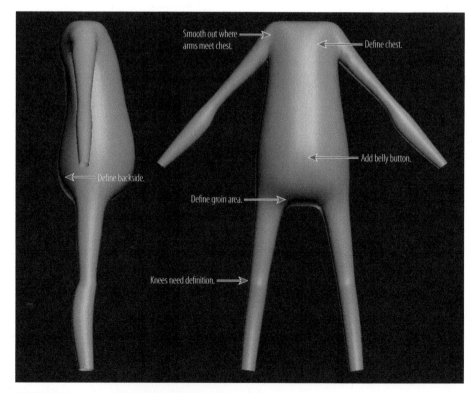

FIGURE 7.22 **Areas to be refined on the model**

Adding Detail to the Knee

The knee doesn't need anything too complicated, just a few extra edges to add some detail.

1. Select the model and enter Edge mode.

2. Select the edge at the front of the knee; double-click on the edge to select all the edges in the loop around the knee.

3. In the Ribbon ➤ Modeling tab ➤ Edges ➤ Chamfer ➤ Chamfer Settings caddy, change the Edge Chamfer Amount to **0.6**, and click OK.

4. Select the Ribbon ➤ Modeling tab ➤ Edit. At the bottom of the tab under Constraints, select Constrain to Edge (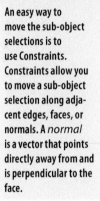).

5. Switch to Vertex mode and, from the Left viewport, move the vertices at the back of the knee closer together, as shown in Figure 7.23. Make sure you drag a selection box around the vertices, because from the Left viewport, you see only the vertex facing the camera, but there is another vertex. You can also turn on See-Through mode so you can see both front and back vertices.

6. Now move the vertices at the front of the knee to the right (from the Left viewport). You want the edges sticking out more, as shown in Figure 7.23. Click the Constrain to None ( ) button to exit Constraints.

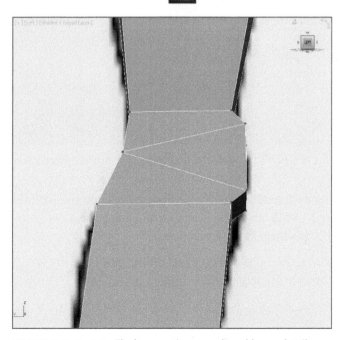

FIGURE 7.23 The knee vertices moved to add more detail

Double-clicking on an edge is a shortcut to the Ribbon ➤ Modeling tab ➤ Modify Selection ➤ Loop tool.

An easy way to move the sub-object selections is to use Constraints. Constraints allow you to move a sub-object selection along adjacent edges, faces, or normals. A *normal* is a vector that points directly away from and is perpendicular to the face.

Refining the Groin Area

The alien doesn't have any sex organs; the area just needs to be smoothed out and a crease needs to be added where the leg meets the body.

1. Using Swift Loop, add an edge to the top of the thigh.

2. Add another edge loop on the torso between the thigh and the center of the body. Refer to Figure 7.24 to see where it needs to be placed.

3. Move the vertices (use the Constrain to Edge tool), as shown in Figure 7.24. These simple edges will add a very subtle crease at this area. To exit Constraints, click the Constrain to None button.

FIGURE 7.24 With vertices added, the groin area is more refined.

4. To see what the model looks like now, turn on Use NURMS. In the Use NURMS tab in the Ribbon ➤ Modeling tab, change Iterations to 2, as shown in Figure 7.25.

5. Exit Vertex mode by selecting the Vertex icon in the Ribbon ➤ Modeling tab ➤ Polygon Modeling.

Use NURMS can also be a floating menu.

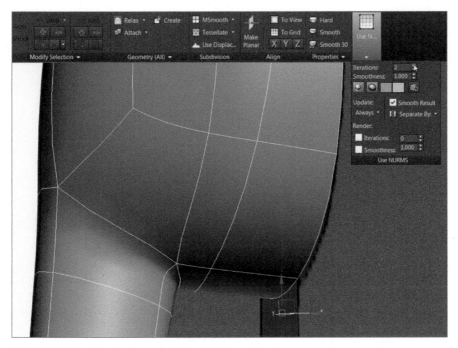

F I G U R E 7 . 2 5 **Groin area with Use NURMS active**

Refining the Backside

The backside looks very similar to the front. To give it some distinction, you will add a backside "crack," a crease to set it apart from the front. Turn off Use NURMS to continue.

1. Select the alien body and enter Isolate Selection mode.

2. Using the ViewCube®, rotate the Perspective view so the backside can be seen.

3. In the Modify panel ➤ Modifier List, select the Symmetry modifier. In the modifier stack, select the Show End Results On/Off toggle (![icon]), which sits directly below the modifier stack. This will allow you to work on the model and see the other side of the model updating.

4. Enter Vertex mode.

5. Select the vertex at the intersection of the backside and leg. Zoom in very close because the vertices are very close together. You will need to select the left side vertex closest to the model center, as shown in Figure 7.26.

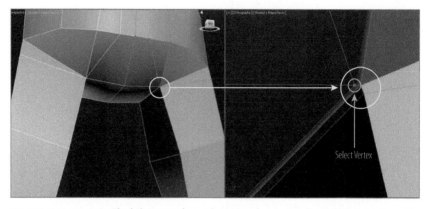

FIGURE 7.26 The left image shows the zoomed-out area; the right image shows the zoomed-in area where you need to select the vertex.

6. In the Ribbon ➤ Modeling tab ➤ Edit ➤ Constraints, select Constrain to Edge.

7. Move the selected vertex toward the center of the model.

8. Repeat the move on the two vertices directly above the vertex moved in step 7, as shown in Figure 7.27.

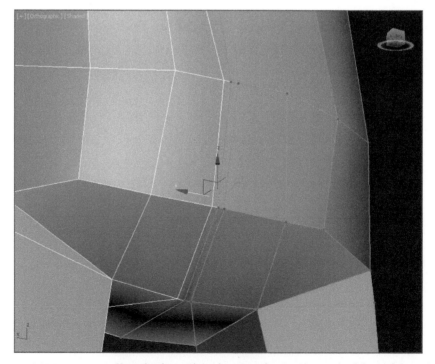

FIGURE 7.27 Move the three selected vertices closer to the center of the model.

9. Select the three vertices at the center of the model.

10. In the Ribbon ➢ Modeling tab ➢ Edit ➢ Constraints, select Constrain to Normal. This will isolate the movement perpendicular to the model.

11. Move the select vertices in toward the inside of the model.

12. Turn on Use NURMS, and exit Vertex mode. Click away from the model to deselect it. The completed backside is shown in Figure 7.28.

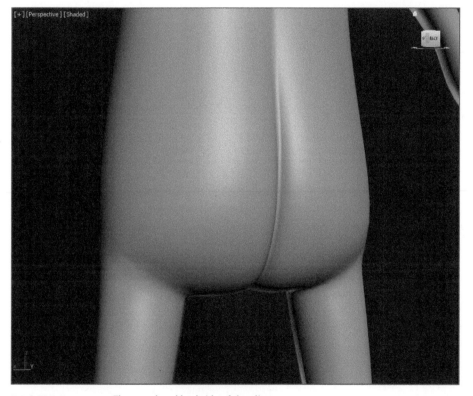

FIGURE 7.28 The completed backside of the alien

Remaining Refinements

At this point, most of the things that need to be refined have been refined. There are a few things you can add using the same techniques used in the previous section. For example, you could add a few extra loops in the elbow area, as shown in Figure 7.29.

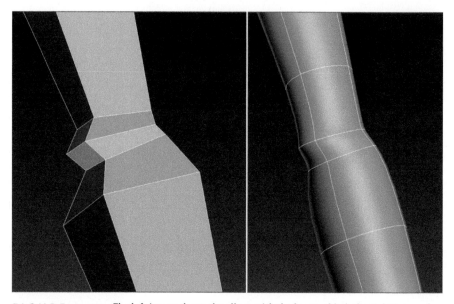

FIGURE 7.29   The left image shows the elbow with the loops added; the right image shows the changes with Use NURMS turned on.

If the Symmetry modifier is active, you won't be able to make some of the changes to the model in separate halves. You will learn how to remedy this in the following chapter. Save your file. To check your final results against the example, open the c07_ex7_body_end.max file in the c07_CharacterModel project folder. The final alien body is shown in Figure 7.30.

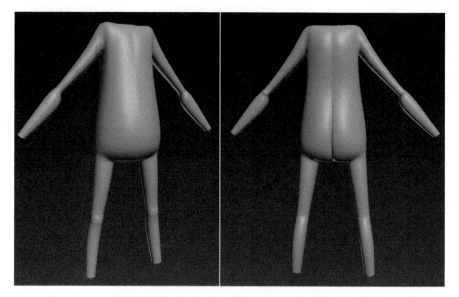

FIGURE 7.30   The final alien body; the left image is the front, and the right image is the back.

Exercise 7.8: Building the Neck

Before you can build the head, you have to build up the neck. Either continue with the exercise scene file from the previous section, or open the c07_ex8_neck_start.max scene file in the scenes folder of the c07_CharacterModel project folder on the book's web page at www.sybex.com/go/3dsmax2016essentials. If you are continuing with your file, make sure to exit Isolate Selection mode.

Certification Objective

1. Select the alien body and go to the Modify panel. In the modifier stack, right-click the Symmetry modifier and choose Delete from the menu.

2. In the Edit tab of the modeling ribbon, turn off Use NURMS.

3. Enter See-Through mode (Alt+X).

4. In the Polygon Modeling tab, enter Polygon mode. Select the two polygons where the neck would be placed, and delete the polygons using the Delete key on the keyboard.

5. In the Polygon Modeling tab, enter Edge mode.

6. Select the edges where the polygons were deleted, as shown in Figure 7.31.

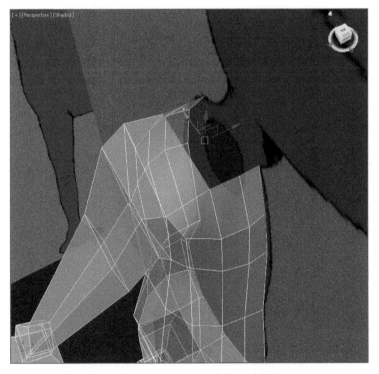

FIGURE 7.31 Select the edges around the neck hole.

7. Switch to the Select and Move tool (W) if it isn't already selected.

8. In the Left viewport, hold down the Shift key; and with the Move tool, move the edges halfway up the neck and slightly forward, following the image plane (the Shift+Move Extrude method). Release the Shift key.

9. Shift+Move again to extrude the edges to the top of the neck, as shown in Figure 7.32. Exit See-Through mode (Alt+X).

F I G U R E   7 . 3 2   Use the Shift+Move Extrude method to create two more sets of polygons for the alien's neck.

10. The neck is too square. To round it out, you will add another edge to the top of the arm and the side of the neck. In the

Ribbon ≻ Modeling tab ≻ Edit tab ≻ Swift Loop, add a loop on the middle top of the arm, as shown in Figure 7.33.

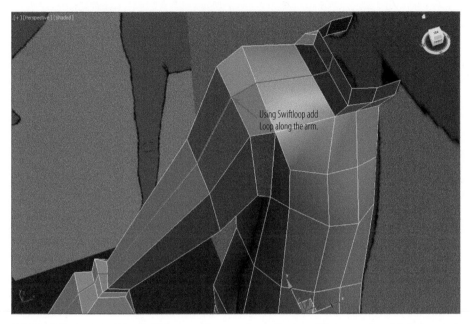

FIGURE 7.33 Using Swift Loop, add a new edge to the top of the arm and neck to help round out the neck.

11. Enter Vertex mode; select and move the vertices at the neck to round out the neck, as shown in Figure 7.34.

12. Switch to the Front viewport, and enter See-Through mode.

13. The area of the neck where it meets the shoulder needs more definition. In the Ribbon ≻ Modeling tab ≻ Edit tab, select Swift Loop and add a loop between the lower loop at the neck and the loop at the shoulder. You can do this while still in Vertex mode. Exit Swift Loop by right-clicking in the selected viewport.

14. From the Front viewport, move the vertices to better follow the neck and shoulder in the image plane, as shown in Figure 7.35. Exit See-Through mode.

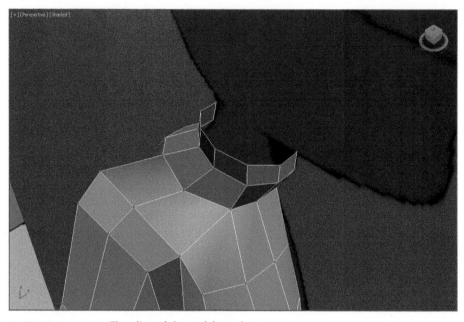

F I G U R E   7 . 3 4   The adjusted shape of the neck

F I G U R E   7 . 3 5   Adjust the vertices to match the neck of the alien in the image plane.

15. The arm needs to be adjusted. The new loop that runs down the arm will flatten it out when NURMS is applied. So, select the vertices running down the outside of the arm and move them up so that the inside edge is higher than the outside edges, as shown in Figure 7.36.

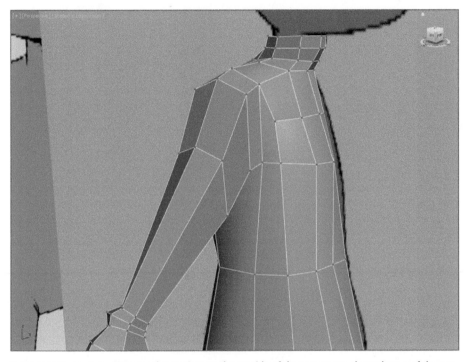

FIGURE 7.36 **Move up the vertices on the outside of the arm to round out the top of the arm.**

16. Exit Vertex mode. Check the model by turning on Use NURMS. The final neck and arm are shown in Figure 7.37.

Save the file. To check your work, open the c07_ex8_neck_end.max scene file in the scenes folder of the c08_CharacterModel project folder.

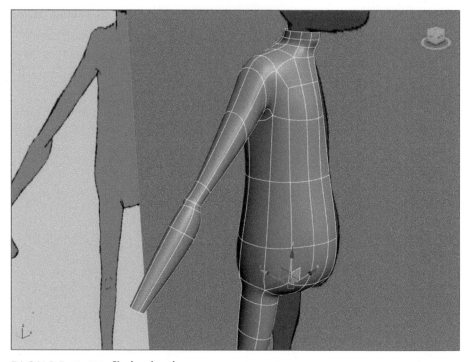

FIGURE 7.37   Final neck and arm

Now You Know

In this chapter, you learned how to begin creating the basic form of the alien character. First, you used reference planes of the alien, and then, from a simple box, you formed a torso to match the general shapes shown in the reference images. You extruded and shaped the arms and legs to match as well. As you can see, the more you model, the easier the process becomes and the more detailed and finessed your models turn out. In the next chapter, you'll create the alien hands, feet, and head, and then add the remaining body refinements.

CHAPTER 8

Character Modeling Part II

Realistic computer-generated (CG) characters are common in television and films; they appear as stunt doubles, as members of vast crowds, and as primary characters. Sometimes using a CG character works better than using a real person. Using a CG stunt double is safer and sometimes cheaper than using a live stunt person, and weird creatures can be created with better clarity by using CG rather than puppetry or special makeup effects.

In this chapter, you will continue with the model of the alien, focusing on using the Editable Poly toolset to create an alien model suitable for character animation and for use in a game engine.

In this chapter, you'll learn to

▶ **Create the alien head**

▶ **Create the alien hands**

▶ **Create the alien feet**

▶ **Complete the alien**

Creating the Alien Head

The alien's head will consist of three parts: the neck, the head shape, and the face (eye and mouth). The easiest way to create these is to start with the head shape.

Exercise 8.1: Blocking Out the Head

Certification
Objective

The head is the most important part of the alien, or any humanoid/anthropomorphic (having human characteristics) character. Its most important feature is the face, which communicates expressions and moods and allows people to relate to this character. The head itself is easy, but the face is another story. The face is more complex and needs more detail than any other part of the alien. Set your project to the c8_CharacterModel project folder that you downloaded to your hard drive from the companion web page at www.sybex .com/go/3dsmax2016essentials. Open the c08_ex1_head_start.max scene file in the scenes folder of the c08_CharacterModel project. This process starts with a simple primitive box.

1. Right-click in the Perspective viewport to select. Go to the Create panel ➢ Geometry ➢ Standard Primitives, and select Box. In the Keyboard Entry rollout, input the following dimensions: Length = 9.0, Width = 9.0, Height = 13.5. Select Create.

2. Go to the Modify panel, and in the Box Parameters rollout, change the following settings: Length Segs = 3, Width Segs = 3, and Height = 3.

3. Enter See-Through mode (Alt+X), and then move the box so it is aligned with the alien head in the Left and Front viewports, as shown in Figure 8.1.

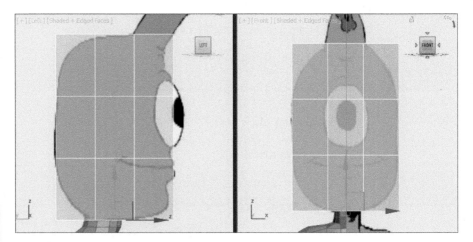

FIGURE 8.1   Align the box with the alien head.

4. Rename the box **Alien Head**.

5. In the Ribbon ➢ Modeling tab ➢ Polygon Modeling, choose Convert to Poly.

6. The edges that are running around the eyes need to be moved so that they surround the eyes. Enter Edge mode, and from the Front

viewport, select the top horizontal edge (make sure the entire edge loop is selected by double-clicking), and move it above the eye. Repeat for all the edges around the eye so it looks like Figure 8.2.

Double-clicking an edge is a shortcut to select the edge loop.

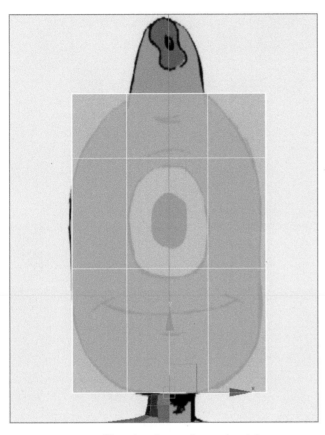

FIGURE 8.2 Move the edges so they surround the eye.

7. Now it's time to make this box more spherical. Enter Vertex mode, and from the Front viewport, select the four vertices at the corners by dragging a selection box around the vertices; this will select the four in front and four in back.

8. Switch to the Scale tool (R), make sure the Transform gizmo is in the center of the box, and scale by centering the cursor inside the scale transform triangle and dragging until the corners are aligned with the image plane.

9. Change to the Left viewport and repeat the process. Then repeat the process from the Top viewport. When finished, the box will look like Figure 8.3. Exit Vertex mode.

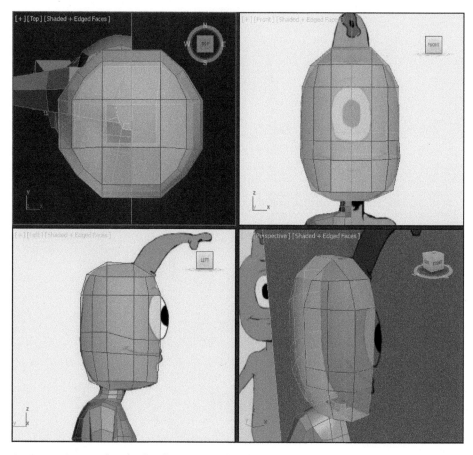

FIGURE 8.3 By selecting the corners and scaling them inward, you make the head more spherical.

Save the file. To check your work, open the c08_ex1_head_end.max scene file in the scenes folder of the c08_CharacterModel project folder.

Exercise 8.2: Building the Nose and Eye

Certification Objective

It's time to build the alien's nose, which is coming out of his forehead. Either continue with the previous file or open the c08_ex2_nose_start.max scene file in the scenes folder of the c08_CharacterModel project folder.

1. Select the alien's head, enter Polygon mode, and select the polygon at the top of the head where the forehead is.

2. In the Ribbon ➤ Modeling tab ➤ Polygons ➤ Bevel ➤ Bevel Settings, set the Bevel Height to **2.5** and the Bevel Outline to **-0.15, press Enter**, and then click the Apply and Continue button.

3. Click the Apply and Continue button again, which will repeat the same setting from step 2.

4. Click the Apply and Continue button again, and then select OK to finish.

5. Switch to Vertex mode and adjust the vertices to follow the alien's nose in the image plane, as shown in Figure 8.4. Exit Vertex mode when you are finished.

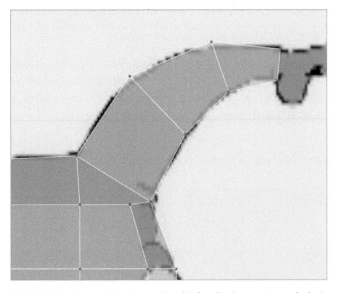

FIGURE 8.4 In Vertex mode, edit the alien's nose to match the image plane.

6. Enter Polygon mode, and select the polygon at the eye.

7. To create the eye socket, go to the Ribbon ➤ Modeling tab ➤ Polygons ➤ Bevel ➤ Bevel Settings. Create three bevels for the eye socket:

   Bevel 1:

   a. Bevel Height: 0.0

   b. Bevel Outline: -0.1

   c. Press Enter

   d. Click the Apply and Continue button (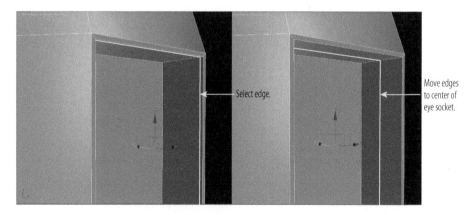).

   Bevel 2:

   a. Bevel Height: -0.1

   b. Bevel Outline: 0.0

   c. Press Enter.

   d. Click the Apply and Continue button.

   Bevel 3:

   a. Bevel Height: -1.5

   b. Bevel Outline: 0.0

   c. Press Enter.

   d. Click OK.

8. To add a bit of a ridge around the eye, you will move around some of the edges that you created in the previous step. Enter Edge mode and double-click the edge on the inside of the eye socket, as shown in Figure 8.5 (left image).

9. Use the Move tool and move the edges about halfway to the inside of the eye socket, as shown in Figure 8.5 (right image).

FIGURE 8.5   Select edges to begin shaping the eye (left image). Move the edge toward the inside of the eye socket (right image).

10. Select the edges shown in Figure 8.6 (left image) and move this edge toward the outside of the eye socket. The eye socket will now resemble Figure 8.6 (right image).

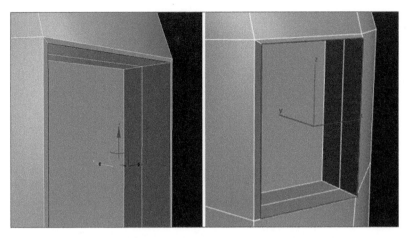

FIGURE 8.6   Move the new edges to create a small ridge around the eye socket.

11. The nose needs to be more defined, so at the base, add another edge loop using Swift Loop (select the Ribbon ➤ Modeling tab ➤ Edit ➤ Swift Loop), and right-click to exit.

12. Enter Border mode and select the edges at the end of the nose. In the Ribbon ➤ Geometry (All), select Cap Poly. This places a new polygon at the end of the nose.

13. Switch to Polygon mode, and select the new polygon at the end of the nose. Then go to the Modeling tab ➤ Polygons ➤ Bevel ➤ Bevel Settings; Create four bevels for the nose

   Bevel 1:

   a. Bevel Height: 0.0

   b. Bevel Outline: 0.2

   c. Press Enter

   d. Click the Apply and Continue button.

   Bevel 2:

   a. Bevel Height: 0.3

   b. Bevel Outline: 0.0

   c. Press Enter

   d. Click the Apply and Continue button.

   Bevel 3:

   a. Bevel Height: 0.0

   b. Bevel Outline: -0.2

    c. Press Enter

    d. Click the Apply and Continue button.

    Bevel 4:

    a. Bevel Height: -0.2

    b. Bevel Outline: -0.15

    c. Press Enter

    d. Click OK.

14. The head started out as a box, and even with all the changes, it still has a hint of the box about it. Deleting a few edges will give the head a more rounded look. Select the edges where the corners of the box were, as shown in Figure 8.7.

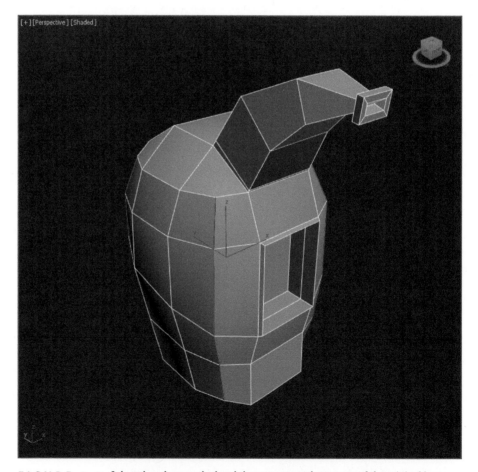

FIGURE 8.7 Select the edges on the head that were once the corners of the original box.

15. To delete the edges, hold down the Ctrl key and press the Backspace key on your keyboard. This is a shortcut for choosing the Ribbon ➤ Modeling tab ➤ Edges ➤ Remove. It is very important to hold down the Ctrl key while using this tool so that the associated vertices will be removed where edges cross the remaining edges.

16. This makes the head thinner than before, so switch to Vertex mode and change to the Front viewport. Move the vertices out to match Figure 8.8. Repeat the process for the Left viewport. Exit See-Through mode.

FIGURE 8.8 From the Front viewport, in Vertex mode, move the vertices so they match the alien's jaw line in the image plane (right). Repeat from the Left viewport (left).

17. To test the head so far, turn on Use NURMS; in the Use NURMS tab, set the iterations to 2. This will show the head smoothed out so you will be able to see any flaws. At this point, you can edit the head to refine and more closely match the image plane, as shown in Figure 8.9.

The head is not complete; the nose tip needs to be refined. This will be addressed later in the chapter. Save the file with which you are working. To check your work, open the c08_ex2_nose_end.max scene file in the scenes folder of the c08_CharacterModel project.

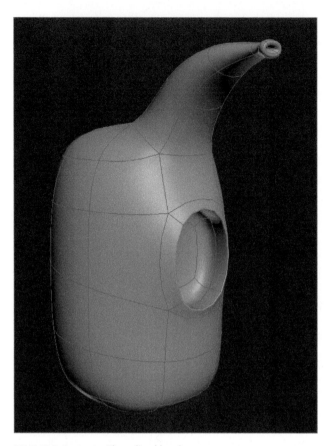

FIGURE 8.9   The refined head

Building the Alien Hand

With just three fingers and a thumb, the alien hand is simple and cartoonish. You won't be adding details such as lines on the palm or nails. In this section, you will create three simple fingers for the alien.

Exercise 8.3: Building the Palm of the Hand

Certification
Objective

Continue with the previous exercise's scene file, or open the c08_ex3_palm_start.max scene file in the scenes folder of the c08_CharacterModel project folder. The first thing to do is to merge in the image plane containing the hand.

1. In the Applications menu, choose Import ➤ Merge.

2. Navigate to the scenes folder of the c08_CharacterModel project folder. Open c08_ex3_hand_image plane.max.

3. In the Merge dialog box, select Hand Image Plane and click OK. The image plane will land in the correct spot, below the arm. If it is not in the correct position, move the image plane so it is beneath the end of the arm, as shown in Figure 8.10.

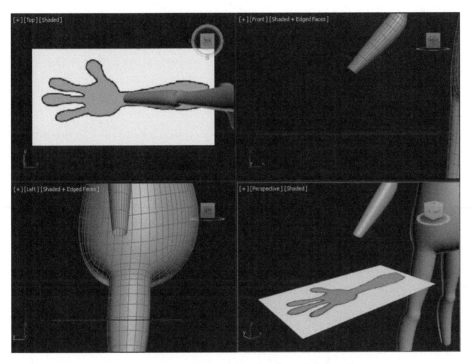

FIGURE 8.10 The hand image plane positioned at the end of the wrist

4. In the Create panel ➤ Geometry ➤ Standard Primitives, in the Top viewport, create a box with the parameters shown in Figure 8.11. Name the box **Alien Hand**.

When you create a box, its color is randomly assigned. So don't be concerned if the color you see is different from the color in the images in this book.

FIGURE 8.11   The parameters for the box that will create the hand

5. In the Ribbon ➤ Modeling tab, choose Polygon Modeling ➤ Convert to Poly.

6. Turn on See-Through mode (Alt+X).

Save the file. To check your work, open the `c08_ex3_palm_end.max` scene file in the scenes folder of the `c08_CharacterModel` project folder.

Exercise 8.4: Beveling the Fingers

Certification
Objective

Using Bevel to create the fingers allows you to extrude and scale the shape of the fingers with a single tool. Continue with the previous exercise's scene file, or open the `c08_ex4_fingers_start.max` scene file in the scenes folder of the `c08_CharacterModel` project folder.

1. Select the Alien Hand object. Enter Vertex mode if you are not already in it. Use the Move tool to rearrange the vertices to match what is shown in Figure 8.12.

2. In Polygon mode, select the three polygons on the front of the hand, where the fingers will be, as shown in Figure 8.13.

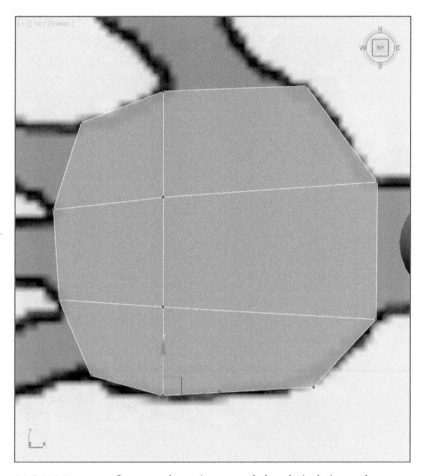

FIGURE 8.12 Rearrange the vertices to match the palm in the image plane.

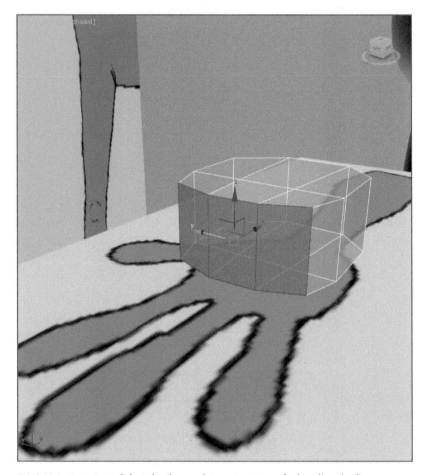

FIGURE 8.13 Select the three polygons to prepare for beveling the fingers.

3. From the ribbon, choose the Modeling tab ➤ Polygons ➤ Bevel ➤ Bevel Settings, set Bevel Type to By Polygon, enter a Height value of 1.2, and press Enter. Set the Outline amount to -0.2 and press Enter. Click the Apply and Continue button. Now enter a Height value of 1.2 and press Enter. Set Outline to 0.3, press Enter, and click the Apply and Continue button. Now enter a Height value of 1.2 and press Enter. Set Outline to -0.3, press Enter, and click OK.

4. Select the polygon on the side of the palm close to the wrist where the thumb will be. In the Modeling tab of the ribbon, choose Polygons ➤ Bevel ➤ Bevel Settings, set Bevel Type to By Polygon,

enter a Height value of **0.6**, and press Enter. Set Outline to **-0.3**, press Enter, and click OK.

5. Switch to Vertex mode; arrange the vertices of the new thumb, and extrude to follow the image plane, as shown in Figure 8.14.

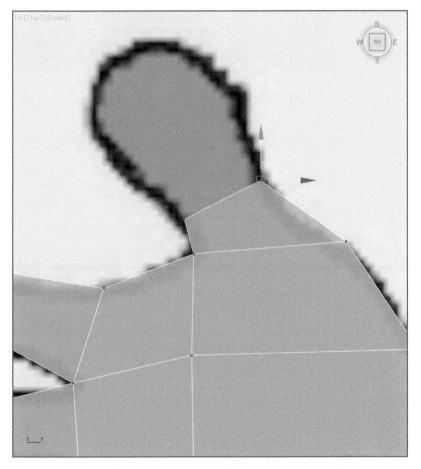

FIGURE 8.14 Rearrange the thumb vertices to follow the thumb in the image plane.

6. Enter Polygon mode and select the polygon at the end of the thumb. Create a new bevel, set the Height to **0.9** and Outline to **0.25**, and press Enter. Then click the Apply and Continue button. Set the Height to **0.9** and Outline to **-0.25**, press Enter, and click OK.

7. In the ribbon, select the Modeling tab ≻ Edit ≻ Use NURMS. In the Use NURMS tab, set Iterations to 2.

8. Enter Vertex mode, and select and move the vertices to better fit the hand in the image plane shown in the Top viewport, as shown in Figure 8.15. Then switch to the Front viewport.

▶

You can edit an object's sub-objects (vertices, edges, polygons) while NURMS is turned on.

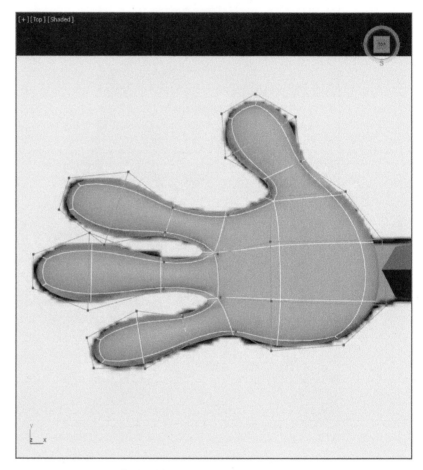

FIGURE 8.15 The hand from the Top viewport

If you continued with the file from the previous exercise, continue with steps 9 through 11. If you started with the c08_ex4_fingers_start.max scene file, skip to step 12.

9. In the Application menu, choose Import ➤ Merge.

10. Navigate to the scenes folder of the c08_CharacterModel project. Open c08_ex4_hand_image plane side.max.

11. In the Merge dialog box, select Hand Image Plane Side and click OK. The image plane will land in the correct spot, under the arm. If it is not in the correct position, move the image plane so it is under the end of the arm and lines up with the hand.

12. Select the hand, enter Vertex mode, and continue to edit the hand to match the hand image plane side. The tops of the fingers need to be flattened out. Make any other changes you think are appropriate.

13. The thumb needs to be angled down. Enter Polygon mode, and select the polygon at the end of the thumb.

14. In the Modeling tab of the ribbon, choose Modify Selection ➤ Grow, and click Grow three times to select the remaining thumb polygons.

15. Switch to the Rotate tool; in the main toolbar, select Local from the Reference Coordinate System drop-down menu, as shown in Figure 8.16.

FIGURE 8.16 Select Local from the Reference Coordinate System drop-down menu.

16. Rotate the polygons 60 degrees along the Y-axis (use the green control handle on the gizmo).

17. Switch to the Move tool, and move the thumb polygons down into a more realistic position. Don't worry if they don't line up perfectly with the thumb in the image plane.

18. Select the polygon at the wrist and delete it. Exit Polygon mode by clicking the Polygon icon.

Oops! The hand was modeled correctly, but the thumb was created on the wrong side. No problem—use the Mirror tool.

◄

19. From the Top viewport and in the main toolbar, select the Mirror tool (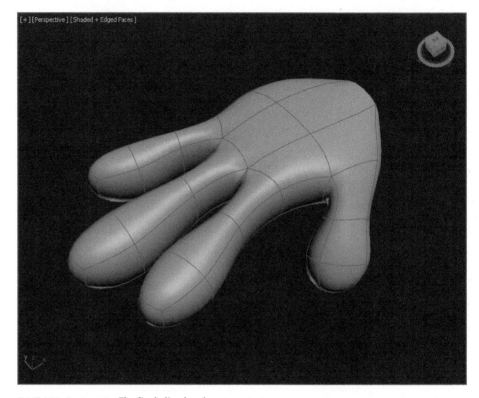). In the dialog box, change Mirror Axis to Y and click OK. Exit See-Through mode (Alt+X). The completed hand is shown in Figure 8.17.

F I G U R E   8 . 1 7   **The final alien hand**

Our alien has very simple hands: no nails, hair, wrinkles, or creases. It is not within the scope of this book to cover the tools to create these details. Use the tools you have been learning and experiment by adding various details to the hands. Perhaps you can start by adding fingernails; you can do this by beveling polygons at the tip of the fingers. Save the file you are working with; to check your work, open the c08_ex4_fingers_end.max scene file in the scenes folder of the c08_CharacterModel project.

Building the Foot

In this section, you will create a simple three-toed foot for the alien. The techniques you will use are very similar to those for modeling the hand. You'll start with a box to block out the foot, and then use Bevel to extrude the toes. Then you'll refine the shape and add NURMS to smooth out the foot.

Exercise 8.5: Blocking Out the Foot

Continue with the previous exercise's scene file, or open the c08_ex5_foot_start.max scene file in the scenes folder of the c08_CharacterModel project.

Certification Objective

In the Application menu, choose Import ➤ Merge, and then navigate to the scenes folder of the c08_CharacterModel project. Open the file c08_ex5_foot_image plane.max. In the Merge dialog box, select Foot Image Plane and click OK. The image plane will land in the correct spot, under the leg. If it is not in the correct position, move the image plane so it is under the end of the leg.

1. Select the alien body, head, hand, the Hand Image Plane object, and the Hand Image Side Plane object. Right-click to access the quad menu, and choose Hide Selection.

2. From the Top viewport, go to the Create Panel ➤ Geometry ➤ Standard Primitives, and create a box with parameters of Length = 8.0, Width = 5.0, Height = 3.0, Length Segs = 3, Width Segs = 3, and Height = 2. Name the box **Alien Foot**.

3. Turn on See-Through mode (Alt+X). From the Left viewport, switch to the Move tool and move the box so it is aligned with the foot in the image plane. Line up the back of the box with the heel in the image plane.

4. Convert the box to an editable polygon (from the Modeling tab of the ribbon, choose Polygon Modeling ➤ Convert to Poly). Enter Vertex mode; from the Top viewport, select the top two rows of vertices, change to the Scale tool, and scale the vertices in the X-axis together until they sit on the sides of the heel, as shown in Figure 8.18 (left images).

5. Now select the second row of vertices from the top and move it down below the heel, as also shown in Figure 8.18 (right images).

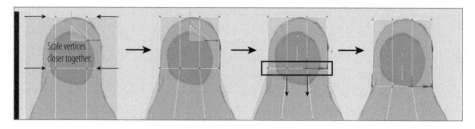

FIGURE 8.18 Select and scale the vertices together to form the heel; then select the second row from the top and move it down below the heel.

6. Switch to the Left viewport. Select and rearrange the middle and top rows of vertices to match the image in Figure 8.19.

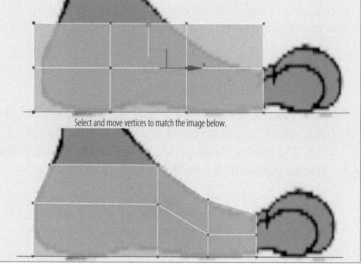

Select and move vertices to match the image below.

FIGURE 8.19 Edit the middle and top rows of vertices to further refine the foot.

7. Switch back to the Top viewport, and arrange the line of vertices at the base of the toes to match the image in Figure 8.20. This will help correctly align the toes for the bevel.

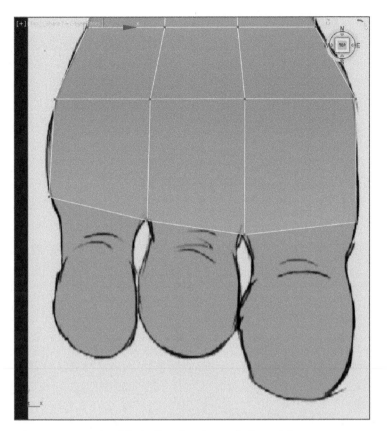

FIGURE 8.20   Edit the line of vertices at the base of the toes.

Save the file. To check your work, open the c08_ex5_foot_end.max scene file in the scenes folder of the c08_CharacterModel project.

Exercise 8.6: Beveling the Toes

As you did when you modeled the fingers, you'll use Bevel. But instead of beveling all the toes at the same time, you will do one at a time, using different settings for each toe. Continue with the previous exercise's scene file, or open the c08_ex6_toes_start.max scene file in the scenes folder of the c08_CharacterModel project.

Certification Objective

1. Select the foot, switch to Polygon mode, and select the polygons at the front of the foot where the smallest toe is.

2. From the Modeling tab of the ribbon, choose Polygons ➤ Bevel ➤ Bevel Settings. In the Bevel caddy, apply these settings:

Setting	Bevel Type	Height	Outline
Bevel 1	Local Normal	0.5	-0.3
Bevel 2	Local Normal	0.9	0.3
Bevel 3	Local Normal	0.9	-0.3

This will build the first toe; use the same technique to build the remaining toes. Don't worry if the geometry overlaps; the geometry smoothing that Use NURMS creates will fix it. The finalized toes are shown in Figure 8.21.

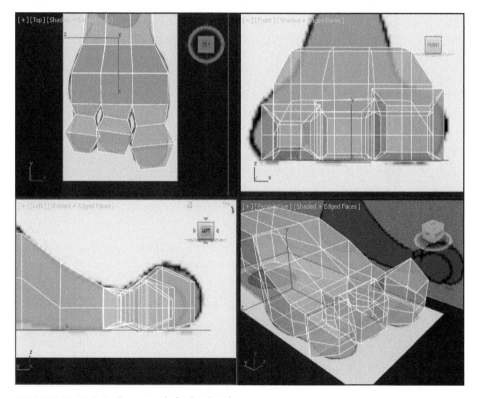

FIGURE 8.21 Toes extruded using Bevel

3. Now select the three polygons on the top back of the foot and delete them.

4. Enter Border mode (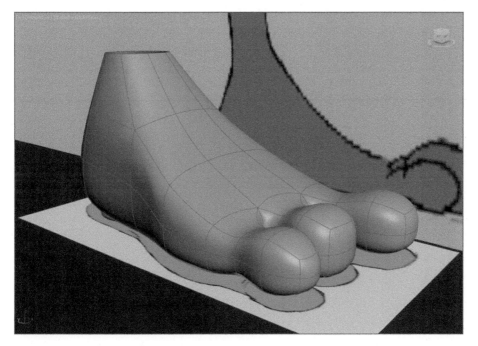). Border mode allows you to select a hole in a mesh so you can modify it with various tools. Select the border of the hole you made when you deleted the polygons in the previous step. This technique allows you to create the ankle.

5. Use the Shift+Move method you used on edges in the previous chapter. From the Left viewport, hold down the Shift key and move the border up along the Y-axis.

6. Switch to Vertex mode. Select and move the vertices at the top of the ankle in toward the ankle in the image plane.

7. Switch to the Front viewport and repeat the process. When you have finished, exit Vertex mode. Exit See-Through mode and select Use NURMS; the results are shown in Figure 8.22.

FIGURE 8.22   The finished foot with the ankle

Save the file. To check your work, open the c08_ex6_toes_end.max scene file in the scenes folder of the c08_CharacterModel project.

Completing the Alien

Now that all the parts of the alien are complete, you need to bring them all together. Once the alien is whole, you can further refine the model if desired. To begin this process, you need to attach the head, hand, and foot to the main alien body.

Exercise 8.7: Attaching to the Body

Certification
Objective

Attaching is easy; just click a button. However, you do need to address some issues before you can get to that point. To attach objects correctly, the objects need to have holes or borders where the objects can attach to each other. Best practice is to have an equal number of edges on both objects going into the border, as shown in Figure 8.23.

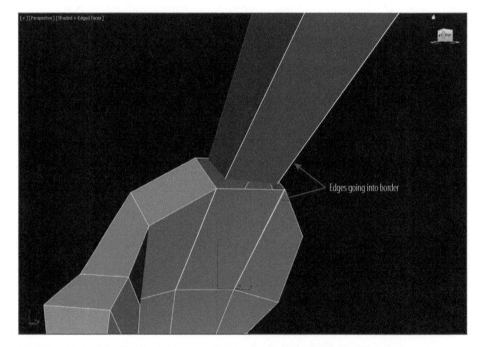

FIGURE 8.23   Hand and lower arm showing the borders meeting and the edges

Figure 8.23 shows the underside of the palm of the hand and the wrist of the alien body. It shows that an equal number of edges are present. Figure 8.24

shows the top side of the same palm and wrist. Notice how the wrist has an extra edge but the palm has two edges, the same as the underside.

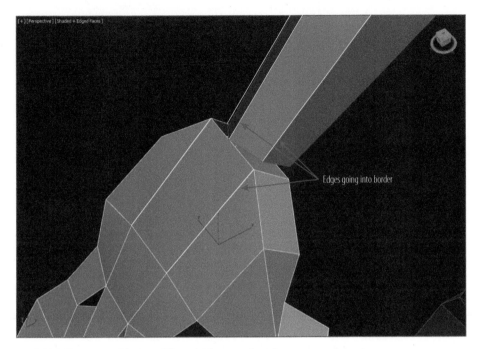

FIGURE 8.24 The top of the wrist has an extra edge.

In order to properly attach, the open edges of the wrist and hand have to have an equal number of edges, so you need to add one edge on the top side of the palm. You could use the Swift Loop tool, but that would add a loop from the top side of the palm to the bottom side. That won't do, so you'll use the Cut tool. Continue with the previous exercise's scene file, or open the c08_ex7_attach_start.max scene file in the scenes folder of the c08_CharacterModel project. If you continue with the file from the previous exercise, you will need to unhide the alien's body, head, and hand. You can either delete the image planes or just keep them hidden. Turn off Use NURMS for the hand and foot.

1. Select the hand and go to the Modeling tab of the ribbon. Choose Edit ➢ Cut. Cut by clicking from the base of the finger to the border opening, as shown in Figure 8.25. Right-click in the viewport to exit the Cut tool.

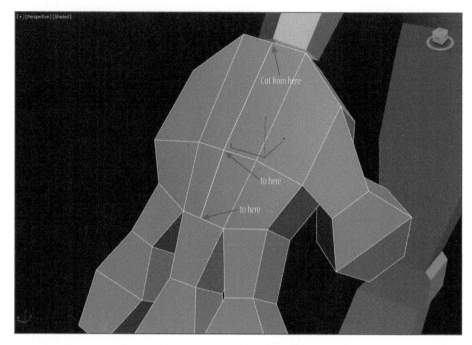

Typically, having an edge dead end in this way is not desirable; it is preferable to have edges loop around an object. On the hand, only one side needed the extra edge.

FIGURE 8.25 Use the Cut tool to create new edges on the top of the hand.

The wrist and hand may be attached, but they are still separate elements within the editable polygon. These separate elements need to be connected. For this, you will use Bridge.

2. Select the Alien Body object, and in the Modeling tab ➤ Geometry (All), click the Attach button, and then click on the hand. Now both the hand and body can be controlled with the same editable polygon parameters.

3. Enter Border mode, and select the borders of the wrist and palm (Ctrl+click to add both borders).

4. In the Modeling tab, choose Borders ➤ Bridge. There's no need to use the Bridge settings or caddy. Just click the Bridge button. You will see the new polygon bridge appear.

5. Enter Edge mode, and double-click on the edge at the wrist.

6. In the main toolbar, change the reference coordinate system to Local, and select Constrain to Edge in the ribbon's Edit panel. Select the Move tool, and move the edge higher on the arm. When you have finished, select Constrain to None (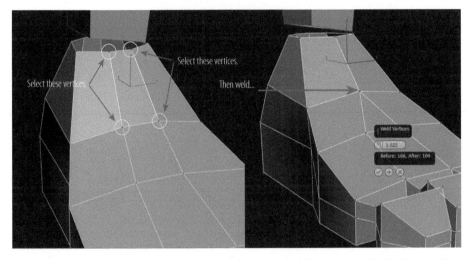). Exit Edge mode by selecting the Edge icon.

7. Time for the foot—it requires a different strategy. Select the foot, enter Vertex mode, and select the vertices shown in Figure 8.26 (left).

8. In the Ribbon ➢ Modeling tab ➢ Vertices ➢ Weld ➢ Weld Setting caddy, set the Weld Threshold to **1.025** (or use whatever value welds the vertices to match the right image in Figure 8.26). Select OK. This will combine the horizontal vertices, as shown in Figure 8.26 (right). Repeat the process on the back of the foot. Exit Vertex mode.

Moving only the edges can be difficult. However, in the Ribbon ➢ Modeling tab ➢ Edit tab, there is a row of constraint buttons at the bottom. These constraints let you use existing geometry to constrain sub-object transformations, making it easier to move edges.

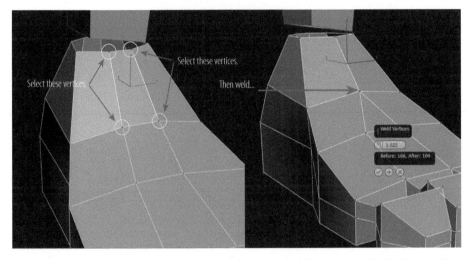

FIGURE 8.26 Select the four vertices on the top front of the foot (left). Use Weld to combine the edges (right).

9. Using the Cut tool, cut an edge on the front of the lower leg to the bottom of the knee, as shown in Figure 8.27. Repeat for the back of the leg.

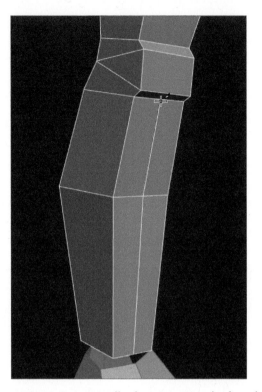

FIGURE 8.27   Use Cut to create an edge from the bottom of the lower leg to the bottom of the knee.

10. Adding the edges to the leg will make the leg less square. Round out the leg by selecting and moving the vertices on the outer edge of the leg, as shown in Figure 8.28.

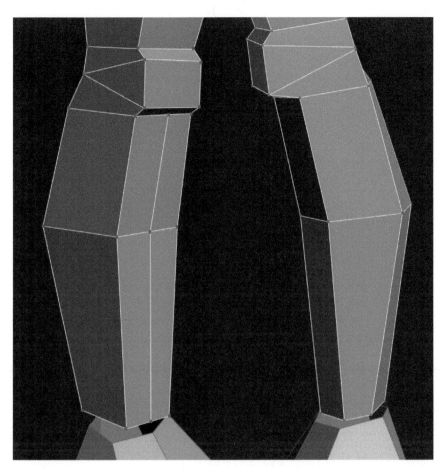

FIGURE 8.28 Select vertices on the outer edge of the leg, and move them so the leg is more rounded.

11. Now the foot is ready to be attached to the leg. In the Modeling tab, choose Geometry (All) ➢ Attach, and then click on the foot.

12. Now you need to bring the two elements together. For the hand, you used Bridge; this time, you'll use something different. In the Modeling tab, choose Vertices ➤ Target Weld (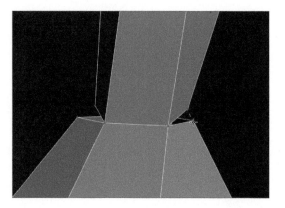 Target). This tool allows you to select a vertex and weld it to a neighboring target vertex. Select the vertex on the end of the leg and then on the neighboring vertex on the foot border, as shown in Figure 8.29. Continue around the ankle until the foot is attached to the leg.

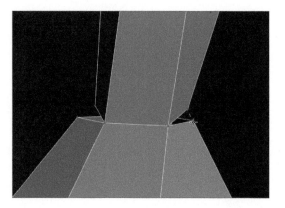

FIGURE 8.29 Attach the foot to the leg using Target Weld.

Save the file. To check your work, open the c08_ex7_attach_end.max scene file in the scenes folder of the c08_CharacterModel project.

Exercise 8.8: Using Symmetry

This part is easy because you have done it before. Continue with the previous exercise's scene file, or open the c08_ex8_symmetry_start.max scene file in the scenes folder of the c08_CharacterModel project.

1. Select the Alien Body model.

2. Choose the Modify panel ➤ Modifier List ➤ Symmetry.

3. In the Symmetry modifier, Mirror Axis group, check the Flip box.

4. You need to combine the two sides of the model, so from the ribbon, choose the Modeling tab ➤ Polygon Modeling ➤ Collapse Stack.

Save the file. To check your work, open the c08_ex8_symmetry_end.max scene file in the scenes folder of the c08_CharacterModel project.

> Collapse Stack collapses the selected object's entire stack into an editable object and preserves the modifiers on the object.

Exercise 8.9: Finishing the Head

The head will require some of the same steps as the hand and foot. First, the edges at the base of the head have to be rearranged, and then some of the edges coming up to the neck need to be merged so that you have an equal number of edges on both objects. You need to do this before you can attach the head. Continue with the previous exercise's scene file, or open the c08_ex9_head_start.max scene file in the scenes folder of the c08_CharacterModel project.

Certification
Objective

1. In the Perspective viewport, zoom close into the underside of the head at the hole in the neck. Make sure you are looking at the front of the face.

2. Select the head, and in the Modeling tab, choose Edit ➣ Cut. Then use the Cut tool to cut from the corner at the chin of the model down to the neck opening. It is important to start the cut from the vertex at the corner but finish in the middle of the edge at the neck, and then repeat on opposite side, as shown in Figure 8.30.

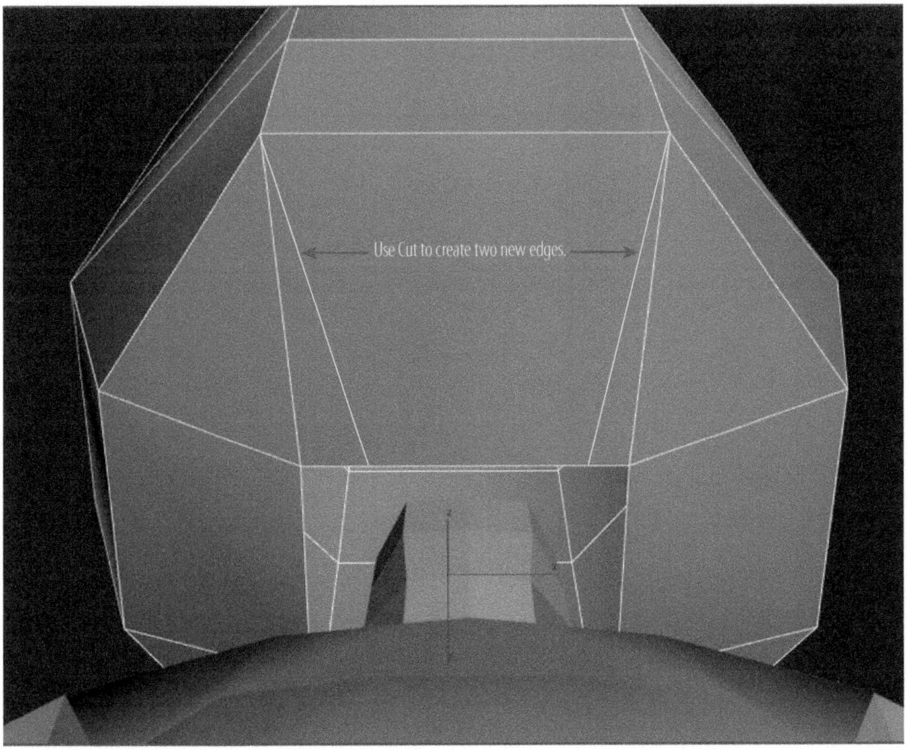

Use Cut to create two new edges.

FIGURE 8.30 Use the Cut tool to add new edges.

3. Enter Edge mode, and select the edges on either side of the new edges created in the previous step. Ctrl+click on the edges to select both.

4. You cannot just delete the edges; you must remove them. In the Modeling tab, choose Edges ➤ Remove (the Backspace key is the keyboard shortcut), as shown in Figure 8.31. This is a simple way to rearrange edges. Repeat the process on the back of the head.

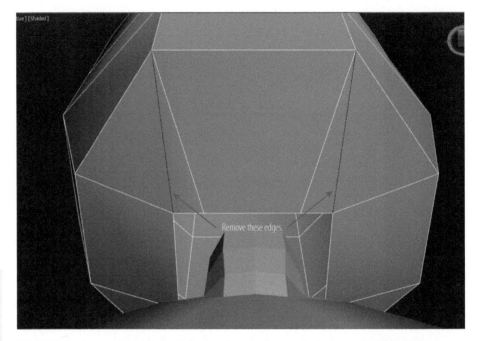

FIGURE 8.31   Select the old edges, and use the Remove tool to properly delete them.

The opening for the neck is square, so you can switch to Vertex mode and just move the vertices around until the opening is round, or ▶

5. Switch to Border mode, select the neck border; and in the Modeling tab, choose Geometry (All) ➤ Cap Poly. This adds a polygon in the hole.

6. Switch to Polygon mode and select the new cap polygon.

7. In the Modeling tab, choose Polygons ➤ GeoPoly. This will rearrange the poly into a more rounded shape, as shown in Figure 8.32.

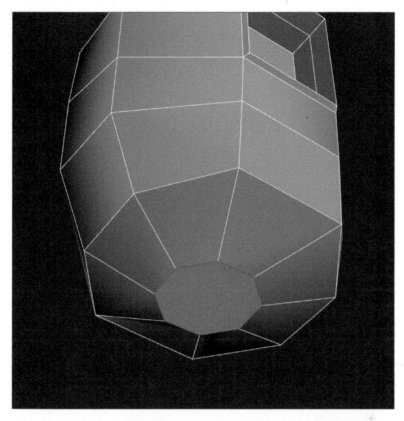

FIGURE 8.32   Use GeoPoly to rearrange the polygon into a circular shape.

8. Delete the selected polygon; exit Polygon mode.

9. As you did with the foot, you will use the Weld tool to combine certain vertices on the body. On the front of the neck, select the top-middle vertex and hold down the Ctrl key; then click on the two vertices on either side, as shown in Figure 8.33 (left).

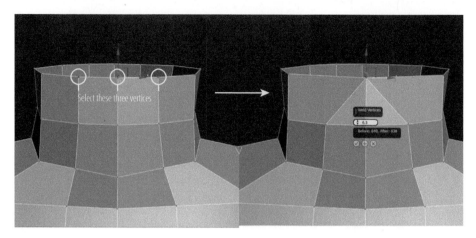

F I G U R E   8 . 3 3   Select the three vertices at the top of the neck (left). Use the Merge tool to combine the vertices (right).

10. Repeat the process on the row below the top row. Then repeat on the row below that until you get to the fourth row down, as shown in Figure 8.34.

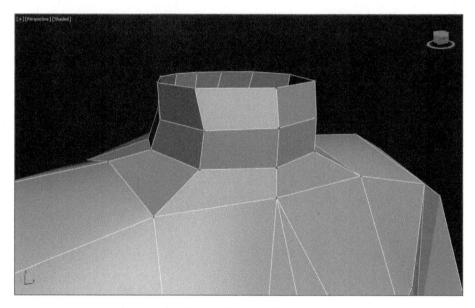

F I G U R E   8 . 3 4   The merged vertices on the front of the neck

11. Repeat the process for the back of the neck.

12. Choose Geometry (All) ➤ Attach; then select the head.

13. Switch to Border mode, and select the border of the head and neck (hold down the Ctrl key to select both).

14. In the Modeling tab ➤ Borders ➤ Bridge ➤ Bridge Settings, keep most of the settings at the default but set Twist 1 to 1. Select OK.

15. There is still some twisting, so switch back to Vertex mode, and in the Edit tab of the modeling ribbon, use Constrain To Edge to help move the vertices, as shown in Figure 8.35. Select Constrain To None before you move on to the next step.

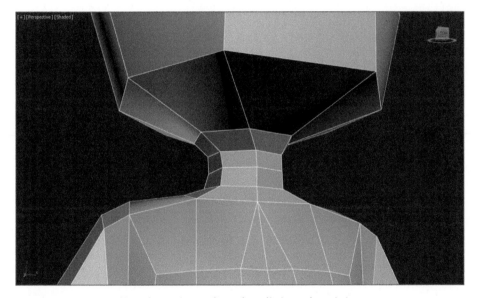

FIGURE 8.35 Move the vertices at the neck to eliminate the twisting.

There is one more thing that you can do. Hidden in the file is an eyeball. Just right-click in the viewport, and from the context menu, choose Unhide All. If you are using your own file, just merge the c08_ex9_eye.max file from the c08_CharacterModeling project folder. Save the file. To check your work, open the c08_ex9_head_end.max scene file in the scenes folder of the c08_CharacterModel project. Turn on Use NURMS to see the final model at its smoothed-out best, as shown in Figure 8.36.

FIGURE 8.36   The completed alien model

Now You Know

In this chapter, you learned how to use more advanced modeling tools to finish modeling the alien from Chapter 7. The first half of the chapter focused on building the alien's head, hand, and foot using many of the same tools from the previous chapter. You also learned to use a few new tools such as Bridge and Cut. The last half of the chapter showed how to put the model together using the Symmetry modifier and the Attach feature.

CHAPTER 9

Introduction to Materials

A material defines an object's look—its color, tactile texture, transparency, luminescence, glow, and so on. *Mapping* is the term used to describe how the materials are wrapped or projected onto the geometry (for example, adding wood grain to a wooden object). After you create your objects, the Autodesk® 3ds Max® 2016 program assigns a simple color to them, as you've already seen. You define a material by setting values for its parameters or by applying textures or maps. These parameters define the way an object will look when rendered. Much of an object's appearance when rendered also depends on the lighting. In this chapter and in Chapter 13, "Introduction to Lighting: Interior Lighting," you will discover that materials and lights work closely together.

In this chapter, you will learn to

▶ **Navigate the Slate Material Editor**

▶ **Identify the Standard material**

▶ **Identify the mental ray material**

▶ **Identify shaders**

▶ **Build materials for the couch**

▶ **Build materials for the lounge chair**

▶ **Build materials for the windows**

Navigating the Slate Material Editor

The Material Editor is the central place where you create and edit all of your material. You can assign materials to any number of objects, as well as have multiple materials assigned to different parts of the same object.

There are two interfaces to the Material Editor: the Slate Material Editor (or Slate) and the Compact Material Editor.

The Slate Material Editor is the interface you will use in this book. It is far superior to the Compact Material Editor and is especially nice when you are first learning to map, because you can see the material structure, as shown in Figure 9.1.

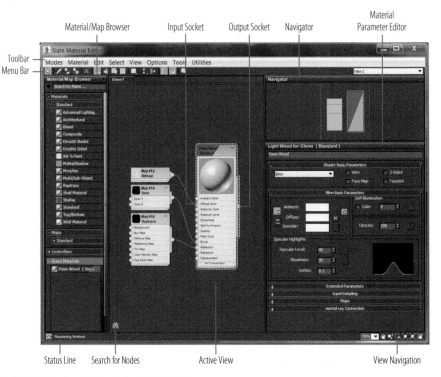

The Slate Material Editor is the default Material Editor. If it opens as the Compact Material Editor, you can switch editors by selecting Modes ➤ Slate Material Editor in the menu bar at the top of the Material Editor.

FIGURE 9.1 **The Slate Material Editor**

You can access the Slate Material Editor by choosing Rendering ➤ Material Editor ➤ Slate Material Editor from the menu bar. You can also click the icon for it on the main toolbar ( ), or you can press the keyboard shortcut (the M key).

The Slate Material Editor's interface uses nodes and wiring to display the structure of materials. It has a simple and elegant layout with the Material/Map Browser on the left for choosing material and map types. The center area is the Active View area, where you build materials by connecting maps or controllers to material components. The area on the right is the Material Parameter Editor; within that area is a Navigator for moving within the Active View area.

Identifying the Standard Material

Different materials have different uses. The Standard material is fine for most uses. However, when you require a more complex material, you can change the material type to one that will fit your needs. To change a material type in the Slate Material Editor, just choose from the list under Materials in the Material/Map Browser. You should see the rollout for Standard. If you are using the NVIDIA mental ray renderer, you will also see a rollout for mental ray. As you can see, the list is extensive; there are not enough pages in this book to cover the multitude of material types, so we will just touch on some of the best as an introduction. You will also see some examples using the Slate Material Editor.

Standard Materials

Standard materials typically use a four-color model to simulate a surface of a single color reflecting many colors. The four colors are known as the material's color components. *Ambient* color appears where the surface is in shadow, *diffuse* color appears where light falls directly on the surface, *specular* color appears in highlights, and *filter* color appears as light shining through an object. Along with the color components, there are parameters that control highlights, transparency, and self-illumination. Some of these parameters are different depending on the shader you are using. With the Standard material, shown in Figure 9.2, you can imitate just about any surface type you can imagine.

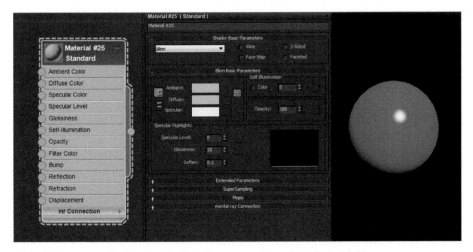

FIGURE 9.2 The Standard material type shown in the Slate Material Editor

Identifying the mental ray Material

3ds Max comes with several materials created specifically for use with the NVIDIA mental ray renderer. These materials are visible in the Material/Map Browser when NVIDIA mental ray is the active renderer. For the sake of time and space, we are going to cover only one here, Arch & Design.

The mental ray Arch & Design material improves the image quality of architectural renderings. It improves workflow and performance in general and performance for glossy surfaces (such as floors) in particular.

Special features of the Arch & Design material include advanced options for reflectivity and transparency, ambient occlusion settings, and the ability to round off sharp corners and edges as a rendering effect. These material types will be explored further in Chapter 15, "mental ray."

Identifying Shaders

The way light reflects from a surface defines that surface to your eye. With the 3ds Max program, you can control what kind of surface you work with by changing the shader type for a material. In either the Compact or Slate Material Editor, you will find the shader type in the material parameters in the Shader Basic Parameters rollout. This option will let you mimic different types of surfaces, such as dull wood, shiny paint, or metal. The following descriptions outline some of the shaders and the differences in how the shader types react to light, as shown in Figure 9.3.

FIGURE 9.3 **Shader types shown on rendered spheres**

Anisotropic Most of the surface types that you will see typically create rounded specular highlights that spread evenly across a surface. By contrast, *anisotropic* surfaces have properties that differ according to direction. This creates a specular highlight that is elliptical in shape and uneven across the surface, changing according to the direction you specify on the surface.

The Anisotropic shader is good for surfaces such as foil wrappers or hair. There are extra controls for how the specular highlights will fall across the surface.

Blinn This is the default shader because it is a general-purpose, flexible shader. The Blinn shader creates a smooth surface with some shininess. If you set the specular color to black, however, this shader will not display a specular highlight and will lose its shininess, making it perfect for regular dull surfaces, such as paper or interior walls.

Metal The Metal shader is not too different from the Blinn shader. Metal creates a lustrous metallic effect, with much the same controls as a Blinn shader but without the effect of any specular highlights.

When you are first starting, it's best to create most of your material looks with the Blinn shader until you're at a point where Blinn simply cannot do what you need.

> The black areas of the shader may throw you off at first, but keep in mind that a metallic surface is ideally black when it has nothing to reflect. Metals are best seen when they reflect the environment. The Metal shader requires a lot of reflection work to make the metal look just right.

Building Materials for the Couch

Now let's dive into creating material for the couch you modeled in Chapter 4, "Modeling in 3ds Max: Architectural Model Part II," to get it ready for lighting and rendering in later chapters.

Study the full-color image of the couch shown in Chapter 4 in Figure 4.1. That will give you an idea of how the couch is to be textured. The couch's material is basically all the same; once you create the material, you can add it to all the couch pieces.

Exercise 9.1: Creating a Standard Material

To begin, set the project to the C09_ArchMaterial project folder, and then open the C09_ex1_standard_start.max file from the scenes folder of the C09_ArchMaterial project folder downloaded from the book's web page at www.sybex.com/go/3dsmax2016essentials. This file has the room with the lounge chair and couch set up. When you open this file, the couch is the only furniture visible; the other models have been hidden. Follow these steps:

1. Open the Slate Material Editor (M). In the Material/Map Browser, open the Materials ➤ Standard rollout, and double-click Standard. This will add the Standard material to the Active View area.

2. Double-click the thumbnail with the sphere showing. This enlarges it and makes your material easier to view.

> **NAVIGATION IN ACTIVE VIEW**
>
> The Active View area uses the same navigation tools as the viewports. In the lower right of the Slate interface are the navigation tools. Keyboard shortcuts and the middle mouse button and wheel also work the same as in the viewports. The Navigator is another way to navigate in the Active View area. The Navigator panel changes the view of your material nodes; the colored box called the Proxy View area corresponds to the currently viewable area in the Active View area.

3. Double-click again on the node title bar; this adds the node parameters to the Material Parameter Editor.

4. In the Material Parameter Editor, at the top of the rollout, change the name to **Gray/Green Woven Fabric**.

5. In the Blinn Basic Parameters rollout, select the color swatch next to Diffuse. This brings up the color selector.

6. Set Red to **35**, Green to **25**, and Blue to **15**. Click OK. In the material node, the sphere in the thumbnail will change color.

Save your file and move onto the next exercise. To check your work, open the C09_ex1_standard_end.max file from the scenes folder of the C09_ArchMaterial project folder.

Exercise 9.2: Applying the Material to the Couch

Continue with the file you are working on or open the C09_ex2_apply_start .max file from the scenes folder of the C09_ArchMaterial project folder. In the scene, select the couch. In Chapter 4, after the couch was merged into the room file, it was grouped. Although grouping objects can save time since you can apply materials to all pieces simultaneously, you don't want to do that in this case. So with the Couch selected, follow these steps:

1. On the menu bar, choose Group ➤ Ungroup. Hold Alt on the keyboard and click on the couch feet to deselect them.

2. Select the Gray/Green Woven Fabric material in the Material Editor; a white highlight appears around the material when it is selected. In the Slate Material Editor toolbar, click the Assign Material to Selection icon (▣). When you compare the material in the viewport to the material on the couch, you should not see a difference, as

> ▶
>
> It is always best to name your materials precisely. Calling the material Couch might be confusing if you want to use the same material on the curtains or a chair.

shown in Figure 9.4, but the best way to view the material is by rendering the viewport.

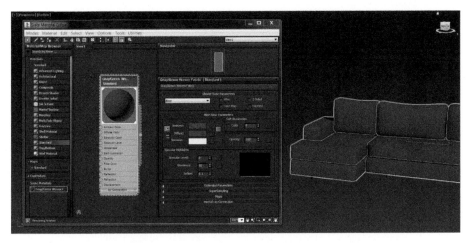

FIGURE 9.4   Material in the Material Editor and on the couch in the viewport

3. In the Perspective viewport, use the keyboard shortcut Z to fit the couch model into the viewport. In the main toolbar, click the Render Production button (   ), or press F9 for Render Last. The result is shown in Figure 9.5.

It is best to judge your material using the render.

FIGURE 9.5   The render of the couch with a Standard material applied

Save your file and move on to the next exercise. To check your work, open the C09_ex2_apply_end.max file from the scenes folder of the C09_ArchMaterial project folder.

Exercise 9.3: Adding a Bitmap

The couch material needs some refinement. It looks flat and too perfect, which in this instance isn't a good thing. A material with only color is not enough; what is needed is a map. Two map types are available, 2D and 3D:

▶ 2D maps are two-dimensional images that are mapped onto the surface of 3D objects; the simplest 2D maps are bitmaps (aka image files).

▶ 3D maps are patterns generated procedurally in three dimensions using the 3ds Max software.

Using a map to replace the diffuse color is a way to create a more realistic material because you are using actual images. You can use maps in other material components to create various effects, such as to make a material look bumpy ort to control its transparency. Continue with the file you are working on or open the C09_ex3_bitmap_start.max file from the scenes folder of the C09_ArchMaterial project folder.

1. In the Slate Material Editor, open the Blinn Basic Parameters rollout and click the small gray box next to the Diffuse color swatch, as shown in Figure 9.6. This is a shortcut to the Diffuse Color Map in the Maps rollout, which you can find if you look lower in the Material Parameter Editor.

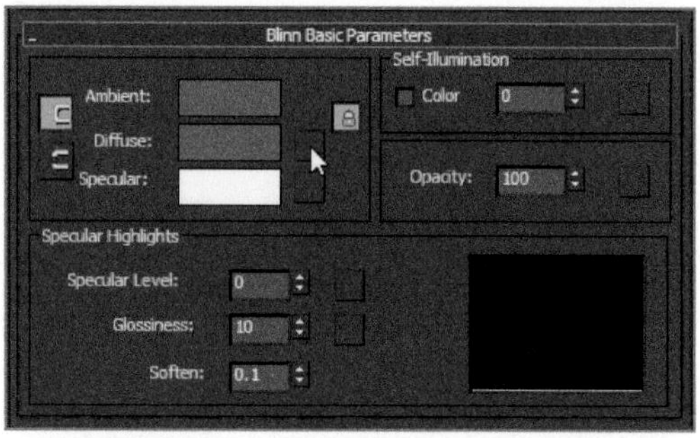

FIGURE 9.6 The Shortcut button used to add an image or bitmap to your material

2. This brings up a separate Material/Map Browser; in the Maps ➢ Standard rollout, choose Bitmap and click OK, as shown in Figure 9.7.

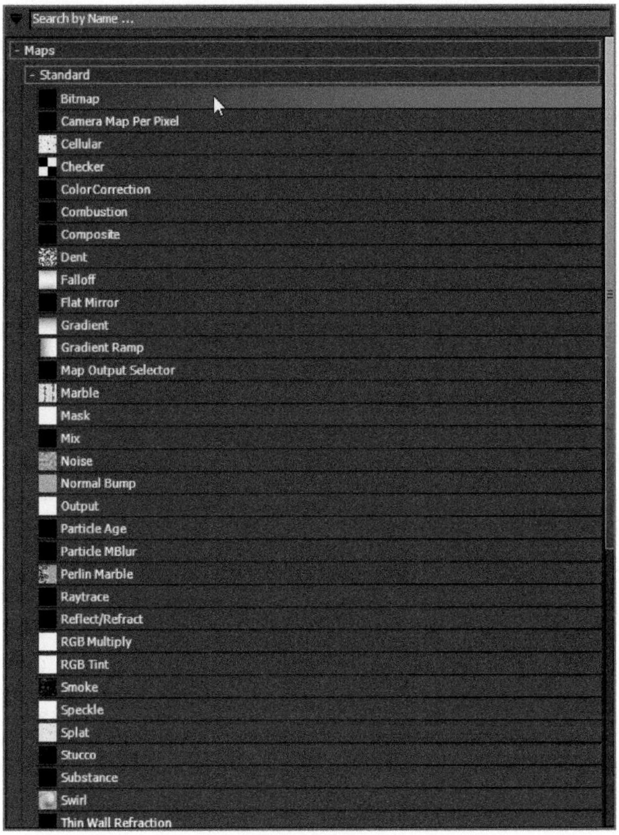

FIGURE 9.7 To add an image to your material, choose Bitmap in the Material/Map Browser ➢ Maps ➢ Standard rollout.

3. Because you set up a project at the beginning of the chapter, you should automatically be in sceneassets\images folder. Select the GrayGreenWovenFabric.tif image file, and click Open.

4. Select the bitmap node, and then in the Slate Material Editor's toolbar, click the Show Shaded Material in Viewport icon (▨). In the viewport, the couch shows the fabric image applied, as shown in Figure 9.8. This improves the color and adds some color variations.

In the Active view area, an additional node has been added to the main material node. The green node is the bitmap node, which holds the fabric image.

◄

◄

If you don't see this map, make sure the Files of Type field is set to TIF Image File or All Formats.

FIGURE 9.8   The couch with the fabric image applied

The image is projected onto the surface of the couch model. How the image looks on the model depends on the *mapping coordinates*. Right now, the bitmap doesn't know how to lay on the surface, so it doesn't look right. Save your file and move on to the next exercise. To check your work, open the C09_ex3_bit-map_end.max file from the scenes folder of the C09_ArchMaterial project folder.

Exercise 9.4: Mapping Coordinates

An image map is two-dimensional; it has length and width but no depth. 3ds Max geometry, however, extends in all three axes. Mapping coordinates define how and where image maps are projected onto an object's surfaces and whether the maps are repeated across those surfaces.

Mapping coordinates can be applied to objects in several ways. When primitive objects are created and the Generate Mapping Coords option is checked at the bottom of the Parameters rollout, the appropriate mapping coordinates are created automatically. Another method is by applying a UVW Map modifier, which is commonly used to apply and control mapping coordinates. You select the type of mapping projection, regardless of the shape of the object, and then set the amount of tiling in the modifier's parameters. The mapping coordinates applied through the UVW Map modifier override any other mapping coordinates applied to an object, and the Tiling values set for the modifier are multiplied by the Tiling value set in the assigned material.

You are going to use a modifier to replace those coordinates on the geometry. The UVW Map modifier allows you to change the bitmap by transforming the UVW Map modifier gizmo. Continue with the file you are working on or open the C09_ex4_mapping_start.max file from the scenes folder of the C09_ArchMaterial project folder.

1. Select the main seat cushion on the couch, and enter Isolate Selection mode ( ) by clicking the icon under the timeline at the bottom of the interface (or press Alt+Q).

   > You can also enter Isolate Selection mode by right-clicking the selected object and choosing Isolate Selection from the quad menu ➢ Display.

2. In the Modify panel, select UVW Map from the Modifier List drop-down.

3. Go to the UVW Map modifier parameters, and in the Mapping section, select Box for the projection type.

   > In the modifier stack, you can see the UVW Map modifier stacked on top of the editable poly. You will also see a flat, orange gizmo running through the seat cushion.

4. In the Alignment section, click the Bitmap Fit button, as shown in Figure 9.9. This will take you to the Select Image dialog box.

FIGURE 9.9   The Alignment section for the UVW Map modifier parameters

5. Navigate to the sceneassets\images folder in the C09_ArchMaterial project folder and select the GrayGreenWovenFabric.tif file. Click Open. This will change the size of the UVW Map gizmo to the size and aspect of the image rather than the geometry.

6. In the modifier stack, click the plus sign in the black box next to the UVW Map modifier and select Gizmo.

   > The UVW Map modifier has also changed the image on the couch. The size is more consistent throughout the couch, but the size of the fabric texture is too big.

7. The Box gizmo will turn yellow when in sub-object Gizmo mode. You will now be able to transform the gizmo to the correct size.

8. Switch to the Select and Uniform Scale tool ( ) or press R, and scale down the gizmo to 60 percent; while you are scaling, watch the Transform type-ins at the bottom of the screen to track the amount scaled.

9. In the modifier stack, click the UVW Map modifier again to exit the sub-object level. Now that the couch fabric is where it should be, it is time to add the UVW Map modifier to the remaining pieces of the couch.

10. Exit Isolate Selection mode.

11. Switch to the Select tool, select one of the back couch cushions, and choose UVW Map modifier in the Modifier List.

12. In the Alignment section, click the Acquire button. Then click on the previous couch seat cushion. The Acquire UVW Mapping dialog will appear. Select Acquire Relative and click OK.

13. Repeat the process on the remaining cushions.

The final results are shown in Figure 9.10.

FIGURE 9.10   The final results of the couch mapping

> Acquire takes the UVW mapping information from the seat cushion and copies it onto the back cushion. This is a great time-saver.

Save your file and move on to the next exercise. To check your work, open the C09_ex4_mapping_end.max file from the scenes folder of the C09_ArchMaterial project folder.

Exercise 9.5: Adding Materials to the Feet

The couch is not finished just yet; look closely at the couch feet. If you compare the current scene couch to the image of the real couch, you'll see that the feet should be a dark wood, not the default material on them now. Continue with the file you are working on, or open the C09_ex5_feet_start.max file from the scenes folder of the C09_ArchMaterial project folder. Then follow these steps:

1. Open the Slate Material Editor if it isn't already open.

2. In the Material/Map Browser, choose Materials, select a Standard material, and drag it into the Active View area.

3. Double-click the title bar of the material to add the material parameters to the Material Parameter Editor.

4. Change the name to **Dark Red Wood**.

5. Expand the Maps rollout, and click the None button across from Diffuse Color. This brings up a separate Material/Map Browser.

6. Choose Bitmap and select OK. In the Select Bitmap Image File dialog box, navigate to the sceneassets\images folder in the C09_ArchMaterial project folder and select the DarkRedWood.jpg image file and select Open.

7. Apply the material by clicking and dragging from the node's output socket to the couch foot, as shown in Figure 9.11.

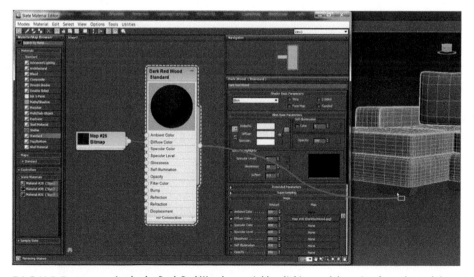

FIGURE 9.11 Apply the Dark Red Wood material by clicking and dragging from the node's output socket to the couch foot.

8. In the Material Editor, select the bitmap node and then click the Show Shaded Material in Viewport icon. The material shows now, but the image has no detail. This is because it needs to have UVW Mapping applied.

9. Select the foot; then, in the Modify panel's Modifier List, add a UVW Map modifier to the couch foot.

10. Change the mapping type to Box, and select Bitmap Fit under Alignment.

11. Navigate to the DarkWood_Grain.jpg image file. Select the image, and then click Open in the dialog box. The material now looks correct on the couch foot.

12. Apply the Dark Red Wood material to the remaining couch feet.

Save your file and move on to the next exercise. To check your work, open the C09_ex5_feet_end.max file from the scenes folder of the C09_ArchMaterial project folder.

Exercise 9.6: Applying a Bump Map

You are almost finished with the couch. One important feature of the couch is the bumpiness on the surface of the fabric, as shown in Figure 9.12. This bumpiness changes all the specular and reflective properties on a surface.

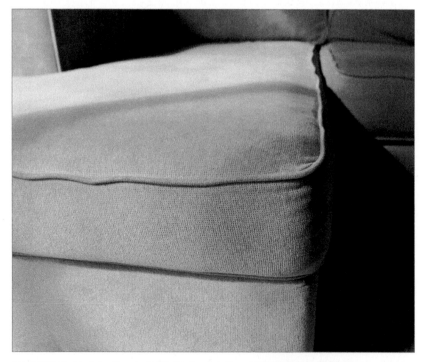

FIGURE 9.12 The couch fabric showing the subtle surface bumpiness

Bump mapping uses the intensity values (the brightness values) of an image or procedural map to simulate bumpiness on the surface of the model without changing the actual topology of the model itself. You can create some surface texture with a bump map; however, you will not be able to create extreme depth in the model. For that, you may want to model the surface depth manually or use displacement mapping instead. Continue with the file you are working on or open the C09_ex6_bump_start.max file from the scenes folder of the C09_ArchMaterial project folder. To add a bump map to the couch, follow these steps:

1. In the Slate Material Editor's Active View area, locate the Gray/Green Woven Fabric material. Double-click the title bar to load the material into the Material Parameter Editor.

2. In the Maps rollout, click the None button next to the Bump map, and in the Material/Map Browser, choose Bitmap.

3. Navigate to the sceneassets\images folder in the C09_ArchMaterial project folder and select the GrayGreenWovenFabric_bmp.tif image file.

4. In the Maps rollout, increase the Bump Amount from 30 (the default) to 60.

5. Render to see the results. You should see a texture on the couch that resembles the real bumpiness, as shown in Figure 9.13.

By creating bumps and grooves in the surface and giving the object a tactile element, bump mapping adds a level of detail to an object fairly easily. It is very common in computer graphics (CG).

No bump map   Bump Map Amount set to 60

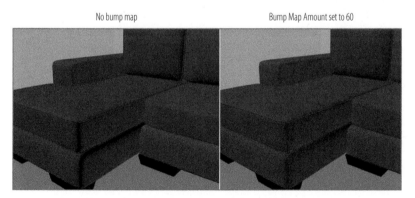
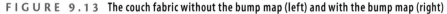

FIGURE 9.13   The couch fabric without the bump map (left) and with the bump map (right)

Save your file and move on to the next exercise. To check your work, open the C09_ex6_bump_end.max file from the scenes folder of the C09_ArchMaterial project folder.

Building Materials for the Lounge Chair

In this section, you will be adding materials to the lounge chair. In some ways, mapping the lounge chair is very much like mapping the couch. Figure 9.14 shows the lounge chair that was modeled in Chapter 4.

FIGURE 9.14 The lounge chair

Exercise 9.7: Creating a Leather Material for the Chair Cushion

The file has the lounge chair centered in the viewports, and the chair group is open so you can select the individual pieces. Start a new 3ds Max file or open the C09_ex7_chair_start.max file from the scenes folder of the C09_ArchMaterial project folder. Using similar techniques as in the previous section you will build a material for the lounge chair cushion. To begin creating follow these steps:

1. In the Slate Material Editor, add a Standard material to the Active View area. Double-click the material title to add it to the Material Parameter Editor.

2. In the Maps rollout, click the None button next to the Diffuse Color map, and in the Material/Map Browser, choose Bitmap.

3. Navigate to the sceneassets\images folder in the C09_ArchMaterial project folder, select the Leather.tif file, and rename the material Leather.

4. Select the lounge chair cushion, and apply the Leather material by clicking the Assign Material to Selection button in the toolbar.

5. On the Material Editor toolbar, click the Show Shaded Material in Viewport icon.

6. In the Specular Highlights group, change the Specular Level to 20 and Glossiness to 9. This will give the leather material a bit of gloss.

7. Repeat steps 2 through 6, but add the bitmap to the Bump map channel.

8. When the Select Bitmap Image File dialog box opens, choose Leather_BMP.tif.

9. In the Modify panel's Modifier List, add a UVW Map modifier.

10. Change the Mapping type to Box, and in Alignment, select Bitmap Fit. Navigate to the Leather.tif bitmap, select the image, and then click OK. This will change the size of the UVW Map gizmo. The size of the map is now the proper height-to-width ratio, but it is too large.

11. In the modifier stack, click the plus sign in the black box and select Gizmo.

12. Using the Scale tool, scale the gizmo until the material looks correct, as shown in Figure 9.15. By selecting the UVW map modifier in the modifier stack while it is in sub-object mode it will exit sub-object mode.

◄

If you double-click the input socket of the Diffuse Color map on the Standard material node, the Material/Map Browser will open.

FIGURE 9.15 The Leather texture is applied to the chair cushion.

Save your file and move on to the next exercise. To check your work, open the C09_ex7_chair_end.max file from the scenes folder of the C09_ArchMaterial project folder.

Exercise 9.8: Creating a Reflective Material

Reflection occurs when light changes direction as a result of "bouncing off" a surface like a mirror. In the following steps, you will create reflections on the lounge chair frame; what you are going to create is a chrome material that has 100 percent reflections. Continue with the file you are working on or open the C09_ex8_reflect_start.max file from the scenes folder of the C09_ ArchMaterial project folder.

1. In the Slate Material Editor, drag a Standard material from the Material/Map Browser to the Active View area.

2. Double-click the title bar of the material to add it to the Material Parameter Editor.

3. Rename the material **Chrome**, and change the diffuse color to black (R: 0, G: 0, B: 0).

4. In the Specular Highlights group, change the Specular Level to **90** and Glossiness to **80**. This will give the chrome material a bit of gloss.

5. In the Material/Map Browser rollout, go to the Maps rollout ➢ Standard, choose Raytrace from the list, and drag the Raytrace map to the Reflection input socket.

6. Apply the Chrome material to the lounge chair frame. You won't be able to see the mirror effect of the chrome in the viewport; you will have to render.

7. To render objects with reflections, there need to be items to reflect. Right-click in any viewport and choose Unhide All from the quad menu.

8. Click the Render Production button. The result of the render is shown in Figure 9.16. In the figure, the chrome doesn't look smooth. It has a noisy, broken-up look to it. You can correct this by controlling the anti-aliasing.

A reflection creates the illusion of chrome, glass, or metal by applying a map to the geometry so the image looks like a reflection on the surface. A Raytrace map provides reflections on a material. Raytrace reflects the actual surroundings in the scene.

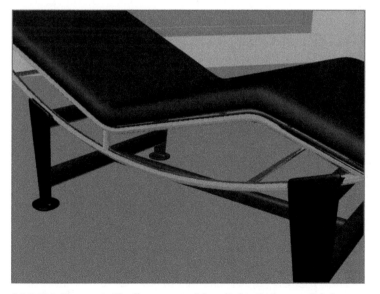

FIGURE 9.16 The Chrome material applied to the lounge chair frame

Anti-aliasing smoothes the jagged edges that occur along the edges of diagonal and curved lines when a scene is rendered. SuperSampling performs an additional anti-aliasing pass on the material and can improve the image quality.

9. In the Chrome material, select the SuperSampling rollout. Uncheck Use Global Settings and check Enable Local Supersampler.

10. Choose Max 2.5 Star from the drop-down menu, and then render. You should see the difference in the reflections, as shown in Figure 9.17.

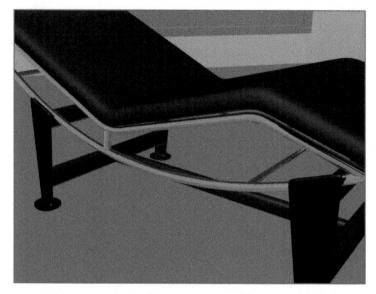

FIGURE 9.17 Final reflections on the chair frame

SUPERSAMPLING FILTERS

The use of SuperSampling Filters is an anti-aliasing technique, the process of eliminating jagged and pixelated edges (aliasing). It is a method of smoothing images rendered in imagery. There are four SuperSampling filters:

Adaptive Halton Samples along both the X- and Y-axes according to a random pattern.

Adaptive Uniform Samples regularly, from a minimum number of four samples to a maximum of 36.

Hammersley Samples regularly along the X-axis, but along the Y-axis, it spaces them according to a random pattern.

Max 2.5 Star The sample at the center of the pixel is averaged with four samples surrounding it.

The last material is the material that is on the base of the chair. This should be a very simple material to create: a matte black material. Follow the steps you've learned throughout this chapter. Use a Standard material and make the diffuse color black. Set the Specular Level to **20** and Glossiness to **15**. Name the material **Base** and apply this material to all the objects from the base, as shown in Figure 9.18.

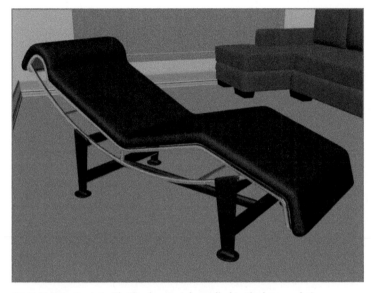

FIGURE 9.18 The final materials applied to the lounge chair

Save your file and move on to the next exercise. To check your work, open the C09_ex8_reflect_end.max file from the scenes folder of the C09_ArchMaterial project folder.

Building Materials for the Window

The window and doors are special 3D primitive objects. They are a collection of multiple objects attached together: a frame, mullions, and glass. You can edit those objects within the Architecture Engineering and Construction (AEC) object's parameters. You also have the ability to add materials to the individual pieces within the attached whole.

Exercise 9.9: Creating a Multi/Sub-Object Material

The Multi/Sub-Object material (MSOM), which is in the Compound Materials category, lets you assign different materials at the sub-object level of your geometry. In the case of the AEC window, it is already divided into separate sub-object levels, so you just have to apply the material and identify the different parts. Continue with the file you are working on or open the C09_ex9_MSOM_start.max file from the scenes folder of the C09_ArchMaterial project folder. Then follow these steps:

Multi/Sub-Object is just a material that gathers other materials together.

▶

The Set Number parameter allows you to control how many materials can be plugged into the Multi/Sub-Object material.

1. In the Slate Material Editor, drag a Multi/Sub-Object material from the Material/Map Browser into the Active View area.

2. Double-click the title bar to add the material to the Material Parameter Editor. Click the Set Number button and change Number of Materials to 5, as shown in Figure 9.19. Change the name to Window/Door.

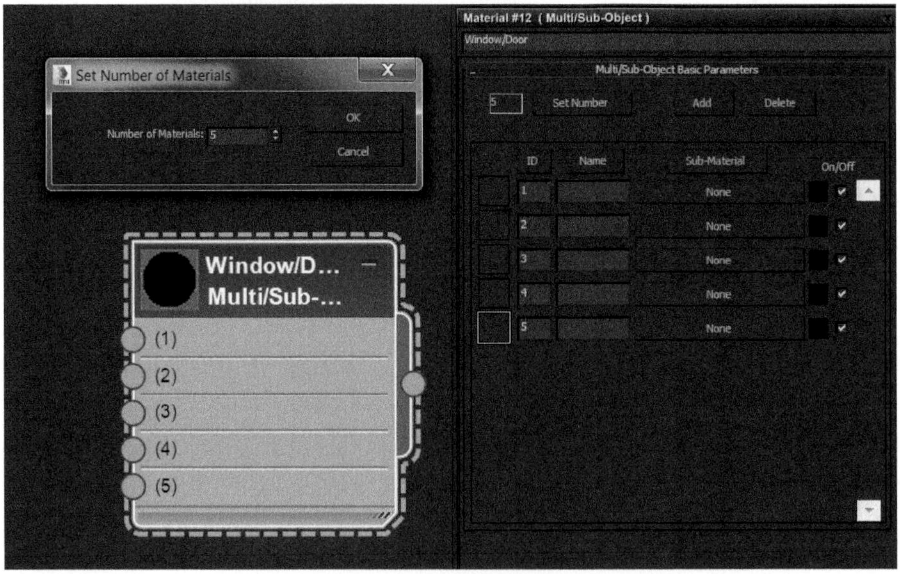

FIGURE 9.19   Multi/Sub-Object material and parameters

3. Drag a Standard material from the Material/Map Browser to the Active View area, and then from the output socket of the Standard material, drag it to the input socket of the MSOM, as shown in Figure 9.20.

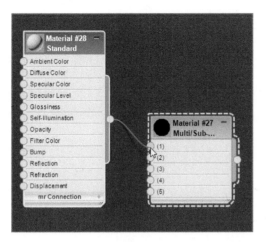

FIGURE 9.20 Adding a Standard material to the Multi/Sub-Object material node

4. Double-click the new Standard material's title bar to add it to the Material Parameter Editor. Click the Diffuse color swatch to open the color selector; create a red color, and click OK.

5. Repeat the process until you have five Standard materials with five different diffuse colors plugged into the 1 through 5 input sockets of the MSOM. The finished node is shown in Figure 9.21. The Standard material nodes have been minimized for the figure. The numbers in the MSOM parameters are material IDs.

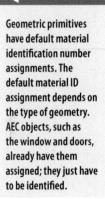

Geometric primitives have default material identification number assignments. The default material ID assignment depends on the type of geometry. AEC objects, such as the window and doors, already have them assigned; they just have to be identified.

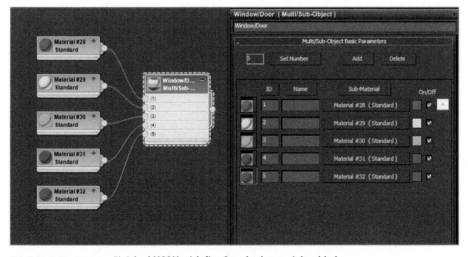

FIGURE 9.21 Finished MSOM with five Standard materials added

6. Apply the MSOM to the window in the living room area, as shown in Figure 9.22. The colors show clearly which section of the window corresponds to which ID number.

FIGURE 9.22 The Multi/Sub-Object material applied to the window object shows the different colors applied to the different parts of the window.

7. Double-click the title of the MSOM to open its parameters. The colored materials that were just created are not needed. Select and delete them.

8. Starting with the window glass, select the material bar that says None for ID #3 in the MSOM parameter from the Material/Map Browser, and then select Standard material.

9. Select the material bar you just loaded the Standard material into. This loads that material's parameters. Rename the material **Window Glass**.

10. In the Blinn Basic Parameters rollout, change the Opacity to 0. If you render, you will see a black hole where the green used to be. That is because you are seeing the default color applied to the background in a render. That means the glass is see-through now.

11. In the Maps rollout, click the Reflection Map button.

12. From the Material/Map Browser, choose Raytrace, and then change the Reflection Amount to **9**.

> When the scene renders, the Reflection amount will appear to be very high; this is a bit of an illusion because of the black in the background.
>
> ◀

13. In the main menu bar, go to the Rendering menu. Choose Environment; then click the color swatch under Background, change it to a light gray, and select OK.

14. Render the Perspective viewport. Now the reflection looks more appropriate. Eventually, an image of an outdoor scene will be placed behind the glass. For now, let's continue with the MSOM for the window. Window frames and mullions come in many colors and textures, but for this example, you are going to use a shiny white plastic.

15. Double-click the MSOM title bar to load the material into the Material Parameter Editor, and then select any of the material IDs (other than #3).

16. Repeat the same process as in step 8 to load the material in the MSOM.

17. Change the diffuse color to White; then in the Maps rollout, add a Raytrace node to the Reflection map, and change the Amount to 10, as you did in step 11. Rename the material **Shiny White Plastic**.

18. Drag from the output socket of the Shiny White Plastic material to the input of the remaining Multi/Sub-Object material's IDs, as shown in Figure 9.23.

This places a clone of the Shiny White Plastic material into the three remaining material slots and completes the window material, as shown in a render in Figure 9.24. Save your file. To check your work, open the C09_ex9_MSOM_end .max file from the scenes folder of the C09_ArchMaterial project folder.

The same technique used for the window can be used for the doors, but if you want the doors to be just a plain solid color or simple wood, you can apply a Standard material to the entire Door object. We'll return to this room in Chapter 13 when we look at lighting. Meanwhile, finish assigning materials to the rest of the scene.

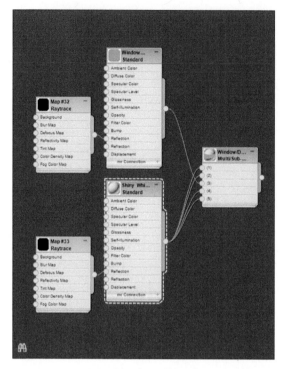

FIGURE 9.23 Drag from the output socket of the Shiny White Plastic material into the input socket of the remaining ID slots of the Multi/Sub-Object material.

FIGURE 9.24 The completed window material

Now You Know

In this chapter, you learned how to build materials using the Material Editor. The Slate Material Editor is the center for material creation in 3ds Max. It begins with identifying the different material types and shaders available. You can apply this information to build materials for the couch, lounge chair, and window. This chapter provided the information to allow you to move forward and create other types of material to complete the room.

CHAPTER 10

Textures and UV Workflow: The Alien

Autodesk® 3ds Max® 2016 materials simulate the natural physics of how you see things by regulating how objects reflect and/or transmit light. You define a material by setting values for its parameters or by applying textures or maps. These parameters define the way an object will look when it is rendered. In this chapter and in Chapter 13, "Introduction to Lighting: Interior Lighting," you will discover that materials and lights work closely together.

In this chapter, you will apply material and maps to the alien model from Chapter 7, "Character Modeling Part I," and Chapter 8, "Character Modeling Part II." You will first set up the model to accept textures properly through a process called UV-unwrap. In contrast to X, Y, and Z Cartesian coordinates, which are the coordinates for the object and scene, another set of 2D coordinates is required to describe the surface of the mesh, so the letters U, V, and W are used to designate those coordinates. This allows you to lay out the colors and patterns for the alien's body and general look. This process essentially creates a flat map that can be used to paint the textures in a program such as Adobe Photoshop. The textures (i.e., the maps) you'll use for the alien have already been created in Photoshop. We will show you how to prepare the model for proper UVs and how to apply the maps you have already painted. We will not demonstrate the actual painting process in Photoshop because that discussion goes beyond the scope of this book.

In this chapter, you will learn to

▶ Define UVs on the alien's body

▶ Unwrap UVs from the alien's body

▶ Build the material and apply it to the alien

Defining UVs on the Alien's Body

Set your project to the c10_UnwrapUV project downloaded from the companion web page at www.sybex.com/go/3dsmax2016essentials. Open the scene file c10_ex1_seam_start.max from the scenes folder of the c10_UnwrapUV project folder.

You will begin by creating seams to define the shapes of the arms so you'll know where to paint the sleeves of the uniform in an image-editing program like Adobe Photoshop. When the c10_ex1_seam_start.max file is opened, the alien will have a new color. Remember that to change the color of any model, you need to use the Name and Color rollout, which appears at the top of all the command panels (other than the Create panel). The new color was added because the unwrap seams that will be added are blue, and another color will highlight the seams much better.

Exercise 10.1: Seaming the Alien's Body

To create the seams to define the alien's body, follow these steps:

1. Change the viewport rendering type to Shaded with Edged Faces (F4) in all the viewports.

2. With your model selected, go to the Modify panel, and from the Modifier List, choose Unwrap UVW.

3. Expand the Unwrap UVW modifier in the modifier stack by clicking the plus sign in the black box next to the Unwrap UVW title. Enter Polygon mode.

4. At the bottom of the Configure rollout, uncheck Map Seams, as shown in Figure 10.1.

FIGURE 10.1   Uncheck Map Seams in the Configure rollout.

5. In the Peel rollout, click the Point-to-Point Seams button, as shown in Figure 10.2. This tool lets you reroute the seams to where you want them.

When you open the file, a Gamma & LUT Settings Mismatch dialog box might appear. You want to adopt the file's gamma and LUT settings, which is the default option, so you only have to click OK.

▶
▶

Keep in mind that any design changes you made to your own alien model may cause discrepancies in the UV unwrapping and mapping steps in the following sections.

Unchecking Map Seams turns off the green highlight on the edges; it is generated by default and is not useful in its current state.

▶

FIGURE 10.2 Click the Point-to-Point Seams button.

A dashed-line "rubber band" appears next to your cursor, letting you know that the tool is waiting for the next point to be selected.

6. With Point-to-Point Seams enabled, click on the center of a pair of intersecting edges about where you want to define the left shoulder, as shown in Figure 10.3 (left image).

7. Select the next intersecting edges in the loop around the shoulder. This creates a blue highlight across the edges, as shown in Figure 10.3 (middle image).

8. Continue around the shoulder until you have a complete loop, ending with the intersection you started with in step 6, as shown in Figure 10.3 (right image).

While Point-to-Point Seams is active, you can navigate using all the viewport navigation tools to look around the model. 3ds Max remembers the last intersection you clicked and draws an accurate seam at the next click.

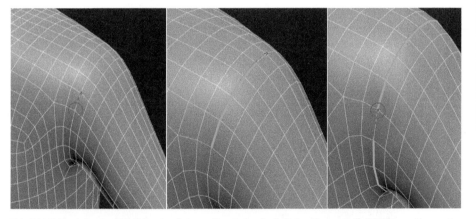

FIGURE 10.3 Pick this edge intersection to begin defining the seam (left). Choose the next point at the upper shoulder (middle).

9. Select the bottommost edge intersection on the underarm and continue selecting edge intersections, as shown in Figure 10.4.

10. Continue all the way to the middle point of the wrist. Right-click to deactivate the Point-to-Point Seams tool's rubber banding, but keep the button active.

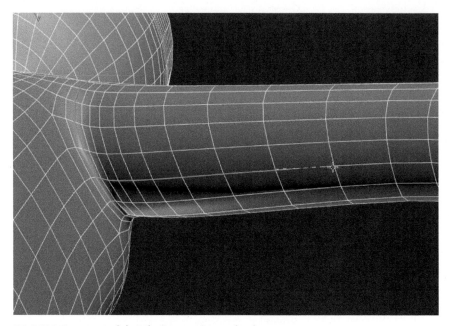

FIGURE 10.4 Select the intersections under the arm.

11. Continue selecting edge interactions around the wrist, as shown in Figure 10.5, until you get back to where you began at the wrist.

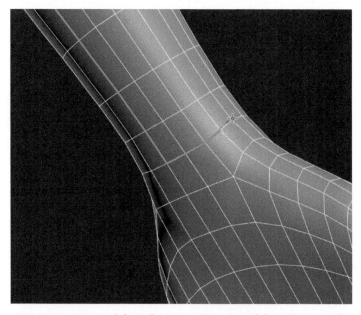

FIGURE 10.5 Select edge intersections around the wrist to complete the forearm/wrist seam.

12. Right-click again, and then continue cutting around the torso area. Go around the arms at the shoulder and also around the top of the legs, as shown in Figure 10.6.

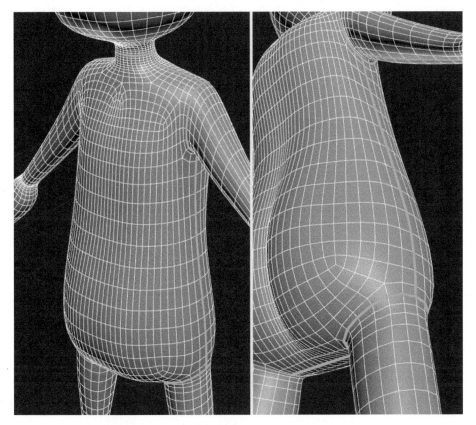

FIGURE 10.6 Add these seams to define the torso area.

13. Using the Point-to-Point Seams tool, cut seams for the hands lengthwise down the middle from wrist to wrist. Begin at the wrist on the side of the thumb and work your way around the fingers to the opposite side of the wrist. You can see this progression for the left hand start in Figure 10.7.

14. Cut another seam from the inside of the left leg down to the ankle. Then continue the seam around the ankle; right-click to complete. The seam is just on the inside of the leg, except where it wraps around the ankle.

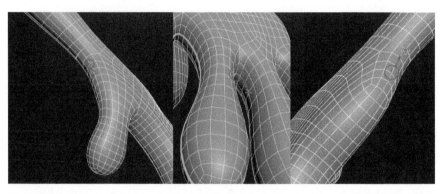

F I G U R E   1 0 . 7   Cut a new seam around the hand, starting as shown in the left image. Cut a seam around the fingers, as shown in the middle image, finishing at the opposite side of the wrist, as shown in the right image.

15. Create the seam for the right leg in the same way; the seams for both legs are shown in Figure 10.8.

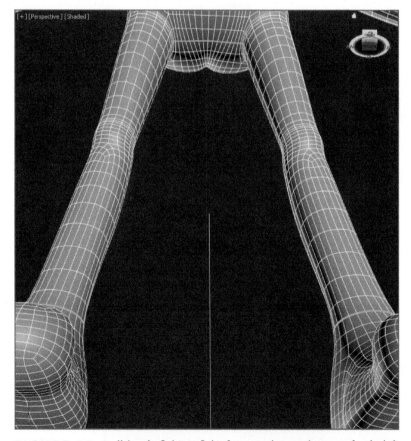

F I G U R E   1 0 . 8   Using the Point-to-Point Seams tool to cut the seams for the left and right legs

16. Continue creating seams for the left foot, using the Point-to-Point Seams tool. Start at the back of the foot and create a seam encircling the foot, as shown in Figure 10.9.

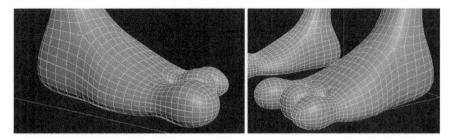

FIGURE 10.9 Cut a seam around the foot.

17. Repeat the same seam on the right foot.

18. Now for the head, start at the base of the back of the neck. Cut a seam up to the base of the nose, shown in Figure 10.10 (right image).

19. Cut the seam around the base of the nose. The head seam is shown in Figure 10.10 (left image).

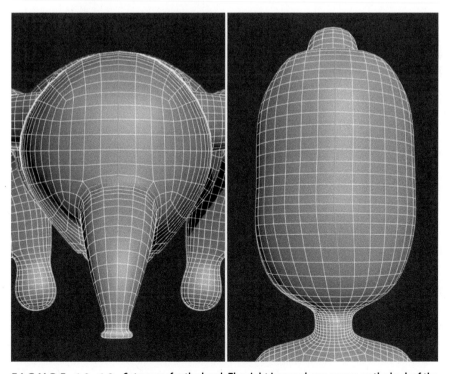

FIGURE 10.10 Cut seams for the head. The right image shows seams on the back of the head; the left image shows the seam that runs around the base of the nose.

20. For the nose, start at the base located at the top of the head. Cut a seam up to the base of the nostril. Cut a seam around the base of the nostril, as shown in Figure 10.11.

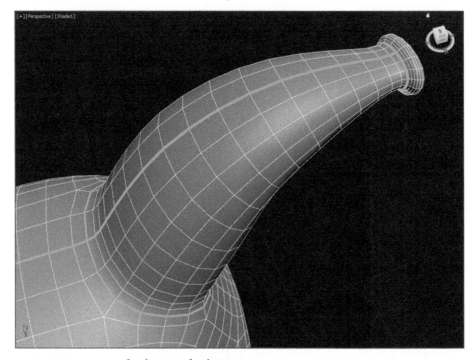

FIGURE 10.11 Cut the seams for the nose.

21. Cut a seam from the top of the nostril into the center of the nostril.

22. Save your work before continuing with the next section. To check your work, open the c10_ex1_seam_end.max file.

Unwrapping UVs on the Alien's Body

Now that the seams are cut for the alien's body, it's time to unwrap the seamed parts. When you are sewing clothing, you cut the fabric from patterns. Similarly, in the next section, you will spread out the patterns so you can paint them to create the texture for the alien surface.

Exercise 10.2: Unwrapping the Alien's Arm

Continue with the scene file from the previous section or open the c10_ex2_
unwrap_start.max from the scenes folder of the c10_UnwrapUV project folder.

1. Select the alien, go to the Modify panel, and in the Unwrap UVW
   modifier in the Edit UVs rollout, select the Open UV Editor button.

2. In the top right of the window, from the drop-down menu, choose
   CheckerPattern (Checker). This will apply a low-contrast checker map
   to the alien, as shown in Figure 10.12.

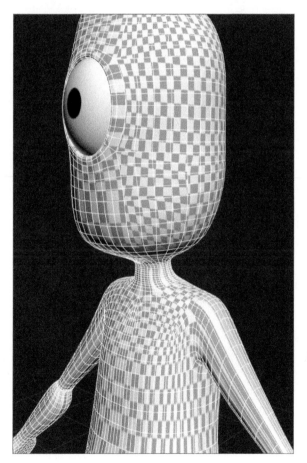

F I G U R E   1 0 . 1 2   A low-contrast checker pattern is added to the alien model.

3. With Polygon mode selected in your Unwrap UVW modifier and Point-to-Point Seams toggled off, click on a polygon on the left forearm of your model; and then in the Peel rollout, click the Expand Polygon Selection to Seams icon (   ). This will select all the polygons that were included when you created the seams for the arm, as shown in Figure 10.13.

The checker pattern applied to the alien will display only if the Edit UVWs dialog box is open. The low-contrast checker will appear only when you select CheckerPattern (Checker) again.

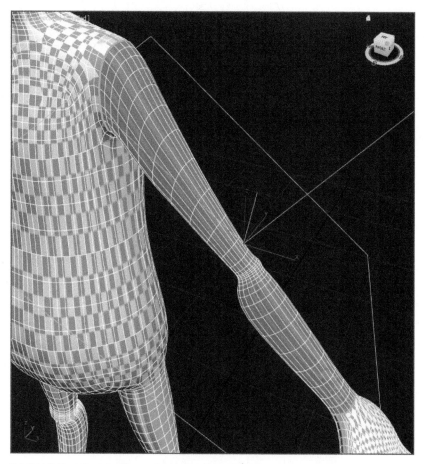

FIGURE 10.13 The arm's polygons are selected.

4. To unfold the UVs into a usable pattern, click the Pelt Map icon (   ) in the Peel rollout. The Pelt Map dialog box opens.

5. In the Edit UVWs dialog box, click the View menu and toggle off Show Grid and Show Map to simplify the UV view. Before moving on,

take a look at the checkerboard pattern on the arm of the alien to recognize how it changes once you pelt, as shown in Figure 10.14.

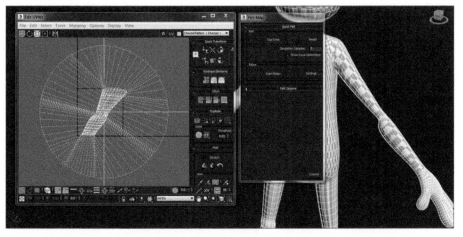

FIGURE 10.14 The Edit UVWs and Pelt Map dialog boxes showing the left arm UVs

6. To unfold the map, click the Start Pelt button in the Pelt Map dialog box. Doing so moves the UVs in the Edit UVWs dialog box in real time, as shown in Figure 10.15.

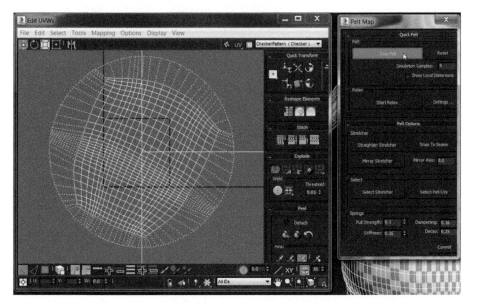

FIGURE 10.15 In the Pelt Map dialog box, use Start Pelt to unfold the UVs of the alien's arm.

7. This procedure keeps unfolding the UVs until you stop it, so wait a couple of seconds for the UVs to stop moving, and then click Stop Pelt. You're almost finished with the arm; however, if you look at the checkerboard texture in your viewport, you can see that some of the checks are bigger than others. To fix this, complete the remaining steps.

8. Click the Settings box next to the Start Relax button in the Pelt Map dialog box. The Relax Tool dialog box opens. Change the drop-down option to Relax By Polygon Angles.

9. Click the Start Relax button in the Relax Tool dialog box. Let Relax run for a good bit until the image matches Figure 10.16.

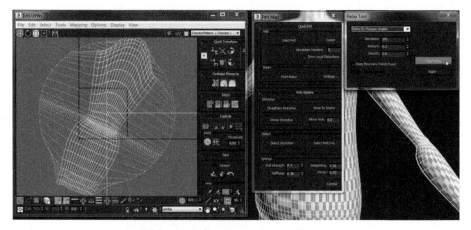

FIGURE 10.16 Use the Start Relax button to relax the UVs.

10. Wait until the UVs stop moving and then click Stop Relax. If it still doesn't match the figure, click Start Relax; then click Apply when it matches the figure.

11. Close the Relax Tool dialog box.

12. Check your texture in the viewport; it now shows the checkerboard the way you want it.

13. Click the Commit button at the bottom of the Pelt Map dialog box, or your changes won't take effect.

14. Close the Edit UVWs dialog box.

15. Repeat steps 1 through 12 for the right arm. You can see in Figure 10.17 that both arms are now laid out—pelted and relaxed.

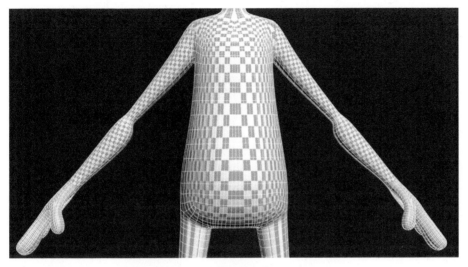

FIGURE 10.17 Both arms are pelted and relaxed.

16. Save your work before continuing with the next section. To check your work, open `c10_ex2_unwrap_end.max`.

Exercise 10.3: Unwrapping the Alien's Body

Now that you have finished the arms, you have an idea about what needs to be done. It's time to unwrap the remaining parts of the body, starting with the alien's torso. Continue with the scene file from the previous section or open `c10_ex3_unwrap_start.max` from the `scenes` folder of the `c10_UnwrapUV` project folder.

1. Select the alien, go to the Modify panel, and enter Polygon mode of the Unwrap UVW modifier.

2. Select a single polygon on the alien's torso (front or back, it doesn't matter). In the Peel rollout, click the Expand Polygon Selection to Seams icon; this will select all the faces that were included when the seams were created for the torso.

3. Click the Pelt Map icon to open the Edit UVWs dialog box and the Pelt Map dialog box. First, click Start Pelt. You will see the UVs moving around. When they stop moving, click the Stop Pelt button.

4. Click the Settings button next to the Start Relax button.

5. Make sure the drop-down menu is set to Relax By Polygon Angles. Click Apply, and then close the Relax Tool dialog box.

6. Click the Start Relax button again, and when the UVs stop moving, click Stop Relax.

7. Click the Commit button. The checker pattern on the torso should look organized and even, as shown in Figure 10.18.

If the checker pattern is not showing, select CheckerPattern (Checker) from the Edit UVWs dialog box so the pattern shows.

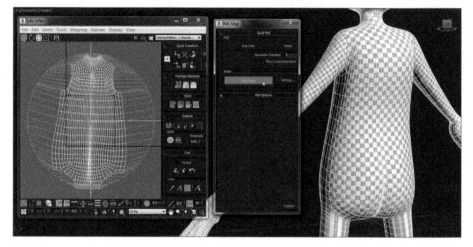

FIGURE 10.18 The alien's backside with its UVs pelted and relaxed, showing the checker pattern evenly laid out

For the remaining objects, you don't have to go into the Relax Tool dialog box—just click Start Relax.

8. Now that you have finished with part of the torso, repeat the process on the part of the torso you didn't do in the previous steps.

9. Repeat the process from steps 2 through 7 until all the remaining body seams on the alien's body are pelted and relaxed.

Save your work before continuing with the next section. To check your work, open c10_ex3_unwrap_end.max.

Exercise 10.4: Arranging the Alien's UVs

When the UVs are unwrapped, the squares in the checker pattern on different parts of the alien are different sizes. They need to be set to the same size, showing that the UVs are uniform. Using the Select by Element UV Toggle tool will help with this process. It allows you to select an individual element's full set of UVs so that you can scale and lay them out separately. Give them some space on the flat blank canvas so they can be used later for painting the textures for those parts of the body. Look in the UV Editor, and you should see the blue-bordered box. It will look like a mess; all of the unwrapped UVs are piled on top of each other.

The UV layout can vary depending on many factors, as we said earlier. The goal is to fit the UVs into this box without going outside it and without overlapping any of them. Anything outside this box ends up tiling (or having no texture at all), and any overlapping UVs share parts of the texture from another element. Either way, that's not good. Once you have the layout, you can select the UVs and move them around.

Continue with the scene file from the previous section or open `c10_ex4_arrange_start.max` from the `scenes` folder of the `c10_UnwrapUV` project folder.

1. Select the alien and go to the Modify panel; enter Polygon mode of the Unwrap UVW modifier.

2. In the Unwrap UVW modifier ➤ Edit UVs, select Open UV Editor.

3. Click the Select by Element UV Toggle button, as shown in Figure 10.19.

FIGURE 10.19   Click the Select by Element UV Toggle button.

4. In the Edit UVWs dialog box, click on the "mess"; one part of the alien will be selected, as shown in Figure 10.20.

In the Edit UVWs dialog box, you can use all the navigation tools you use in the viewports to pan and zoom.

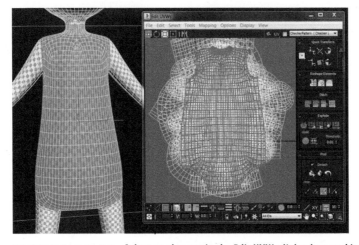

FIGURE 10.20   Select an element in the Edit UVWs dialog box, and it will appear as selected on the model.

5. In the Edit UVWs dialog box, drag a selection box around all the UVs.

6. From the Arrange Elements rollout on the right side of the Edit UVWs dialog box, change the Padding type-in field to 0.0 and then click the Pack Normalize button, as shown in Figure 10.21. The results of the Pack Normalize command are shown in Figure 10.22.

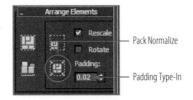

FIGURE 10.21   The Arrange Elements rollout

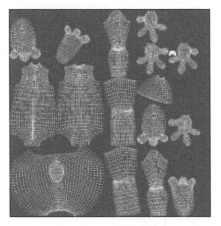

FIGURE 10.22   UVs placed within the UV space

7. In the Edit UVWs dialog box, select Tools ➢ Render UVW Template to open the Render UVs dialog box.

8. Click the Render UV Template button in the UVs dialog box to create an image of your UVs, as shown in Figure 10.23. Remember, the layout of the UV rendered image can vary.

FIGURE 10.23 The UV layout image

9. Save the UV layout image by clicking the Save Image icon in the Render Map dialog box, as shown in Figure 10.24.

10. In the Save Image dialog box, name the UV layout image **AlienUV_ new**, and change Save As Type to TIF Image File (*.tif, *.tiff). Save the UVs in the sceneassets/images folder.

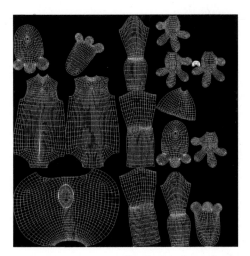

FIGURE 10.24 Use the Save Image button to create the UV layout image.

The more you practice unwrapping UVs for models, the easier it will become to anticipate how to paint the textures.

Once the UVs are saved, close the Edit UVWs dialog box. Now you can open this image in your favorite image editor, and you can use the pieces as guides to paint the alien's textures. Save your work before continuing with the next set of steps. To check your work, open c10_ex4_arrange_end.max from the scenes folder of the c10_UnwrapUV project folder.

Building and Applying Material to the Alien

With the UV layout image saved, we loaded the UV image into Photoshop and used painting to create the final map for the alien, as shown in Figure 10.25.

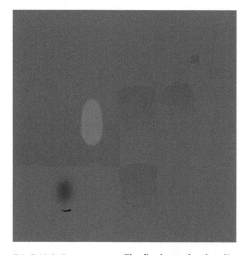

FIGURE 10.25 The final map for the alien

The texture map, as you can see, places painted parts of the alien's body according to the UV layout you just created. For example, you can clearly see the alien's eye socket painted in middle of the texture image file.

Exercise 10.5: Applying the Color Map

Now it is time to use the map that you put so much effort into creating. Continue with the scene file from the previous section or open c10_ex5_color-map_start.max from the scenes folder of the c10_UnwrapUV project folder.

1. Open the Slate Material Editor (M).

2. In the Material/Map Browser, expand the Materials rollout, and on the Standard rollout, drag and drop a Standard material onto the View1 window. Double-click the material node title bar to load the parameter into the Material Parameter Editor. Rename the material **Alien**.

3. Double-click the Diffuse Color input socket of the material to open the Material/Map Browser.

4. In the Maps rollout, expand the Standard rollout and double-click Bitmap.

5. When the Select Bitmap Image File dialog box appears, navigate to the \sceneassets\images folder for the c10_UnwrapUV project, select the Alien_ColorMap.tif file, and then select Open.

6. Apply the material to the alien, and click Show Shaded Material In Viewport.

   The result is shown in Figure 10.26. Now wasn't all that hard UV work worth it? If the blue seams are showing, go back to the Modify panel and select the Unwrap UVW modifier. Go to the Configure rollout and uncheck Peel Seams.

Save your work before continuing with the next set of steps. To check your work, open c10_ex5_colormap_end.max from the scenes folder of the c10_UnwrapUV project folder.

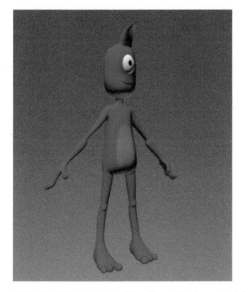

FIGURE 10.26 The alien with the material applied

Exercise 10.6: Applying the Bump Map

Bump mapping makes an object appear to have a bumpy or irregular surface by simulating surface definition. When you render an object with a bump-mapped material, lighter (whiter) areas of the map appear to be raised on the object's surface, and darker (blacker) areas appear to be lower on the object's surface; Figure 10.27 shows an example of the alien color map turned into a bump.

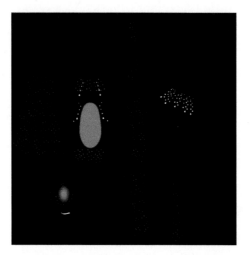

FIGURE 10.27 The Bump map was created in Photoshop by desaturating the original color map to create light and dark areas that conform to the original color texture.

You can use this mapping technique to create additional surface detail. Bump maps are simple to create because you can usually take the color map and just desaturate it to make a grayscale image file. You will continue with the Alien material you created in the previous exercise as you add the new map. Continue with the scene file from the previous section, or open c10_ex6_bumpmap_start .max from the scenes folder of the c10_UnwrapUV project folder.

1. Double-click the Bump input socket of the material to open the Material/Map Browser.

2. Under the Maps rollout, expand the Standard rollout and choose Bitmap.

3. When the Select Bitmap Image File dialog box appears, navigate to the \sceneassets\images folder of the c10_UnwrapUV project folder and select the Alien_BumpMap.tif file.

4. Double-click the material's title bar to show the main material parameters.

5. In the Maps rollout, set Bump Amount to 30.

The bump map is applied and finished. See Figure 10.28 for an image with the bump map. You may notice that the bump map has created a lot more detail in the alien's body. You will notice the difference even better in your own renders.

Save your work before continuing with the next set of steps. To check your work, open c10_ex6_bump_end.max from the scenes folder of the c10_UnwrapUV project folder.

FIGURE 10.28   Alien rendered with the bump map

Exercise 10.7: Applying the Specular Map

Highlights in objects are reflections of a light source. *Specular* maps are maps you use to define a surface's shininess and highlight color, without the complex calculations of reflections in the render. The higher a pixel's value (from black to white, or 0 to 1, respectively), the shinier the surface will appear at that location. You will be adding a specular map to the alien to increase the amount of detail you can get from the render, as shown in Figure 10.29.

FIGURE 10.29   The specular map for the alien

Continue with the scene file from the previous section or open `c10_ex7_spec_start.max` from the `scenes` folder of the `c10_UnwrapUV` project folder.

▶

Placing the map into the Specular Color slot allows for iridescence and flexibility.

1. Double-click the Specular Color input socket of the material to open the Material/Map Browser.

2. Under the Maps rollout, expand the Standard rollout and choose Bitmap.

3. When the Select Bitmap Image File dialog box appears, navigate to the `\sceneassets\images` folder for the `c10_UnwrapUV` project and select the `Alien_SpecularMap.tif` file.

4. Double-click the material's title bar to show the main material parameters.

5. In the Specular Highlights group, set Specular Level to **50** and Glossiness to **40**.

6. Render the alien in the Perspective viewport.

The final render of the alien is shown in Figure 10.30. You can see the improvement to the appearance of the alien's bumps with the added specular color map.

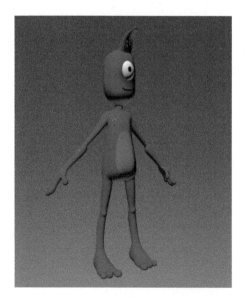

FIGURE 10.30 The final render of the alien with the specular map applied

Save your work. To check your work, open `c10_ex7_spec_end.max` from the scenes folder of the `c10_UnwrapUV` project folder.

Now You Know

In this chapter, you learned how to set up the alien model to accept textures properly through a process called UV-unwrap, which allowed you to lay out the maps onto the alien's body using the Unwrap UVW modifier. Once the model was prepared with proper UVs, you saw how to apply the painted maps to the model.

CHAPTER 11

Character Studio: Rigging

At one time or another, almost everyone in the 3D community wants to animate a character. This chapter examines the toolsets used in the process of setting up for character animation using Character Studio, a full-featured package that is incorporated into the Autodesk® 3ds Max® 2016 software and used mostly for animating bipedal characters, including humans, aliens, robots, and anything else that walks on two feet—although you can have characters with more than two feet in certain situations.

In this chapter, you'll learn to:

▶ **Utilize the Character Studio workflow**

▶ **Associate a biped with the alien model**

▶ **Skin the alien model**

Character Studio Workflow

Character Studio is a system built into the 3ds Max program to help automate the creation and animation of a character, which may or may not be exactly a *biped* (two-footed creature). Character Studio consists of three basic components: the Biped system, the Skin modifiers, and the Crowd system. Biped and Skin are used to pose and animate a single character, and the Crowd system is used to assign similar movements and behaviors to multiple objects in your 3ds Max scene. This chapter covers the Biped and Skin features; the Crowd system is beyond the scope of this book.

The first step in the Character Studio workflow is to build or acquire a suitable character model. The second step is to *skin* (bind) the character model to the skeleton so the animation drives the model properly.

Models should typically be in the reference position known as the da Vinci pose, where the feet are a shoulder's width apart and the arms are extended to the sides with the palms down, as shown in Figure 11.1. This allows the animator to observe all of the model's features, unobstructed by the model itself, in at least two viewports.

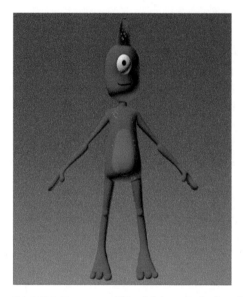

FIGURE 11.1 A bipedal character in the reference position

In 3ds Max parlance, a *biped* is a predefined, initially humanoid structure. It is important to understand that you animate the biped that is associated with your model and not the model itself. Once the model is bound to the skeleton, the biped structure *drives* the model. You use the Skin modifier to create that relationship between the skeleton and the model.

General Workflow

You can choose from four different biped types: Skeleton, Male, Female, and Classic, as shown in Figure 11.2. They all consist of legs, feet, toes, arms, hands, fingers, pelvis, spine, neck, and head. After your model is ready, you will create a biped and, using its parameters and the Scale transform, fit the biped closely to the model.

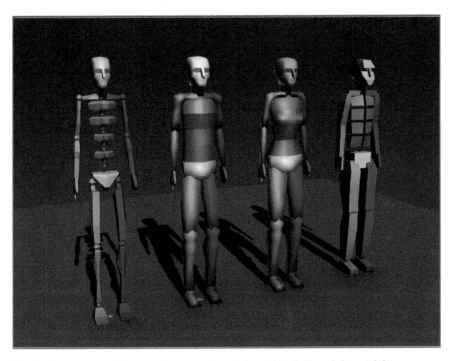

FIGURE 11.2 Skeleton, Male, Female, and Classic bipeds (from left to right)

The better the biped-to-model relationship, the easier the animation will be.

Once the biped is fit snugly to the model, you select all the components of the model, not the biped skeleton, and apply the Skin modifier in a process often referred to as *skinning*. It may take a while to properly test and refine the relationship between the model and the biped to get it to an acceptable level.

The final step is animating your character. You can accomplish this by adding to the biped any combination of default walk, run, and jump cycles included with Character Studio; applying any kind of freeform animation to the character; and finally, refining the animation keyframes in the Dope Sheet.

Don't expect the default walk, run, and jump cycles to create realistic motion, though. They are just starting points and must be tweaked to achieve acceptable movements.

The best way to start is to jump in and examine the tools available. In the next sections, you will work with a biped and adjust the parameters and components to modify it.

The Dope Sheet displays animation keys over time on a horizontal graph. It simplifies editing animation timing by displaying them in a spreadsheet format.

Associating a Biped with the Alien Model

The purpose of a biped is to be the portal through which you add animation to your model rather than animating the model itself using direct vertex manipulation or deforming modifiers. Any motion assigned to a biped is passed through it to the nearest vertices of the associated model, essentially driving the surfaces of the model. For this reason, it is important that the biped fit as closely as possible to the model.

Exercise 11.1: Creating and Modifying the Biped

In the following steps, you'll create and adjust a biped to fit to a character model. Set your project to the c11_CharacterRigging project available for download from this book's web page at www.sybex.com/go/3dsmax2016essentials. You can then open the c11_ex1_biped_start.max file from the scenes folder of the c11_CharacterRigging project folder. It contains a completed alien model in the reference position.

1. With the alien model file open, select the Perspective viewport, and set the viewport rendering type to Shaded + Edged faces (F4). Repeat for the Front viewport.

2. Select the alien, and use Alt+X to make the model see-through.

3. Right-click in a viewport and choose Freeze Selection. This will prevent you from inadvertently selecting the alien instead of the biped.

VIEWING FROZEN OBJECTS

If your background color is similar to the default shade of gray used to depict frozen objects, the model may seem to disappear against the background. There are several solutions to this situation:

▶ Before you freeze the model, go to Object Properties, turn off Show Frozen In Gray, turn on See-Through, and set all viewports to Realistic or Shaded mode.

▶ To access Object Properties, right-click over the model, and from the menu, choose Object Properties. This will open the dialog box.

▶ You can change the viewport background color in the Customize User Interface dialog box (Customize ➤ Customize User Interface ➤ Colors tab).

---

4. From the command panel, select Create ➤ Systems (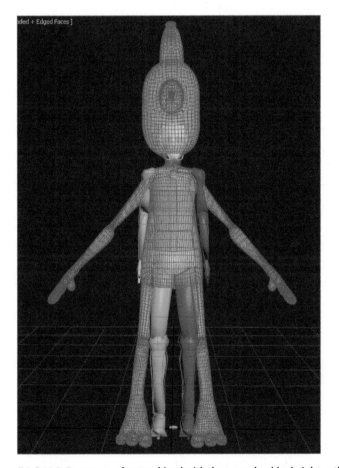) ➤ Biped. When you click Biped, the parameters will appear below.

5. Go to Body Type, and from the drop-down menu, choose Male.

6. In the Perspective viewport, click at the alien's feet and drag to create the biped.

7. Create a biped with a shoulder height the same as the alien's. This will make most of the biped's parts similar in size to those of the alien, as shown in Figure 11.3.

The first click sets the insertion point. Dragging defines the height of the biped system and defines all of the components. All of the biped's components are sized relative to the Height parameter.

F I G U R E   1 1 . 3   Create a biped with the same shoulder height as the alien model's.

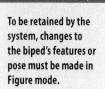

To be retained by the system, changes to the biped's features or pose must be made in Figure mode.

8. With the biped still selected, in the command panel, click the Motion tab (), and in the Biped rollout, enter Figure mode, as shown in Figure 11.4.

9. Then in the Structure rollout, change the parameters to match Figure 11.5. The number of Spine Links should be set to 3. Change the number of Toes to 3 and Toe Links to 3. Change the number of Fingers to 4 **and Finger Links to 3.** For the alien's nose, you will use the Ponytail; set the Ponytail Links to 3.

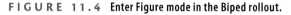

FIGURE 11.4   Enter Figure mode in the Biped rollout.

FIGURE 11.5   Change the biped from the Structure rollout.

10. Use the Body Vertical and Body Horizontal buttons in the Track Selection rollout and the Move Transform gizmo to position the biped's pelvis in the same location as the model's pelvis, as shown in

Figure 11.6. With the pelvis located properly, scaling the legs or spine to match the model's proportions will be much easier.

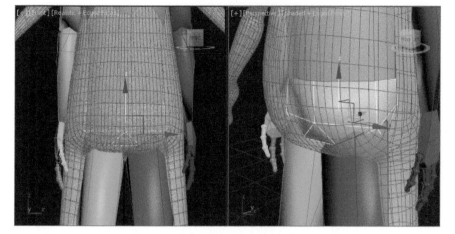

When you're creating a biped skeleton, remember these two important tips: Place the joints accurately at the 3D mesh's joints; and modify only one side of the biped and then use Copy/Paste to update the other side, if the model is symmetrical.

FIGURE 11.6 Match the positions of the biped's pelvis and the alien's pelvis.

11. Check to make sure the location is correct in all of the viewports.

12. Select Uniform Scale in the main toolbar; make sure the reference coordinate system is set to Local on the Reference Coordinate System drop-down menu in the main toolbar, as shown in Figure 11.7. This will be set for the Scale tool only.

FIGURE 11.7 Set the reference coordinate system to Local.

13. In the Front viewport, select the pelvis and scale its width so that the biped's legs fit inside the alien's legs. Scale the pelvis in the Left viewport so that it roughly encompasses the alien's lower region, as shown in Figure 11.8.

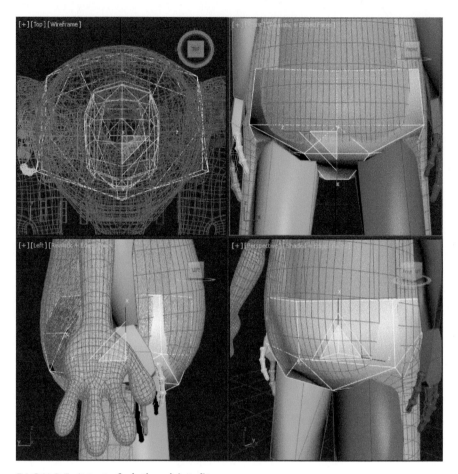

FIGURE 11.8 Scale the pelvis to fit.

14. Select the biped's left thigh (the blue leg), and then scale it along the X-axis until the knee aligns with the alien's knee. Scale it on the Y- and Z-axes until it is similar in size to the alien's thigh.

15. Select the biped's left calf. Switch to the Right viewport, rotate the calf to match the model (move the calf if necessary), and then scale it on the X-axis until the biped's ankle matches the alien's ankle. Scale the calf to match the proportions of the alien's calf. You may need to select the left foot and use the Move transform, in the Front viewport, to orient the calf to the model.

16. Continue working down the leg by scaling the biped's foot to match the alien's. Be sure to check the orientation of the foot in the Top viewport.

17. Scale and move the biped's toes to match the alien's toes. Be sure to scale the toe links on the Z-axis. The finished leg and foot are shown in Figure 11.9.

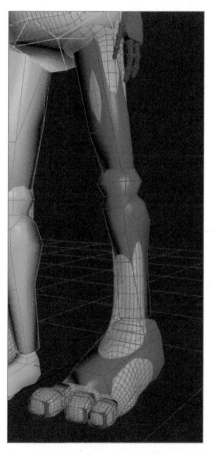

FIGURE 11.9 Match the biped's leg, foot, and toes with the alien's.

18. Double-click the left upper leg to select it and all of the objects below it in the hierarchy, from the thigh down to the toes.

19. Open the Copy/Paste rollout.

20. Postures must be saved as collections prior to being pasted. Click the Create Collection button, as shown in Figure 11.10, and then rename the collection from the default Col01 to **Left Leg**.

21. Click the Copy Posture button just below the Posture button to copy the selected posture to the Clipboard. A preview of the copied posture will appear in the Copied Postures area of the command panel, as shown in Figure 11.11.

FIGURE 11.10 Create the collection to paste the left leg hierarchy.

FIGURE 11.11 Copy the posture. The selected objects will appear in red in the preview.

22. Click the Paste Posture Opposite button ( ). The size, scale, and orientation of the selected objects will be applied to the reciprocal objects on the opposite side of the biped.

Save your work before continuing with the next set of steps. To check your work, open c11_ex1_biped_end.max from the scenes folder of the c11_CharacterRigging project folder.

Exercise 11.2: Adjusting the Torso and Arms

Similar to the method used to adjust the legs, you will use the Scale and Rotate transforms to fit the biped to the model. The locations of the arms rely on the scale of the spine links. Continue with the file from the previous exercise or open the c11_ex2_biped_start.max file from the scenes folder of the c11_CharacterRigging project folder.

1. Select the biped and then access Figure mode if needed.

2. Ctrl+click to select each of the spine links in turn, and then rotate and scale them to fit the alien's torso. Each spine link should be scaled up slightly to match the model, as shown in Figure 11.12.

> Only the lowest spine link can be moved, and this will move all of the links above it as well.

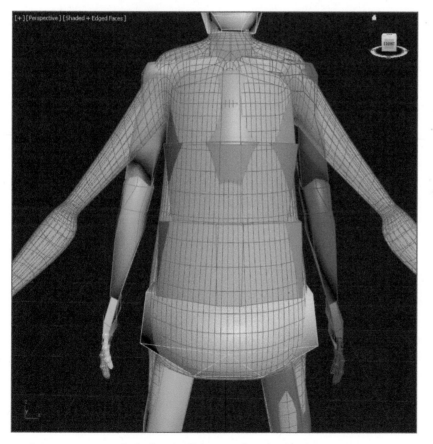

FIGURE 11.12 Scale the spine links up to place the clavicles in position.

3. Move, rotate, and scale the left clavicle as required, placing the biped's shoulder joint in the proper location.

4. Scale and rotate the left upper arm and left forearm to fit the arm to the model using the same techniques you used to adjust the biped's legs. Pay close attention to the placement of the elbow and wrist joint, as shown in Figure 11.13.

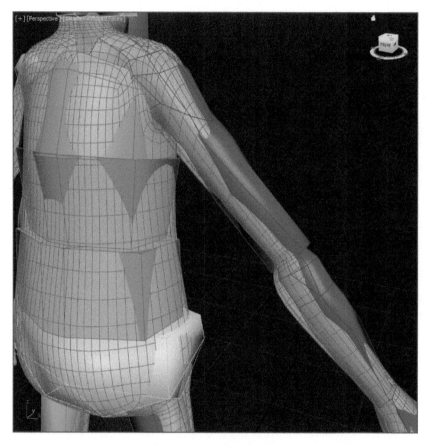

FIGURE 11.13   Arm positioned within the 3D mesh

Once the fingers have been adjusted, you cannot go back and change the number of fingers or finger links. If you do, all of the modifications to the fingers will be lost.

5. Scale and rotate the left hand as required to fit the model.

6. The hands need to have only three fingers and one thumb (the fourth finger is actually the thumb) and three links each. Adjust the biped's fingers to match the model's fingers, as shown in Figure 11.14.

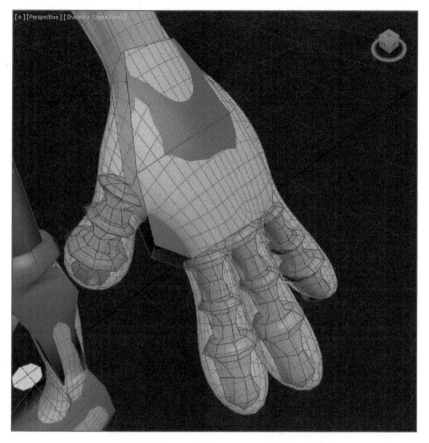

FIGURE 11.14 Match the biped's fingers to the model's fingers.

Matching the fingers to the model can be one of the most tedious tasks in character animation, depending on the complexity and orientation of the model's fingers. Take your time and get it right.

7. When you have finished, create the collection, copy and then paste the posture to the right side of the biped, and make any required changes.

Save your work before continuing with the next set of steps. To check your work, open c11_ex2_biped_end.max from the scenes folder of the c11_CharacterRigging project folder.

Exercise 11.3: Adjusting the Neck and Head

When compared to the hands, the neck and head will seem easy to adjust. You need to make sure the neck links fill the alien's neck area and scale the head to fit. Continue with file from previous exercise or open the c11_ex3_biped_start .max file from the scenes folder of the c11_CharacterRigging project folder.

1. Select the model and go to the Motion panel. In the Structure rollout, increase the number of neck links to 2.

2. Move, scale, and rotate the neck links to match the proportions of the model's neck.

3. Move and scale the head to the approximate size of the alien's head, as shown in Figure 11.15.

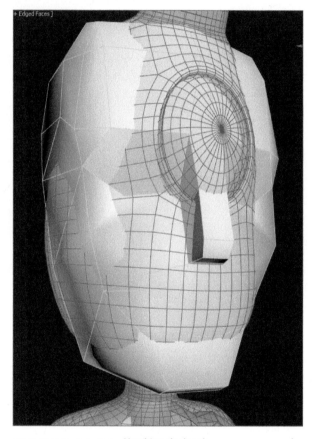

FIGURE 11.15   Matching the head

4. Now for the nose. The ponytail links need to be selected and moved into position at the nose. Using Move, Rotate, and Scale, adjust the ponytail links to match the nose, as shown in Figure 11.16.

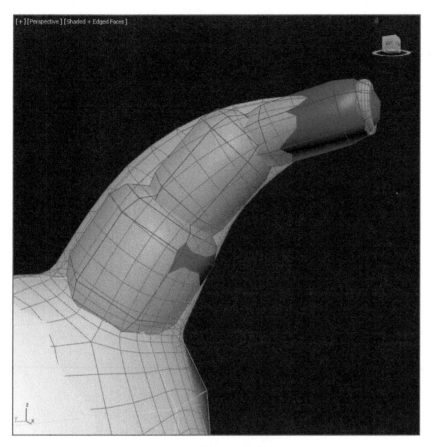

FIGURE 11.16 Match the ponytail links with the nose.

That's it. The biped has been created and adjusted to fit the 3D model, and half the battle is over. Next, you will tie the biped to the model and make adjustments to the skinning process. Save your work before continuing with the next set of steps. To check your work, open c11_ex3_biped_end.max from the scenes folder of the c11_CharacterRigging project folder.

Skinning the Alien Model

The Skin modifier is the tool used to skin the 3D model to the biped so that all of the biped's animation is passed through to the model. It's important to remember that the modifier is applied to the model and not to the biped.

Exercise 11.4: Applying the Skin Modifier

Continue with the previous exercise's file or open the c11_ex4_skin_start.max file from the scenes folder of the c11_CharacterRigging project folder.

1. Right-click in any viewport, and select Unfreeze All from the quad menu to unfreeze the alien model.

2. Select the alien, use Alt+X to exit See-Through mode, and turn off Edged Faces (F4) in all viewports.

3. In the Modify panel, expand the Modifier List and select the Skin modifier.

4. In the Skin parameters, click the Add button next to Bones. In the Select Bones dialog box, click the Select All button ( ) in the toolbar, and then click the Select button at the bottom on the dialog box.

Save your work before continuing with the next set of steps. To check your work, open c11_ex4_skin_end.max from the scenes folder of the c11_CharacterRigging project folder.

Exercise 11.5: Testing the Model

The most time-consuming part of the process is complete. You have created a biped and adjusted all of its component parts to fit your model. The next step is to add animation that will allow you to test the skinning once it has been applied.

Before we get into fixing the skin, you need to add a little extra animation. Continue with the previous exercise's file or open the c11_ex5_skin_start.max file from the scenes folder of the c11_CharacterRigging project folder.

1. Select the model, right-click, and from the quad menu, choose Hide Selection.

2. Move the time slider to frame 0. Turn on the Auto Key button ( ) below the time slider.

3. Select the entire biped: The best way to do this is to use the Scene Explorer, which is docked on the left of the interface. If it is not, you can open a floating Explorer dialog box by going to the Main Menu ➤ Tools ➤ Scene Explorer. In the Scene Explorer, go to the Select menu and choose Select All.

4. From the Scene Explorer, select the Bip001 object, then go to the Motion panel (Auto), and click the Figure Mode button (⊚) to exit.

◀

You cannot animate a biped in Figure mode.

5. Select the Move tool and move the biped just a bit. The purpose of this is to create a keyframe of this original pose so that when you add animation, this pose won't be lost. The biped should still be in the same position as before—just give the Move tool a wiggle.

6. Select the right upper arm, Ctrl+click the left upper arm on the biped, and then set the reference coordinate system for the Rotate tool to Local.

7. Move the timeline to frame 15, and rotate the arms –55 degrees on the Y-axis (the green wire in the Rotate gizmo).

8. Now select the right and left lower arms on the biped and rotate –55 degrees on the Z-axis.

9. Move the timeline to frame 30 and select the upper arms again; this time rotate 45 degrees on the Z-axis (blue wire).

10. Now move to frame 50 and select the lower arms and upper arms. In the timeline, Shift+click the keyframe at frame 0, and then drag it to frame 50. This copies the keyframe at frame 0 to frame 50.

11. Continue adding keyframes to the animation to fill 100 frames.

Using the same technique, add animation to the legs, chest, and head. The animation does not have to be elaborate. The purpose of the animation is to test the skinning when applied to the model. When you have finished, turn off the Auto Key button, unhide the alien, and play the animation. Most likely, you will see some problem with the skin—mostly around the feet, upper arms, and groin. To see the model clearly, hide the biped objects, as shown in Figure 11.17.

Save your work before continuing with the next set of steps. To check your work, open c11_ex5_skin_end.max from the scenes folder of the c11_CharacterRigging project folder.

FIGURE 11.17 **The problem areas with the skinning**

Exercise 11.6: Tweaking the Skin Modifier

Each element in the biped has an area of influence, called an *envelope*. It determines which parts of the model it affects. The biped's left foot, for instance, should control the movement of only the model's left foot and the lower part of the ankle. In this case, the envelopes extend to affect some of the vertices on the opposite side of the model.

The biped bone is represented in the viewport as a straight line with vertices at either end. Envelopes are represented by two concentric capsule-shaped volumes; vertices within the inner volume are fully affected by that bone, and then the weighting falls off increasingly for vertices that lie outside the inner volume and inside the outer volume. The weight values appear as a colored gradient using red for the higher weights and blue for the lowest values, with orange, yellow, and green in between.

Continue with the previous exercise's file or open the c11_ex6_skin_start .max file from the scenes folder of the c11_CharacterRigging project. The animation might be a bit different if you are using your own file, but it will still work to check the Skin modifier.

1. Select the alien model. Then in the Modify panel, go to the Skin parameters and click the Edit Envelopes button. You will see a color gradient around the pelvis. The gradient shows how heavily weighted the vertices on your mesh are to a given envelope, as shown in Figure 11.18.

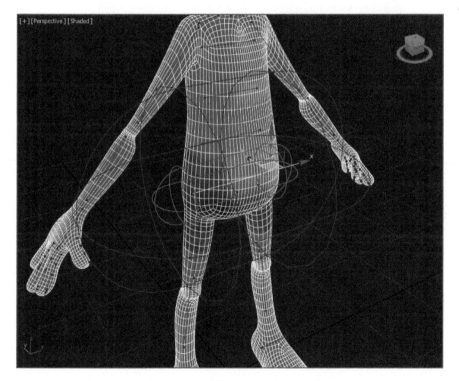

FIGURE 11.18   The alien with the Edit Envelopes button active

2. Select the Bip001 R UpperArm object. You can select the object from the name list in the Skin parameters or just click on the representation of the bone on the model. Select the vertex at the end of the bone near the elbow and move it toward the clavicle to make the

envelope smaller (change the reference coordinate system to Local to make the move easier), as shown in Figure 11.19.

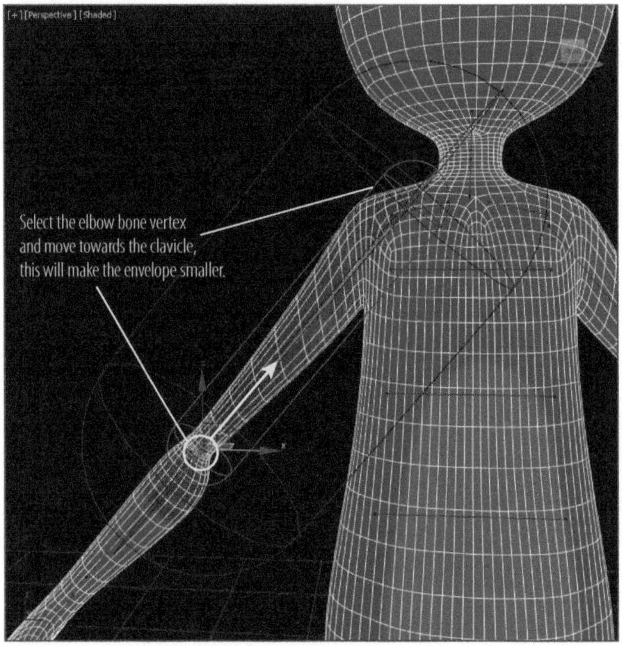

Select the elbow bone vertex and move towards the clavicle; this will make the envelope smaller.

FIGURE 11.19 Select the bone vertex and move it to make the envelope smaller.

3. As the vertex moves, the gradient that represents the influence changes so the yellow-red color moves up the arm. You want the influence to be on the upper arm only. Repeat this step on the other end of the bone near the clavicle, bringing it in toward the center of the bone.

4. Select the points on the inner envelope and move them in on both ends of the bone.

5. Select the points on the outside envelope and move them in on both ends of the bone, as shown in Figure 11.20.

6. Move to frame 30 in the animation. In this frame, you can really see the problem with the arm. Even though you edited the envelope for the upper arm, you can't see any improvement in the deformity. The previous steps showed how to edit the envelope; now let's figure out

where the trouble really lies with the upper arm: Bip001 Spine 2 and Bip001 Spine 1. Select each one and see how the inner envelope is crossing the upper arm.

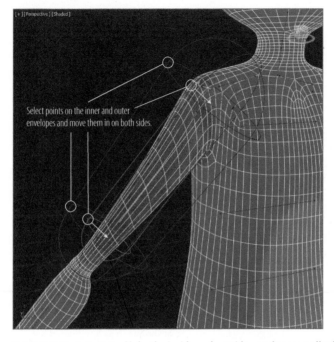

FIGURE 11.20   Make the inside and outside envelopes smaller by selecting and moving the points.

7. Select the Bip001 Spine 2 bone. This bone's envelope is huge! It is influencing almost the whole upper body. Select a vertex on either end of the bone and move it in; immediately, you will see the arms reacting. Repeat the process on Bip001 Spine 1.

8. Now scale down the size of the outer envelope so that the gradient has some yellow on the inside and blue between the capsules, as shown in Figure 11.21.

9. Now select and edit the remaining two spine bones. Fixing the remaining bones will also fix the issue with the Bip001 R Forearm bone.

10. Select the BIP001 R UpperArm bone, and in the Mirror Parameters rollout of the Skin modifier, click the Mirror Mode button.

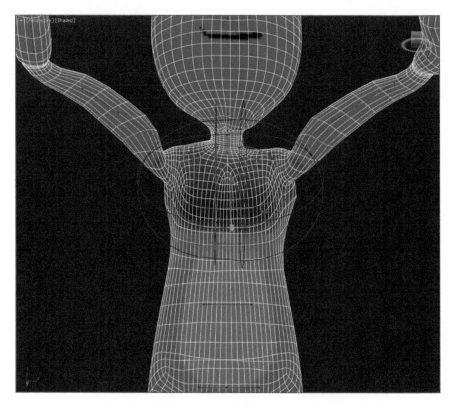

FIGURE 11.21 The Bip001Spine2 bone after the envelope has been edited.

11. Click the Paste Green to Blue Bones button. This pastes the envelope settings from the green bones to the blue bones ( ).

12. In the Skin parameters, click the Edit Envelopes button to exit.

13. Play the animation again, and pay attention to any areas where you see parts of the mesh pulling or distorting.

14. Go back to that area's envelope, and edit until you are happy with the results.

Save your work before continuing with the next set of steps. To check your work, open c11_ex6_skin_end.max from the scenes folder of the c11_CharacterRigging project folder.

Exercise 11.7: Testing the Alien Model Rig

Continue with the previous exercise's file or open the c11_ex7_skin_start .max file from the scenes folder of the c11_CharacterRigging project folder.

The animation might be a bit different if you are using your own file, but it will still work to check the Skin modifier.

1. To delete any animation, select all the biped bones, drag a selection around the keyframes, and delete them in the timeline.

2. Select away from the model and then select any element of the biped and click the Motion tab of the command panel.

3. Enter Footstep mode (![]). The rollouts change to display the tools for adding and controlling a biped's motion.

4. In the Footstep Creation rollout, make sure the Walk button (![]) is selected, and then click the Create Multiple Footsteps button (![]) to open the Create Multiple Footsteps dialog box. In the dialog box that appears, you will assign Footstep properties for the number of steps you want, the width and length of each step, and which foot to step with first.

5. Set Number of Footsteps to 8, leave the other parameters at their default values, and click OK.

6. Zoom out in the Perspective viewport to see the footsteps you just created. Look at the time slider, and note that the scene now ends at frame 123; that's 23 more frames than the 100 frames the scene had at the beginning of this chapter. The 3ds Max software recognized that it would take the biped 123 frames, or just over 4 seconds, to move through the eight steps that it was given.

7. Click the Play Animation button in the Playback Controls area. What happens? Nothing. The biped must be told explicitly to create animation keys for the steps that you have just added to the scene.

8. Stop the animation, and drag the time slider back to frame 0.

9. In the Footstep Operations rollout in the command panel, click the Create Keys for Inactive Footsteps button (![]). The biped will drop its arms and prepare to walk through the footsteps that are now associated with it. Select Footstep Mode button to exit.

10. Select the alien model and right-click to access the quad menu. Choose Hide Unselected; this will hide the biped. Click the Play Animation button again. This time, the alien model walks through the footsteps with its arms swinging and its hips swaying back and forth.

You cannot be in both Footstep mode and Figure mode at the same time.

Watch the animation play; it won't be perfect. Notice that the arms are in too close to the body and the alien is walking a bit stiffly. Chapter 12, "Character Studio: Animation," will cover the finer points of animating with Character Studio. Save your work before continuing with the next set of steps. To check your work, open c11_ex7_skin_end.max from the scenes folder of the c11_CharacterRigging project folder.

Exercise 11.8: Controlling the View

Now the problem is that if you zoom in on the model and play the animation, it walks off the screen so you cannot see the end of the walk cycle. What good is that? Motion cycles can be very linear and difficult to track, so Character Studio provides the In Place mode to follow a biped's animation. In the In Place mode, the biped will appear to stay in place while the scene moves around it in relation. Continue with the previous exercise's file or open the c11_ex8_test_start.max file from the scenes folder of the c11_CharacterRigging project folder.

To set up In Place mode, follow these steps:

1. Right-click and choose Unhide All; then select a part of the biped. Go to frame 0, and zoom in on the biped in the Perspective viewport.

2. At the bottom of the Biped rollout, click the Modes and Display text with the plus sign to the left of it. This is a small rollout located inside another rollout that expands to show additional display-related tools. It is hidden and difficult to find, as shown in Figure 11.22.

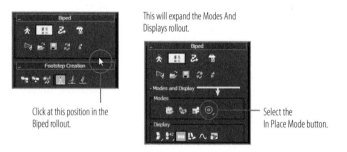

FIGURE 11.22   In the Biped rollout, click at the bottom to reveal the Modes and Display rollout.

3. In the Modes and Display rollout, click the In Place Mode button (![icon]), as shown in Figure 11.22.

4. Click the Play Animation button again. This time, the biped will appear to be walking in place while the footsteps move underneath it.

5. Stop the animation playback when you're ready.

6. Select the entire biped by double-clicking Bip001. If it is too difficult to do, use the Scene Explorer, which is docked on the left of the interface. If it is not, you can open it by going to the Main Menu ➤ Tools ➤ Scene Explorer.

7. Right-click in any viewport and choose Hide Selection from the quad menu to hide the biped and obtain an unobstructed view of the model.

8. Click the Play Animation button.

   Your alien will walk through the scene. It should be similar to the rendered alien shown in Figure 11.23.

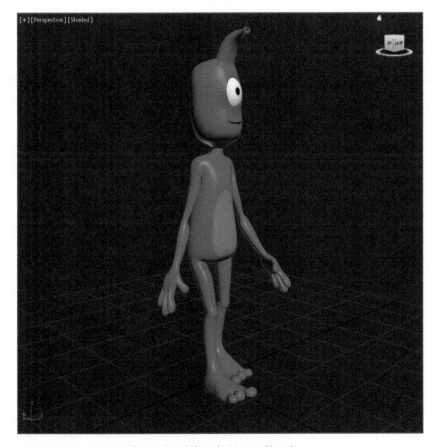

FIGURE 11.23 The rendered alien during a walk cycle

The Character Studio tutorials and help system that ship with the 3ds Max program are very thorough, and you should find the information there to expand your skills once you have a solid footing with the basics.

Skinning a character is a detail-oriented task, and it requires lots of experimentation and trial and error—and patience. Character Studio is a complete character-animation package, and we've barely scratched the surface here. There are tools for saving biped configurations and sequences of animation. You can mix animation sequences from different files to create an entirely new motion. When the model does not skin as well as you need, you can use envelopes to refine the skinning process further, define vertices to be excluded from a specific Biped object's influence, or include bulge conditions to define the model's behavior depending on the angle between subsequent biped elements. The list goes on.

It's important to realize that animation requires nuance, and the best animation with the simplest rig and setup will beat a mediocre animation created with a more wonderful, complicated, and ingenious setup. Save your work. To check your work, open c11_ex8_test_end.max from the scenes folder of the c11_CharacterRigging project folder.

Now You Know

In this chapter, you were introduced to the basics of Character Studio and the Biped setup for the alien character. The Skin modifier was introduced to apply the Biped setup to the geometry of the alien and was used to adjust the envelopes for the best animation results.

CHAPTER 12

Character Studio: Animation

Character animation is a broad and complex field; in fact, the character-animation computer-generated specialty is one of the toughest specialties to master. To use one word, good character animation comes down to *nuance*. When you animate a character, you have to have a keen eye for detail and an understanding of how proportions move on a person's body. Setting up a computer-generated character to walk *exactly* like a human being is amazingly complicated.

Character systems such as Character Studio make it a breeze to outfit characters with biped setups and have them moving in a walk cycle very quickly.

This chapter introduces you to the basics of using Character Studio and bones for animation. If you want your animation to be full of life and character, further investigation into these tools is a must.

In this chapter, you'll learn to

▶ **Animate the alien**

▶ **Use freeform animation**

▶ **Modify animating using the Dope Sheet**

Animating the Alien

Bipeds can be animated in several ways, including footstep-driven animation and freeform animation. With *footstep-driven animation*, you add visible Footstep objects to your scene and direct the biped to step onto those footsteps at particular points in time. Footsteps can be added individually or as a set of walk, run, or jump steps; they can be moved or rotated to achieve the desired result and direction. When you use footstep-driven animation, the legs and feet of the biped are not the only things animated; the hips, arms, tails, and all other components are animated as well. However, this approach is rarely the complete solution to your animation needs.

Freeform animation means that you animate the components of the biped manually, as you would animate any other object, such as a bouncing ball.

Animation keys that are added to the selected biped objects appear in the track bar, just like other objects, where they can be moved, modified, or deleted to adjust the animation.

Exercise 12.1: Adding a Run-and-Jump Sequence

At the end of the previous chapter, you finished rigging the alien model and added footsteps to check the model. New footsteps can be appended to any existing footsteps. In the next exercise, you will add footsteps to the existing animation cycle.

Set your project to the c12_CharacterAnimation project available for download from this book's web page at www.sybex.com/go/3dsmax2016essentials. Open the c12_ex1_run_start.max file in the scenes folder. This file has most of the biped bones hidden. The objects that are visible in the file are for the alien model; Bip001 is the diamond shape that sits at the pelvis area of the alien character and acts as the center for your biped rig.

If you have trouble, you can either press the H key or click the Select by Name icon ( ) found on the main toolbar, which opens the Select from Scene dialog box.

When you add the run steps, the arms will change position.

The Actual Stride Height parameter in the Create Multiple Footsteps dialog box determines the height difference from one footstep to the next. This is how to make the biped climb stairs.

1. Select the Bip001 object from the Scene Explorer panel on the left of the interface; if it is not docked in the interface, open it by going to the main menu bar and choosing Tools ➢ Scene Explorer.

2. On the Motion panel, select Footstep mode ( ).

3. Click the Run icon ( ) in the Footstep Creation rollout. This will apply a run gait to any footsteps you add to your current footsteps using the Create Multiple Footsteps dialog box.

4. Click the Create Multiple Footsteps icon ( ) to open the Create Multiple Footsteps dialog box.

5. Change Number of Footsteps to 10 and click OK.

6. In the Footstep Operations rollout, click the Create Keys for Inactive Footsteps icon ( ) to associate the new footsteps with the biped.

7. Click the Play Animation button. The In Place Mode icon (⊙) is active in this file. The biped will appear to stay in place while the scene moves around it. The biped walks through the first 8 steps and then runs through the next 10. Click the Stop Animation button to turn off the animation.

8. Click the Jump button in the Footstep Creation rollout, and then click the Create Multiple Footsteps button.

9. In the Create Multiple Footsteps dialog box, set the number of footsteps to 4 and click OK.

10. Click the Create Keys for Inactive Footsteps icon to associate the new jump footsteps with the biped.

11. Click the Play Animation button. The biped will walk, run, and then end the sequence with two jumps, as shown in Figure 12.1.

◀

The run sequence meets the definition of a run, but it is far from realistic. In the next exercise, you'll learn how to add to or modify a biped's motion with freeform animation to make a better run cycle.

◀

Because a jump is defined as a sequence with either two feet or zero feet on the ground at a time, four jump steps will equal two actual jumps.

FIGURE 1 2 . 1 Alien model with the jump sequence added

Save your work before continuing with the next set of steps. To check your work, open c12_ex1_run_end.max from the scenes folder of the c12_CharacterAnimation project folder.

Freeform Animation

When you set your keys initially, you will need to edit them to suit good timing and form. When one part of the body is in one movement, another part of the body is in an accompanying or supportive or even opposite form of movement. When you are walking and your right leg swings forward in a step, your right arm swings back and your left arm swings forward to compensate.

You can easily add or modify the biped's existing animation keys with freeform animation using the Auto Key button and the Dope Sheet. The following exercises contain examples of freeform animation.

Exercise 12.2: Moving the Head

The following steps will guide you through the process of creating head movement for your biped. Continue with the previous alien model or open the c12_ex2_head_start.max file in the scenes folder of the c12_CharacterAnimation project on the book's web page. Because you will be working with the biped a lot in this exercise, the biped components have been unhidden and the alien model has been hidden. If you are using your own file, you need to do the same.

1. Select any Biped object, and if necessary, exit Footstep mode by clicking the Footstep Mode icon.

2. Drag the time slider to frame 50, approximately the point when the biped lifts its left foot off footstep number 2.

3. Select the biped's head and note the animation keys that appear in the track bar, as shown in Figure 12.2.

4. In the track bar, select the two keys on either side of the current frame. You can do that using either of the following methods:

   ▶ Drag a selection box around both keys directly on the track bar.

   ▶ Select one key, and then hold down the Ctrl key while selecting the other key.

> Footsteps are numbered, starting with the number 0 and initially alternating from the left to the right side. They are also color coded, with blue footsteps on the left and green footsteps on the right.

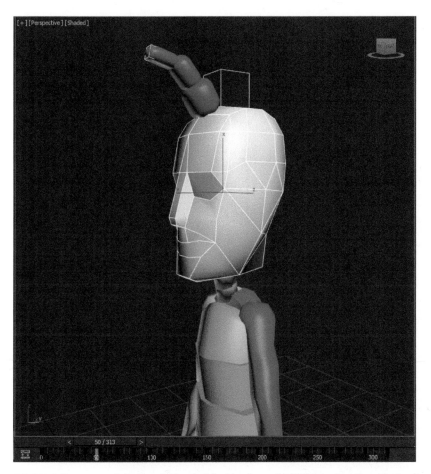

FIGURE 12.2 Selecting the head of the biped reveals all of that object's animation keys in the track bar.

5. Once the two keys are selected, right-click over either key and then choose Delete Selected Keys, as shown in Figure 12.3.

Key Properties	▶
Controller Properties	▶
Delete Key	▶
Delete selected keys	
Filter	▶
Configure	▶
Go to Time	

FIGURE 12.3 Delete the keys on either side of frame 50.

6. Click the Auto Key button or press the N key to turn it on. This will allow you to begin creating the animation.

7. Click the Rotate tool and rotate the head, to the left and up, as shown in Figure 12.4, as if the character sees somebody in a second-floor window off-screen. A new key will be created at frame 50, recording the time and value of the head's rotation.

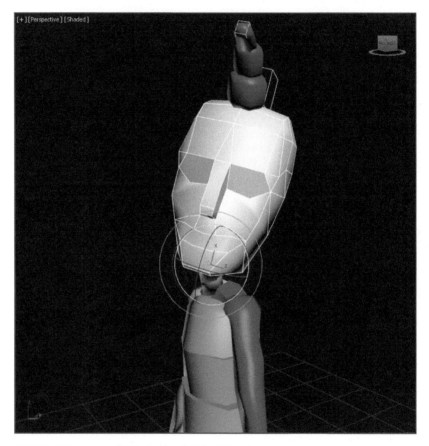

FIGURE 12.4 Rotate the head to the left and up.

If animation keys are too close together, the animation could appear jerky.

▶

8. Scrub through the time slider by moving it back and forth, watching the head rotate from a neutral position to the orientation that you created and then back to the neutral position.

9. Select both keys between frame 50 and frame 100 (but not the keys at frames 50 and 100), and delete them. Doing so will make room for the new key that you are about to create.

10. Select the key at frame 50, hold down the Shift key, and drag a copy of the key to frame 90, as shown in Figure 12.5. Use the readout at the bottom of the window to drag the key with precision. Copying the key will cause your biped to hold that neck pose for 40 frames, or about 1 1/3 seconds.

FIGURE 12.5 Shift and drag to copy the key.

11. Scrub the time slider to review the animation.

Save your work before continuing with the next set of steps. To check your work, open c12_ex2_head_end.max from the scenes folder of the c12_CharacterAnimation project folder.

Exercise 12.3: Moving the Arms

Continue with the previous alien model or open the c12_ex3_arm_start.max file in the scenes folder of the c12_CharacterAnimation project folder.

1. Select the biped's left upper arm.

2. In the track bar, select and delete the key frames between frames 50 and 100. If you scrub the time slider or play the animation, the biped will hold its arm unnaturally stiff for 60 frames because you deleted the animation keys between two points where it moves its hand forward.

3. Move the time slider to frame 60. This is the location for the first new animation key. Now it's time to animate the arms, which are essential components in any walk cycle.

4. Turn on Auto Key (N) and then rotate the upper arm upward, so that it points to the location at which the head is looking.

5. Continue adjusting the biped's left arm, hand, and fingers until they appear to be pointing at something, as shown in Figure 12.6.

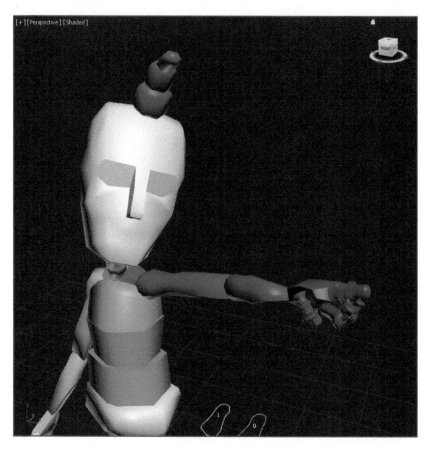

FIGURE 12.6 Rotate the biped's arm, hand, and fingers to assume a pointing posture.

6. Double-click the left upper arm to select it and all of the components below it in the hierarchy.

7. In the track bar, select the key at frame 60, hold down the Shift key, and drag it to frame 90 to create a copy.

8. Drag the time slider and watch the Perspective viewport. The biped will walk for a bit, notice something off-screen, point at it, and drop its arm while looking forward again before breaking into a run and then a jump.

9. Click the Auto Key button to turn it off.

Save your work before continuing with the next set of steps. To check your work, open c12_ex3_arm_end.max from the scenes folder of the c12_CharacterAnimation project folder.

Exercise 12.4: Completing the Motion Sequence

Continue with the previous alien model or open the c12_ex4_motion_start.max file in the scenes folder of the c12_CharacterAnimation project folder.

For additional practice, add keys to the animation of the biped's arms when it jogs through the run cycle. For example, when the left foot is fully extended and the heel plants on the ground, the right arm should be bent at the elbow and swung forward and slightly in front of the biped's body. As the right foot swings forward during the next step, the right arm should swing backward and assume a nearly straight position. Bend each of the spine links and swing both arms backward to prepare the biped for each of the jumps. Use the Body Vertical button in the Track Selection rollout to lower the pelvis into a prelaunch position, as shown in Figure 12.7, before the biped launches into its upward motion.

Make sure the Auto Key button is turned on to record all the changes that you make as you animate your character.

F I G U R E 1 2 . 7   Use the Body Vertical button to position the biped for a jump.

Save your work before continuing with the next set of steps. To check your work, open `c12_ex4_motion_end.max` from the `scenes` folder of the `c12_CharacterAnimation` project folder.

Modifying Animation in the Dope Sheet

▶

The only way to edit the footstep keys is to use the Dope Sheet.

To change the animation that is generated with Character Studio, you will edit the keyframes of the biped once you are happy with the base animation cycle. For this, you need to use the Track View - Dope Sheet. The Track View - Curve Editor, as you have already seen in Chapter 5, "Introduction to Animation," is used to edit the function curves between animation keys; however, the Track View - Dope Sheet interface is cleaner and is used to edit the specific value and position of the keys. It is not a different set of keyframes or animation; it's just a different way of editing them.

In the next exercise, you will add individual footsteps and modify the footstep timing in the Dope Sheet to make the biped dance and jump.

Exercise 12.5: Adding Footsteps Manually

For this exercise, you will need a file with no animation applied, so start with the `c12_ex5_steps_start.max` file in the `scenes` folder of the `c12_CharacterAnimation` project folder. This is the rigged and skinned alien biped with no footsteps applied.

1. Select a biped component and enter Footstep mode.

2. In the Footstep Creation rollout, click the Walk button and then the Create Footsteps (At Current Frame) icon ( ).

3. In the Top viewport, click in several locations around the biped to place alternating left and right footsteps to your liking.

4. Change the gait to Jump, and then click the Create Footsteps (Append) icon to create additional footsteps. Create about 13 footsteps in all.

5. When you have finished, use the Move and Rotate transforms to adjust the footstep locations and orientations as desired. Your Top viewport should look similar to Figure 12.8.

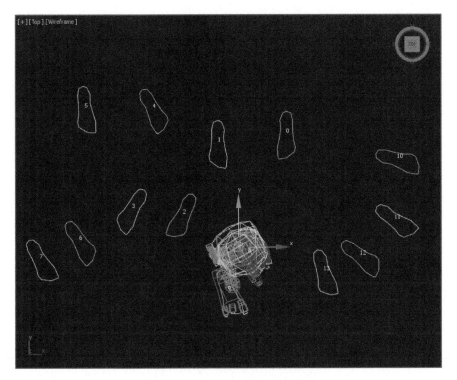

FIGURE 12.8 **Manually place the footsteps in the Top viewport.**

6. Select the Perspective viewport. In the Footstep Operations rollout, click the Create Keys for Inactive Footsteps icon, and then play the animation.

Character Studio doesn't have a collision-detection feature, so it is very possible that limbs will pass through one another, which would be quite uncomfortable in real life. If this happens, the footsteps must be modified to eliminate these conditions. If necessary, move any footsteps that cause collisions or other unwanted conditions during the playback. Save your work before continuing with the next set of steps. To check your work, open c12_ex5_steps_end.max from the scenes folder of the c12_CharacterAnimation project folder.

Exercise 10.6: Using the Dope Sheet

In Chapter 5, you experimented with the Track View - Curve Editor and learned how to adjust the values of animation keyframes. When the Track View is in Dope Sheet mode, frames are displayed as individual blocks of time that may or may not contain keys. Although you cannot see the flow from key to key that the Curve Editor displays with its curves, the Dope Sheet mode has its advantages. For one, the Dope Sheet has the ability to add Visibility tracks to control the display of an object, as well as Note tracks for adding text information regarding the keys as reminders.

Using the Track View - Dope Sheet, you can adjust the point in time when a foot plants on or lifts off the ground, how long the foot is on the ground, and how long the foot is airborne. Rather than appearing as single-frame blocks in the Dope Sheet as other keys do, footstep keys appear as multiframe rectangles that identify each foot's impact time with the footstep. Continue with the previous alien model or open the c12_ex6_dope_start.max file in the scenes folder of the c12_CharacterAnimation project folder.

1. Make sure you are in Footstep mode.

2. In the main toolbar, choose Graph Editors ➢ Track View - Dope Sheet. The Dope Sheet will open.

3. In the Navigation pane on the left, scroll down until you find the Bip001 Footsteps entry and expand it.

4. Click the Zoom Region icon ( ) in the lower-right corner of the Dope Sheet window, and drag a zoom window around the footstep keys, as shown in Figure 12.9. The region will expand to fit the Key pane. Right-click to exit the Zoom Region tool.

> The footstep keys appear as rectangles in the Key pane. As expected, the left keys are colored blue and the right keys are colored green.

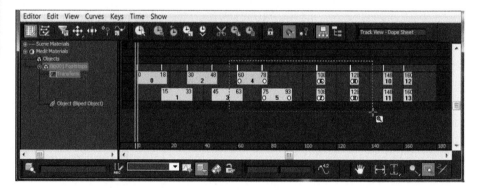

FIGURE 12.9 Zoom to the footstep keys.

5. Select a few footsteps in the viewport or select the green- and blue-colored rectangles (holding Ctrl to select multiple footsteps). The white dot on the left side of a selected key identifies the frame when the heel of the biped's foot first impacts the footstep. The white dot on the right side of a selected key, as shown in Figure 12.10, identifies

when the biped's foot lifts off a footstep. A blue key (rectangle) over-lapping a green key (rectangle) indicates that both feet are on the ground. A vertical gray area with no footstep indicates that the biped is airborne and neither foot is on the ground.

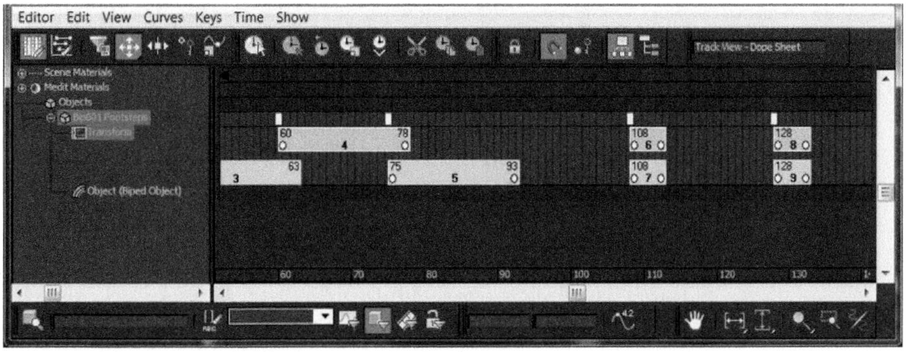

FIGURE 12.10 The dots indicate when contact begins and ends. You can drag a dot to change the duration of contact.

6. Place the cursor over the right edge of the key, and then drag the dot to the right to extend the length of time the biped's foot is on the ground.

7. Drag the Dope Sheet's time slider to a point in time when the biped is airborne. Increasing the airborne time by increasing the gap between footsteps will also boost the height to which the biped rises, acting against the gravitational force pushing it downward.

8. Select the four jump keys, and drag them to the right to create a gap approximately 40 frames wide, as shown in Figure 12.11. Doing so will cause the biped to be airborne for about one second.

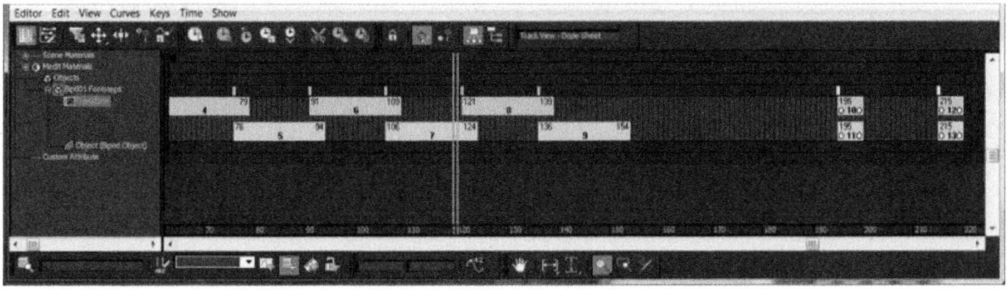

FIGURE 12.11 Create a key gap to get your biped airborne.

You can't move the end of one footstep key beyond the beginning of another one, and you must maintain a one-frame gap between same-side footsteps.

◄

The double vertical line in the Dope Sheet's Key pane is another time slider that allows you to scrub through the animation.

It is possible to move a footstep beyond the limits of the active time segment in the Dope Sheet. Use the Alt+R key combination to extend the active time segment to include all existing keys.

9. Move the time slider to the frame when both feet are planted before a jump starts, and turn on Auto Key mode.

10. Deselect any keys by clicking a blank area in the Key pane.

11. Prepare the biped to leap as follows:

    a. Exit Footstep mode, and then select the Bip001 object and move it downward, causing the biped to bend its knees more.

    b. Be sure to choose Local as the reference coordinate system for the Rotate transform.

    c. Rotate the spine links, neck, and head to bend the torso forward and tuck the chin.

    d. Rotate both arms backward into a pre-jump posture, as shown in Figure 12.12.

FIGURE 12.12   Prepare your biped to jump.

12. Move the time slider forward until the biped is at the apex of the jump.

13. Rotate the biped's components into positions you like, such as the split shown in Figure 12.13.

FIGURE 12.13 **Position your biped in mid-jump.**

14. Delete any animation keys that may interfere with your desired motion, and turn off Auto Key.

    The c12_ex6_dope_end.max file in the scenes folder of the c12_ CharacterAnimation project folder contains the completed exercise so you can check your work. This file has the alien model unhidden and the biped hidden.

15. Play the animation and see how it looks; modify it where needed.

As you saw, there are several ways to animate a biped, including the footstep-driven method, the freeform method, and a combination of techniques. You can also modify the animation in the track bar, with the Auto Key button, and with Track View - Dope Sheet.

Now You Know

In this chapter, you learned how to animate characters with Character Studio. Using the Biped system, you can quickly create and adjust the substructure that controls a 3D model. Once the Skin modifier associates or skins the model to the biped, character animation can be added using footstep-driven or freeform animation.

CHAPTER 13

Introduction to Lighting: Interior Lighting

Light reveals the world around us and defines shape, color, and texture. Lighting is the most important aspect of computer graphics (CG), and it simply cannot be mastered at a snap of the fingers. The trick to correctly lighting a CG scene is to understand how light works and to see the visual nuances it has to offer.

In this chapter, you will study the various tools used to create light in the Autodesk® 3ds Max® 2016 software. This chapter will serve as a primer on this important aspect of CG. It will start you on the path by showing you the tools available and giving you opportunities to begin using them.

In this chapter, you will learn to

▶ **Recognize 3ds Max lights**

▶ **Light a still life**

▶ **Select shadow types**

▶ **Create atmospheres and effects**

▶ **Utilize the Light Lister tool**

Recognizing 3ds Max Lights

The 3ds Max program has two types of light objects: photometric and standard. *Photometric lights* are lights that possess specific features to enable a more accurate definition of lighting, as you would see in the real world. Photometric lights have physically based intensity values that closely mimic the behavior of real light. *Standard lights* are extremely powerful and capable of realism, but they are more straightforward to use than photometric lights and less taxing on the system at render time. In this chapter, we will discuss only the standard lights.

Standard Lights

The 3ds Max lights attempt to mimic the way real lights work. For example, a lightbulb that emits light all around itself would be an *omni* light in 3ds Max terminology. A desk lamp that shines light in a specific direction in a cone shape would be a spotlight. Each of the different standard lights casts light differently. We will look at the most commonly used lights.

The 3ds Max program has a total of eight light types in its Standard Light collection:

> Target spotlight
>
> Target direct light
>
> Free spotlight
>
> Free direct light
>
> Omni light
>
> Skylight
>
> mr area omni light
>
> mr area spotlight

The last two on this list begin with *mr* to signify that they are mental ray–specific lights (see Chapter 15, "mental ray," for more about mental ray). An advanced renderer, mental ray is commonly used in production today. It offers many sophisticated and frequently complex methods of lighting that enhance the realism of a rendered scene. In this chapter, we will cover only the first five standard lights.

Target Spotlight

A *target spotlight*, as shown in Figure 13.1, is one of the most commonly used lights because it is extremely versatile. A spotlight casts light in a focused beam, similar to a flashlight. This type of lighting allows you to light specific areas of a scene without casting any unwanted light on areas that may not need that light. You can control the size of the *hotspot*, which is the size of the beam before it starts losing intensity.

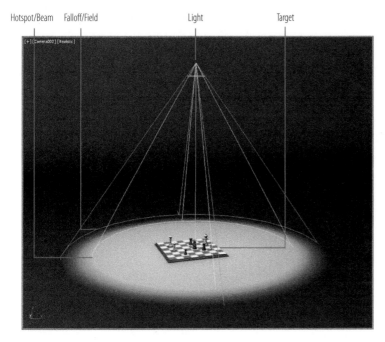

FIGURE 13.1 A target spotlight

The light is created with two nodes: the light itself (*light source*) and the target node (at which the light points at all times). This way, you are easily able to move the light following the subject of the scene, as a spotlight would follow a singer on stage. Select the target and move it as you would any other object. The target spot rotates to follow the target. Similarly, you can move the light source, and it will orient itself accordingly to aim at the stationary target. To see the Spotlight Parameters, select the light source, go to the Modify panel, and open the Spotlight Parameters rollout, shown in Figure 13.2.

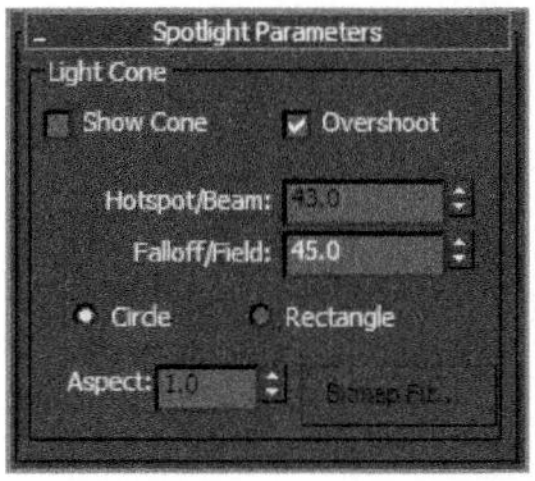

FIGURE 13.2 The Spotlight Parameters rollout

The falloff, which pertains to standard lights in 3ds Max software, is represented in the viewport by the area between the inner, lighter yellow cone and the outer, darker yellow cone, shown in Figure 13.1. The light diminishes to 0 by the outer region, creating a soft area around the hotspot circle (where the light is the brightest), as shown in Figure 13.3.

FIGURE 13.3 The falloff of a spotlight

Target Direct Light

A *target direct light* has target and light nodes to help you control the direction of the light. It also has a hotspot and beam, as well as a falloff, much like the target spot. However, whereas the target spot emits light rays from a single point (the light source) outward in a cone shape, the target direct light casts parallel rays of light within its beam area. This helps simulate the lighting effect of the sun because its light rays (for all practical purposes on Earth) are parallel. Figure 13.4 shows a target direct light in a viewport.

> Because the directional rays are parallel, the target direct lights have a beam in a straight cylindrical or rectangular box shape instead of a cone.

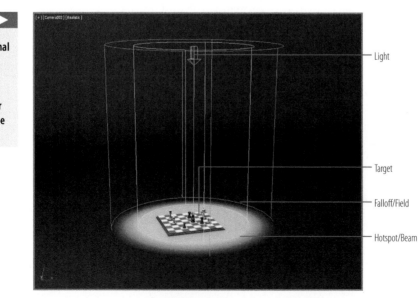

FIGURE 13.4 A target direct light

You can create and select/move parts of a target direct light in much the same way as a target spot. In the Directional Parameters rollout, you'll find the similar parameters for the target direct light. Although the spotlight and the directional light don't seem to be very different, the way they light is strikingly different, as you can see in Figure 13.5. The spotlight rays cast an entirely different hotspot and shadow than the directional light, despite having the same values for those parameters.

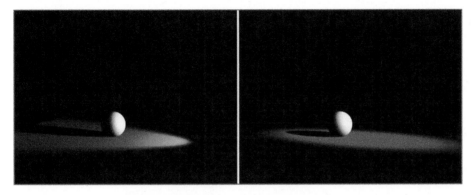

FIGURE 13.5 A target spot (left) and a target direct (right)

Free Spot or Free Direct Light

Free spotlights and *free direct lights* are virtually identical to target spots and target direct lights, respectively, except that the free spot and direct lights have no Target object. You can move and rotate the free spot however you want, relying on rotation instead of a target to aim it in any direction, as shown in Figure 13.6.

FIGURE 13.6 Free spot (left) and free direct (right) lights

Another difference between a free spot or direct light and a target spot or direct light is that while the length of the target spotlight is controlled by its target, a free spot or direct light instead has, in the General Parameters rollout, a parameter called Targ. Dist: The default is 240 units.

Because they are very easy to control and give a fantastic sense of direction, free spot and free direct (as well as target spot and target direct) lights are great for creating the main lighting in your scene. When a light is selected, go to the Modify tab and go to the General Parameters rollout; you'll find a drop-down menu that will allow you to change your chosen light type to another type. You can also change a free light to a target light by checking the Targeted box.

> Adjusting the length of the target for a free spot or free direct light will not affect the final render; however, seeing a longer light in the viewports can help you line up the light with objects in the scene.

Omni Light

The 3ds Max *omni light* is a point light that emanates light from a single point in all directions around it. Figure 13.7 shows an omni light. Unlike the spot and directional lights, the omni light does not have a special rollout, and its General Parameters rollout is much simpler.

FIGURE 13.7 An omni light is a single-point-source light.

Omni lights are not as good for simulating sunlight as directional lights are. In Figure 13.8, the omni light in the image on the left creates different shadow and lighting directions for all the objects in the scene, and the directional light in the image on the right creates a uniform direction for the light and shadow, as would the sun here on Earth.

F I G U R E   1 3 . 8   Omni light (left) and directional light (right)

Omni lights are good for fill lights, which are supplementary lights used in photography or filming that do not change the character of the main light and are used chiefly to lighten shadows.

Lighting a Still Life

Lighting a still life can be approached using the three-point lighting setup. Three-point lighting is a traditional approach to lighting a television shot. After all these years, the concepts still carry over to CG lighting. In this setup, three distinct roles are used to light the subject of a shot. The scene should, in effect, seem to have the following elements:

> ► Only one primary or key light to define lighting direction and create primary shadows

> ► A softer light to fill the scene and soften the shadows a bit

> ► A back light to make the subject pop out from the background

This does not mean there are only three lights in the scene. Three-point lighting suggests that there are three primary angles of light for your shot, dependent on where the camera is located.

Three-point lighting ensures that your scene's main subject for a particular shot is well lit, has highlights, and has a sense of lighting direction using shadow and tone. Figure 13.9 shows a plan view of the three-point lighting layout. The subject is in the middle of the image.

◄

Try to avoid casting shadows with omni lights, because they use a lot more memory than spotlights when casting shadows.

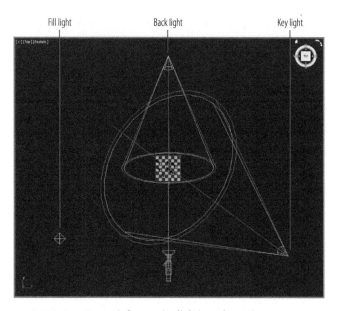

Fill light   Back light   Key light

FIGURE 13.9   **A three-point lighting schematic**

Exercise 13.1: Setting Up the Basic Lights for the Scene

Now that you have an overview of how lights work in a 3ds Max scene, let's put them to good use and light the room from Chapter 3, "Modeling in 3ds Max: Architectural Model Part I," and create a basic light setup for the scene. Set your current project to the **c13_IntroLight** you copied to your hard drive from this book's web page, www.sybex.com/go/3dsmax2016essentials. Open c13_ex1_basic_start.max from the scenes folder of the c13_IntroLight project folder.

c13_ex1_basic_start .max is a version of the room built in Chapter 3. Models and more materials have been added to beef up the file.

1. Go to the Create panel and select the Lights icon ( ) to bring up the selection of lights you can create.

2. Click the drop-down menu and choose Standard, as shown in Figure 13.10.

FIGURE 13.10   **Choose Standard from the Lights drop-down menu.**

3. Select Target Spot and go to the Front viewport.

4. Click and drag from the ceiling above the dining room table to the floor below the table. In the command panel, rename the light **Key Light**.

The click will create the light, and the mouse drag places the target.

5. In the Top viewport, use the Move tool to select the light and the target by dragging a selection box around both. Use the Zoom tool if needed to see the light selected.

6. Move the light and target so they are over the dining room table in the Top viewport, as shown in Figure 13.11.

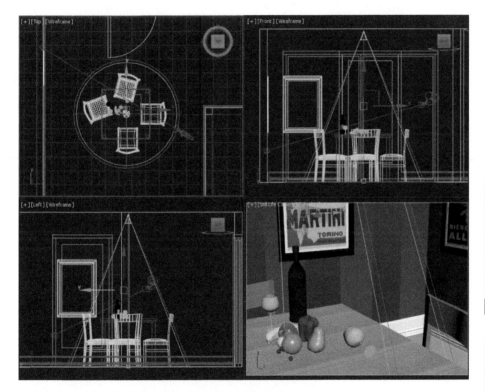

FIGURE 13.11 The spotlight's position in the room

The multiplier acts as a dimmer switch for the key light. This light will have shadows and give the scene its main source of light and direction.

7. Click away from any objects in the scene to deselect the light; then select just the source of the light object. Go to the Modify panel. In the Intensity/Color/Attenuation rollout, set Multiplier to 1.2.

8. In the Still Life Camera viewport, click the Shading viewport label menu to expand it. Choose Realistic from the list.

Take advantage of the Nitros display driver that is available; it is turned on by default. It gives the most information in the Camera viewport about lights, cameras, and shadows without the need for rendering.

9. Click the Shading viewport label menu again, go down to Lighting and Shadows, and choose Illuminate With Scene Lights, as shown in Figure 13.12. Now the Still Life camera can be used to judge the lights and shadows for this scene.

> Keep in mind that rendering a viewport is always the most accurate way of testing lights and shadows.

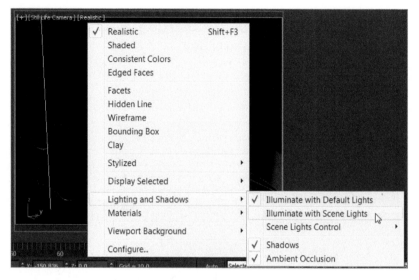

FIGURE 13.12 The Shading viewport label menu

10. Go to the Modify panel and expand the Spotlight Parameters rollout.

11. Set Hotspot/Beam to 40 and Falloff/Field to 100. As you can see in the Still Life Camera viewport, the light spreads out farther toward the walls.

12. Now render by clicking the Render Production button ( ), which is on the main toolbar; the rendered image is shown on the right in Figure 13.13.

> The Realistic viewport setting is fairly accurate. The reflections and transparencies that can be seen in the rendered image on the right are not shown with the Realistic viewport shading.

FIGURE 13.13 The Still Life Camera viewport set to Realistic, with the new Hotspot/Beam and Falloff/Field settings (left image). The rendered scene is shown in the image on the right.

Save your file and move on to the next exercise. To check your work, open the c13_ex1_basic_end.max file from the scenes folder of the c13_IntroLight project folder.

Exercise 13.2: Adding Shadows

Using shadows intelligently is important in lighting your scenes. Without the shadows in the scene, the still life would float and have no contact with its environment.

Continue with the file you are working on or open c13_ex2_shadows_start .max from the scenes folder of the c13_IntroLight project folder.

1. Select the key light, if it isn't already selected.

2. In the Modify panel, go to the General Parameters rollout ➤ Shadows area and check the On box.

3. In the Still Life Camera viewport, a low-resolution version of the shadows appears, but a render of the scene will show it more accurately.

4. Render the scene. The result is shown in Figure 13.14.

FIGURE 13.14   It looks good, but the scene shadows are too soft.

5. Go to the Shadow Map Params rollout and change Size to 2048. This parameter adds more pixels to the shadow, which makes it more defined and less diffused.

6. Render the Still Life Camera viewport, as shown in Figure 13.15.

F I G U R E 1 3 . 1 5   The render showing more defined shadows

Save your file and move on to the next exercise. To check your work, open the c13_ex2_shadows_end.max file from the scenes folder of the c13_IntroLight project folder.

Exercise 13.3: Adding a Fill Light

In the viewport, the shadow already looks better, but in the render, because the glasses are transparent, the shadow looks a bit weird—too dark and solid for a shadow for a transparent glass. To fix this issue, the shadow's density needs to be lowered. Adding a light to fill in the very dark shadows will correct this issue. A fill light simulates the indirect light seen in the real world. A fill light should not have any shadows or specular highlights; without them, you can make sure the render looks as if there is only one light in the room. Continue with the file you are working on or open c13_ex3_fill_start.max from the scenes folder of the c13_IntroLight project folder.

1. In the Create panel, select Lights ➤ Omni. In the Top viewport, click to create the omni light in the lower-right corner of the dining room.

2. In the Front viewport, move the omni light up so it is just below the ceiling of the dining room, and change the name to **Fill Light**.

3. In the Intensity/Color/Attenuation rollout, change Multiplier to 0.2. By default, shadows are always off, but you must turn off specular highlights manually.

4. With the omni light selected, go to the Modify panel and, under the Advanced Effects rollout, uncheck Specular.

5. Render again (press F9), and you'll see that the render looks better, but the still life's shadows are still dark, as shown in Figure 13.16. To fix the darkness of the shadow, the density of the shadow needs to be adjusted.

FIGURE 13.16 Interior room with key light and fill light

6. Select the key light, go to the Modify panel, and in the Shadow Parameters rollout, change the Object Shadows Dens parameter to 0.8.

7. Render the Still Life Camera viewport again by selecting the Render Production icon (F9) in the main toolbar. The shadows look much better, as shown in Figure 13.17.

FIGURE 13.17   Shadows with Density set to 0.8

Save your file and move on to the next exercise. To check your work, open the c13_ex3_fill_end.max file from the scenes folder of the c13_IntroLight project folder.

Exercise 13.4: Setting Up the Fill Light Attenuation

The omni light needs to have *decay* or *attenuation* applied. This means that light over distance loses its intensity or energy. Standard lights don't do this by default; it has to be simulated within the parameters. Continue with the file you are working on or open c13_ex4_attenuation_start.max from the scenes folder of the c13_IntroLight project folder.

1. Select the omni light. In the Intensity/Color/Attenuation rollout, click the Use and Show check boxes under Far Attenuation, as shown in Figure 13.18. The Start value defines the start of the decay of the light. The End value defines when the light drops off to zero. This is best seen in the Top viewport, as shown in Figure 13.19.

When the Use box is checked for Far Attenuation, the circles that appear when the light is selected show the start and end of the attenuation. Show makes them appear whether it is selected or not.

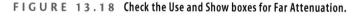

FIGURE 13.18   Check the Use and Show boxes for Far Attenuation.

Start   End

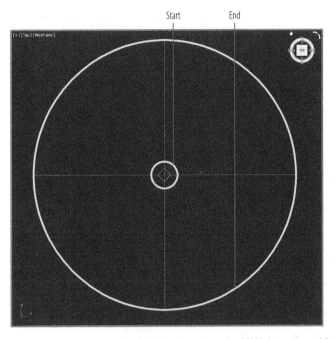

FIGURE 13.19 Far Attenuation set on the fill light as viewed from the Top viewport with all the scene objects hidden

2. Set the Start value to **120.0** and the End value to **200.0**; this gives some variation to the fill light, as shown in Figure 13.20.

FIGURE 13.20 A still life rendered with Far Attenuation

Save your file and move on to the next exercise. To check your work, open the c13_ex4_attenuation_end.max file from the scenes folder of the c13_IntroLight project folder.

Selecting a Shadow Type

To get shadows to respond to transparencies, you will need to use raytraced shadows instead of shadow maps.

You can create the following types of shadows using the 3ds Max program:

▶ Advanced Ray Traced

▶ mental ray shadow map

▶ Area shadows

▶ Shadow map

▶ Ray Traced shadows

Each type of shadow has its benefits and its drawbacks. The two most-frequently used types are shadow map (which you've already seen) and raytraced shadows.

Shadow Maps

Using a shadow map is often the fastest way to cast a shadow. However, shadow map shadows do not show the color cast through transparent or translucent objects.

When you are close to a shadow, to avoid jagged edges around it, use the Size parameter to make the resolution higher. The following parameters are useful for creating shadow maps:

Bias   The shadow is moved, according to the value set, closer to or farther away from the object casting the shadow.

Size   Detailed shadows need detailed shadow maps. Increase the Size value, which in turn will increase the detail of the shadow cast. Figure 13.21 compares using a low Shadow Map Size setting to using one four times larger. Notice how the shadows on the left (Size = 1024) are somewhat mushy and less noticeable, and the shadows on the right (Size = 4096) are crisp and clean. A size around 2048 is good for most cases. Scenes like this chessboard that have a large scale require higher Size values, such as the 4096 that was used.

Setting the Shadow Map Size too high will increase the render time for little to no effect. The rule of thumb is to use the lowest size value that will get you the best result for your scene.

FIGURE 13.21   The Shadow Map Size setting affects the shadow detail.

Sample Range   This option creates and controls the softness of the edge of shadow map shadows: the higher the value, the softer the edges of the shadow.

Raytraced Shadows

Raytracing involves tracing a ray of light from every light source in all directions and tracing the reflection back to the camera lens. You can create more accurate shadows with raytracing than with other methods, at the cost of longer render times. Raytraced shadows are realistic for transparent and translucent objects. Figure 13.22 shows the still life rendered with a plane object casting a shadow over it. The plane has a checker pattern mapped to its Opacity map channel, so it has alternating transparent and opaque areas defining the solid and transparent parts of the logo. On the left side of the image in Figure 13.22, the light is casting shadow map shadows; and on the right, the light is casting raytraced shadows.

FIGURE 13.22   The image on the left shows the shadow maps, which do not show transparencies. The image on the right shows raytraced shadows and how they react to transparencies.

Use raytraced shadows when you need highly accurate shadows or when shadow map resolutions are just not high enough to get you the crisp edges you need. You can also use raytraced shadows to cast shadows from wireframe rendered objects.

The Ray Traced Shadow Params rollout controls the shadow. The Ray Bias parameter is the same as the Shadow Map Bias parameter in that it controls how far the shadow is from the casting.

Atmospherics and Effects

Atmospherics provides effects such as parallel beams of fog seen within light rays and glows. Atmospheric effects with lights, such as fog or volume lights, are created using the Atmospheres & Effects rollout in the Modify panel for the selected light. Using this rollout, you can assign and manage atmospheric effects and other rendering effects that are associated with lights.

Exercise 13.5: Creating a Volume Light

Volume Light is a light effect based on the interaction of a light with the atmosphere. In the real world, this effect is visible when there's a lot of dust in an enclosed space.

1. Open the c13_ex5_volume_start.max file from the scenes folder of the c13_IntroLight project folder.

2. Go to the Create panel, select Lights, and in the drop-down list, select Standard, and then select the Target Direct light.

3. Go to the Left viewport and, clicking from the left outside of the room, position the light at an angle from the window. Drag toward the living room window and click to set the light on the floor inside the room.

4. Select the Move tool and then, in the Top viewport, click the line that connects the light and its target, which will select both easily. Move the light so it is aligned with the living room window, as shown in Figure 13.23.

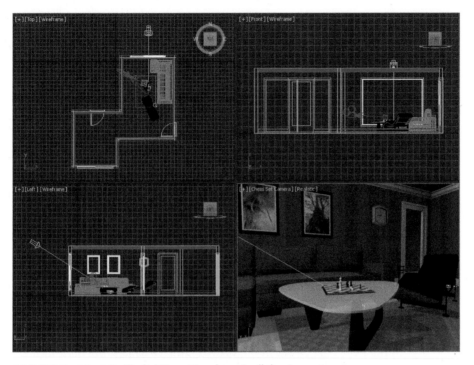

FIGURE 13.23   The light's position shown in all the viewports

5. Select the light source only and name the light **Sunlight**.

6. In the Chess Set Camera viewport, select the Shading viewport label menu to expand it. Choose Realistic from the list. Click the Shading viewport label menu again, go down to Lighting and Shadows, and choose Illuminate with Scene Lights.

7. Select the Sunlight object and go to the Modify panel. In the General Parameters rollout, check On in the Shadows group. Use the default Shadow type, which is Shadow Map.

8. In the Intensity/Color/Attenuation rollout, change the Multiplier to **1.2**.

9. In the Directional Parameters rollout, change Hotspot/Beam to **60.0** and Falloff/Field to **63.0**. Looking at the Chess Set Camera viewport, you will see the light coming in through the window, but it is very dark everywhere else, as shown in Figure 13.24. More lights need to be added.

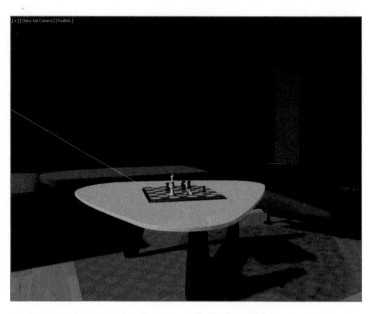

FIGURE 13.24 Interior room with the direct light in place as the sun

10. In the Create panel, select Lights ➤ Omni, and place the light near the Sunlight's position. Name the light **Fill Light 1**.

11. With the omni light selected, go to the Modify panel and, in the Intensity/Color/Attenuation rollout, change Multiplier to 0.5.

12. In the Intensity/Color/Attenuation rollout, in the Far Attenuation section, check Use and set Start to **150.0** and End to **400.0**.

13. In the Advanced Effects rollout, uncheck the Specular check box. This keeps the light on but does not show any specular highlights from this light.

14. In the Create panel, select Lights ➤ Omni and place the light behind the Chess Set Camera.

15. Move the light so it is just below the ceiling. Name the light **Fill Light 2**.

16. With the omni light selected, go to the Modify panel and, in the Intensity/Color/Attenuation rollout, change Multiplier to 0.3.

17. In the Advanced Effects rollout, uncheck the Specular check box.

18. In the Intensity/Color/Attenuation rollout, in the Far Attenuation section, check Use and set Start to 48.0 and End to 400.0.

19. Select the Sunlight light. In the Sunlight's parameters, go to the Atmospheres and Effects rollout.

20. Select Add from the rollout to open the Add Atmosphere or Effect dialog box, select Volume Light, and click OK to add the effect to the light. Volume Light will be added to the rollout.

21. Render the scene. You should see a render similar to Figure 13.25.

FIGURE 13.25 Ooh! Volume light!

22. To adjust the volume light, go back to the Atmospheres and Effects rollout, select the Volume Light entry, and click the Setup button. This will bring up the Environment and Effects dialog box.

23. Scroll down to the Volume Light Parameters section to access the settings for the volume light, as shown in Figure 13.26.

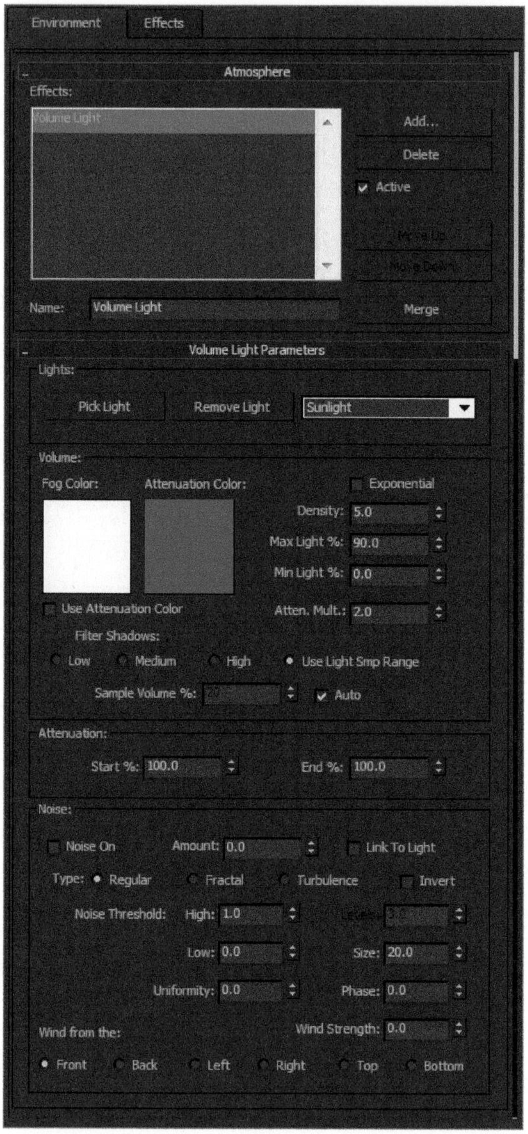

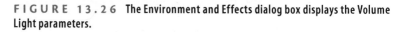

FIGURE 13.26   The Environment and Effects dialog box displays the Volume Light parameters.

24. In the Volume section, change Density to .25. This lessens the intensity of the volume and makes it more realistic.

25. Change Max Light % to **10.0**.

26. Render the Chess Set Camera viewport; the results are shown in Figure 13.27.

FIGURE 13.27 The final results of the volume light in the interior room

Save your file. To check your work, open the c13_ex5_volume_end.max file from the scenes folder of the c13_IntroLight project folder.

Volume Light Parameters

The default parameters for a volume light will give you some nice volume in the light for most scenes, right off the bat. If you want to adjust the volume settings, you can edit the following parameters:

Exponential   The density of the volume light will increase exponentially with distance. By default (Exponential is off), density will increase linearly with distance. You will want to enable Exponential only when you need to render transparent objects in volume fog.

Density   This value sets the fog's density. The denser the fog is, the more light will reflect off the fog inside the volume. The most realistic fog can be rendered with about a 2 to 6 percent density value, depending on the scene.

Most of the parameters are for troubleshooting volume problems in your scene if it is not rendering very well. Sometimes you just don't know what the problem is, and you have to experiment with switches and buttons.

The Noise settings are another cool feature to add some randomness to your volume:

Noise On   This toggles the noise on and off. Render times will increase slightly with noise enabled for the volume.

Amount   This is the amount of noise that is applied to the fog. A value of 0 creates no noise. If the amount is set to 1, the fog renders with pure noise.

Size, Uniformity, and Phase   These settings determine the look of the noise and let you set a noise type (Regular, Fractal, or Turbulence).

Adding atmosphere to a scene can heighten the sense of realism and mood. Creating a little bit of a volume for some lights can go a long way to improve the look of your renders. However, adding volume to lights can also slow your renders, so use it with care.

The Light Lister

If several lights are in your scene, and you need to adjust all of them, selecting each light and making one adjustment at a time can become tedious. This is where 3ds Max Light Lister comes in handy. Accessed through the menu bar by choosing Tools ➤ Light Lister, this floating palette gives you control over all of your scene lights, as shown in Figure 13.28.

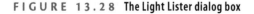

FIGURE 13.28   The Light Lister dialog box

You can choose to view or edit all the lights in your scene or just the ones that are selected. When you adjust the values for any parameter in the Light Lister dialog box, the changes are reflected in the appropriate place in the Modify panel for that changed light.

Now You Know

In this chapter, you learned the key concepts in CG lighting. You learned about the various types of lights that the 3ds Max program has to offer, from default lights to target spots, and how to use them. You explored the common light parameters to gauge how best to control the lights in your scene before moving on to creating various types of shadows. You ran through a set of short exercises in which you created a Volume light, and you finished with a peek at the Light Lister window.

CHAPTER 14

3ds Max Rendering

Rendering is the last step in creating your CG work, *but it is the first step to consider when you start to build a scene.* During rendering, the computer calculates the scene's surface properties, lighting, shadows, and object movement and then it saves a sequence of images. To get to the point where the computer takes over, you'll need to set up your camera and render settings so that you'll get exactly what you need from your scene.

This chapter will show you how to render your scene using the Scanline Renderer in the Autodesk® 3ds Max® 2016 software and how to create reflections and refractions using raytracing.

In this chapter, you'll learn to

▶ **Navigate the Render Setup dialog**

▶ **Render a scene**

▶ **Work with cameras**

▶ **Raytrace reflections and refractions**

▶ **Render the interior and furniture**

Navigating the Render Setup Dialog

Certification Objective

Your render settings and the final decisions you make about your 3ds Max scene ultimately determine how your work will look. If you create models and textures with the final image in mind and gear the lighting toward elegantly showing off the scene, the final touches will be relatively easy to set up.

The Render Setup dialog box is where you define the scene render output. You can open this dialog box by taking one of the following actions:

▶ Click the Render Setup icon (▣) in the main toolbar.

▶ Select Rendering ➤ Render Setup.

▶ Press F10.

You've already seen how to render ( ) a frame in your scene to check your work. The settings in the Render Setup dialog box are used even when the Render Production button is invoked, so it's important to understand how this dialog box works.

Common Tab

The Render Setup dialog box is divided into five tabs; each tab has settings grouped by function. The Common tab stores the settings for the overall needs of the render—for example, image size, frame range to render, and type of renderer to use. Some of the most necessary render settings are described here:

Time Output   In this section, you can set the frame range of your render output by selecting one of the following options:

> **Single**   Renders the current frame only.
>
> **Active Time Segment**   Renders the current range of frames.
>
> **Range**   Renders the frames specified.
>
> **Every Nth Frame**   Allows you to render every nth frame, where n is a whole number, so you can specify how many frames to skip.

Output Size   The image size of your render, which is set in the Output Size section, will depend on your output format—that is, how you want to show your render.

> **Resolution**   By default, the dialog box is set to render images at a resolution of 640×480 pixels, defined by the Width and Height parameters, respectively.
>
> **Image Aspect**   Changing the Image Aspect value will adjust the size of your image along the Height parameter to correspond with the existing Width parameter. For example, regular television is 1.33:1 (simply called 1.33) and a high-definition (HD) television is a wide screen with a ratio of 1.78:1 (simply called 1.78). The resolution of your output will define the screen ratio.

In addition to turning down the resolution for a test render, you can use a lower-quality render or turn off certain effects, such as atmospherics.

In the Output Size section of the Render Setup dialog box, there is a drop-down menu for choosing presets from different film and video resolutions. The image quality and resolution of a render affect how long a render will take.

Options   The Options section lets you access several global toggles. You can toggle the rendering of specific elements in your scene. For example, if you are using atmospherics (volume light) or effects (lens flare) and don't want them to render, you can clear the appropriate boxes.

Render Output   Use the Render Output section to indicate that the file should be saved. The image format can be selected to be a single image file or a sequence of image files (such as Targa or TIFF files) that form a sequence, or it can be a movie file such as QuickTime.

Choosing a Filename

To specify a location and file type for the render, click the Files button in the Render Output section. This will open the Render Output File dialog box shown in Figure 14.1. Select the folder to which you want to render, and set the filename. You can set the file type using the Save As Type drop-down menu.

Name your rendered images according to the scene's filename. This way, you can always know from which scene file a rendered image was produced.

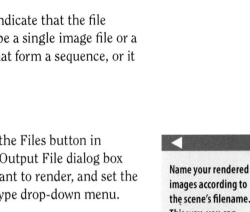

FIGURE 14.1   The Render Output File dialog box defines how the render saves to disk.

Rendered Frame Window

When you click the Render button at the top of the Render Setup dialog box, the Rendered Frame window opens and the selected viewport is rendered, as shown in Figure 14.2.

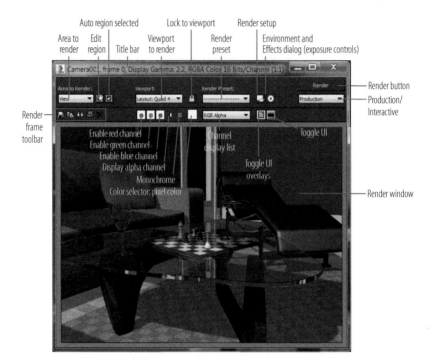

FIGURE 14.2 **The Rendered Frame window**

The Rendered Frame window shows you how the frames look as the renderer processes through the sequence of frames. A collection of quick-access buttons on the frame is also available in the Render Frame window.

Render Processing

When you click Render, a Rendering progress dialog, shown in Figure 14.3, shows the parameters being used, and it displays a progress bar indicating the render's progress. You can pause or cancel the render by clicking the appropriate button.

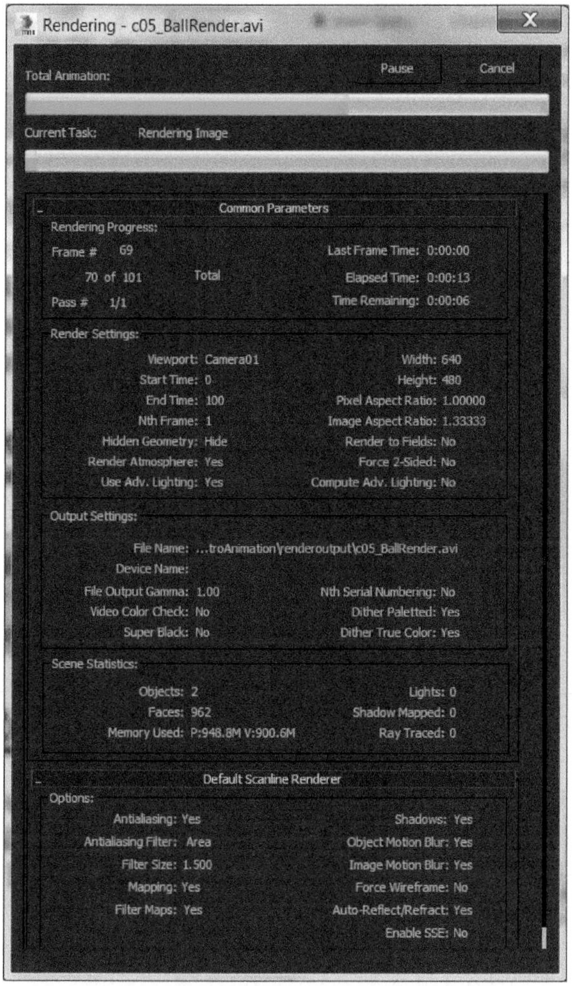

FIGURE 14.3 The Rendering processing dialog shows you everything you want to know about your current render.

Assign Renderer

Five types of renderers are available by default (without any additional plug-ins installed). The Default Scanline Renderer is the default renderer. It is already assigned and appears in the Assign Renderer rollout, which you will find back in the Render Setup dialog box. To access the Choose Renderer dialog box, click the ellipsis button (**...**). Because the NVIDIA mental ray renderer is already assigned, only four renderers appear. Rendering with mental ray is covered in Chapter 15, "mental ray."

The Render Setup dialog box contains preset and menu controls. This is also an alternative area to choose a renderer from a drop-down menu, as shown in Figure 14.4.

FIGURE 14.4 **Renderer drop-down menus enable you to easily choose between different renderers.**

Rendering a Scene

3D rendering is the 3D computer graphics process of automatically converting 3D wireframe models into 2D images with 3D photorealistic effects or nonphotorealistic rendering on a computer.

Exercise 14.1: Rendering the Bouncing Ball

Seeing is believing, but doing is understanding. In this exercise, you will render the bouncing ball animation from Chapter 5, "Introduction to Animation," to get a feel for rendering an animation using the 3ds Max program. Just follow these steps:

1. Set your project folder to the c14_Rendering project that you downloaded to your hard drive from the companion web page at www.sybex.com/go/3dsmax2016essentials.

2. Open the c14_ex1_render.max file in the scenes folder. If a *File Load: Gamma & LUT Settings Mismatch* dialog box shows up, select

Adopt the File's Gamma and LUT Settings? and then select OK. Now, let's render a movie to see the animation.

3. Open the Render Setup dialog box and, in the Time Output section, select Active Time Segment: 0 To 100.

4. In the Output Size section, select the 320×240 preset button and leave the Image Aspect and Pixel Aspect at their current settings.

5. Leave the Options group at the defaults, and skip down to the Render Output section.

6. Click the Files button to open the Render Output File dialog box, and navigate to where you want to save the output file, preferably into the renderoutput folder in your c14_Rendering project.

7. Name the file **c14_ex1_render**, and click the drop-down menu next to Save As Type to choose MOV QuickTime File (*.mov) for your render file type.

8. After you select MOV QuickTime File and click the Save button, the Compression Settings dialog box, shown in Figure 14.5, opens.

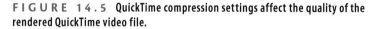

FIGURE 14.5 QuickTime compression settings affect the quality of the rendered QuickTime video file.

By default, the 3ds Max program renders your files to the renderoutput folder in the current project directory.

Normally, you would render to a sequence of images rather than a movie file; however, for short renders and to check animation, a QuickTime file works out fine.

Apple's QuickTime movie file format gives you a multitude of options for compression and quality. The quality settings for the QuickTime file are not the same as the render quality settings.

9. Set the parameters for the QuickTime file as indicated:

   ▶ Compression Type: Photo - JPEG

   ▶ Frames Per Second: 30

   ▶ Compressor Depth: Color

   ▶ Quality: High

Click OK to close the Compression Settings dialog box.

10. At the top of the Render Setup dialog box in the View to Render drop-down menu, select Quad 4 - Camera01.

11. Set the Target drop-down menu to Production Rendering Mode and the Renderer drop-down menu to Default Scanline Renderer, and then click the Render button.

12. After the render is complete, navigate to your render location (by default, it is set to the renderoutput folder for the c14_Rendering project).

13. Double-click the QuickTime file to see your movie.

To see an already rendered QuickTime movie of the ball animation and to check your work, navigate to your render location; it is set to the renderoutput folder for the c14_Rendering project. To check the Render Setup dialog, open the c14_ex1_render_end.max file in the c14_Rendering project folder.

Certification
Objective

Working with Cameras

The 3ds Max cameras, as shown in the Perspective viewport in Figure 14.6, capture and output all the fun in your scene. In theory, 3ds Max cameras work as much like real cameras as possible.

The *camera* creates a window through which you can see and render your scene. You can have as many cameras in the scene as you want. You can use the Perspective viewport to move around your scene as you work, leaving the render camera alone.

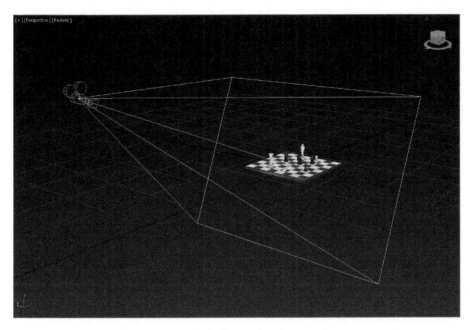

[+][Perspective][Realistic]

FIGURE 14.6 A camera as seen in the Perspective viewport

There are three types of cameras:

Physical Camera   The *Physical camera* is the camera to use for photorealistic rendering because it includes sophisticated framing with exposure controls.

Target Camera   A *Target camera,* much like a target spotlight, has a target node that allows it to look at a spot defined by where the target is placed (or animated). A Target camera is easier to aim than a Free camera because once you position the Target object at the center of interest, the camera will always aim there.

Free Camera   *Free cameras* have only one node, so they must be rotated to aim at the subject, much like a free spotlight. If your scene requires the camera to follow an action, you will be better off with a Target camera.

You can create a camera by clicking the Cameras icon (▣) in the Create panel and selecting one of the three camera types:

- ▶ To create a Free camera, click in a viewport to place it.
- ▶ To create a Physical camera or Target camera, click in a viewport to lay down the camera node, and then drag to pull out and place the target node.

A camera's main feature is the *lens*, which sets the *focal length* in millimeters and also sets the *field of view (FOV)*, which determines how wide an area the camera sees, in degrees. By default, a Target/Free camera lens is 43.456mm long with an FOV of 45 degrees. A Physical camera has a lens with a focal length of 40 and Specify FOV of 47.654 degrees. To change a lens, you can change the Lens or FOV parameters, or if you're using a Target/Free camera, you can pick from the stock lenses available for a camera in its Modify panel parameters, as shown in Figure 14.7.

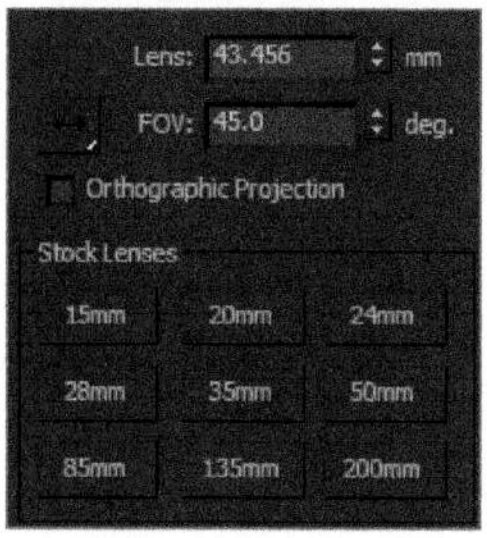

You can also change a camera by selecting the Camera object and using the transform tools, just as you would any other object. The movement depends on the camera type.

FIGURE 14.7　Target/Free camera stock lenses make it easy to pick the right lens for a scene.

The most interactive way to adjust a camera is to use the viewport navigation tools. The Camera viewport must be selected for the viewport camera tools to be available to you in the lower-right corner of the user interface (UI). You can move the camera or change the lens or FOV.

Exercise 14.2: Creating a Camera

The best way to explain how to use a camera is to create one. Open the c14_ex2_cameras_start.max scene file in the scenes folder. If a *File Load: Gamma & LUT Settings Mismatch* dialog shows up, select *Adopt The File's Gamma And LUT Settings?* and then select OK.

This scene is without a camera. Creating a camera is similar to creating a light. It's easier to create a camera in the Top viewport so you can easily orient it in reference to your scene objects.

1. In the Create panel, click the Cameras icon, select the Target camera, and go to the Top viewport. Click from the window inside the room and drag toward the gap between the coffee table and the couch. The camera is created along the ground plane. You need to move the entire camera up.

The first click creates the Camera object. The mouse drag-and-release sets the location of the target, just like creating a target light.

2. Right-click to exit Create mode. Select both the camera and the target by clicking the line that connects the camera and target in the Top viewport, and then in the Front viewport, use the Move tool to relocate the camera higher in the scene.

3. To see the Camera viewport, select a viewport and press the C key. This changes the viewport to whatever camera is currently selected. In Figure 14.8, you can see Camera001 in all viewports.

If there are multiple cameras in your scene and none are selected, when you press C, you will get a dialog box that lists the cameras from which you can choose.

FIGURE 14.8 The camera shown in the Top, Front, Left, and Camera001 viewports

4. Now render the scene—press F9 or click the teapot icon in the main toolbar—through the camera you just created and positioned.

▶

Zooming a lens (changing the Lens parameter) is not the same as a dolly in or dolly out. The field of view changes when you zoom, and it stays constant when you dolly. These lens parameters will yield different framing, or they will focus on the subject.

Now that the camera is set up, take some time to move it around and see the changes in the viewport. To move the camera, select the Camera object. Use the Select and Move tool. Moving a camera from side to side is known as a *truck*. Moving a camera in and out is called a *dolly*. Rotating a camera is called a *roll*. Also change the Lens and FOV settings to see the results. Save the file. To check your work, open the c14_ex2_cameras_end.max file in the c14_Rendering project folder.

Exercise 14.3: Animating a Camera

Camera animation is done in the same way as animating any object. You can animate the camera, the target, or both. You can also animate camera parameters such as Lens or FOV. Open the c14_ex3_animate_start.max scene file in the scenes folder in the c14_Rendering project folder.

1. Select the camera.

2. Move the time slider to frame 60.

3. Press the N key to activate Auto Key, or select the Auto Key button.

4. In the Top viewport, use the Move tool to move the camera farther away from the chess set; watch the Camera001 viewport to be sure you don't go outside the room. The direction or distance doesn't really matter, just as long as it is different from the previous camera position.

5. Look in the Camera001 viewport, and then move the time slider through the animation. Press the N key again to turn off Auto Key. The camera position is shown in Figure 14.9. Don't worry if your camera position isn't the same as in the figure.

Save the file. To check your work, open the c14_ex3_animate_end.max file in the c14_Rendering project folder.

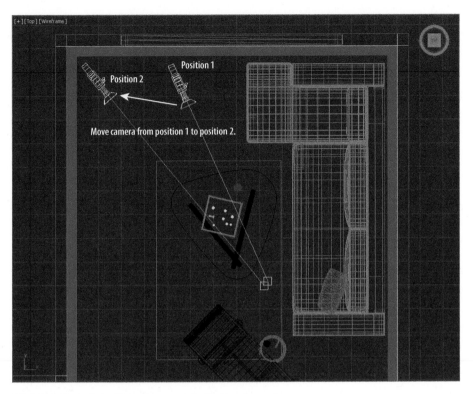

FIGURE 14.9 Move the camera in the Top viewport.

Clipping Planes

In a huge scene, you can exclude, or *clip*, the geometry that is beyond a certain distance from the camera by using *clipping planes*. This helps minimize the amount of geometry that needs to be calculated. Each camera has a clipping plane for distance (Far Clip), as shown in the left image in Figure 14.10, and for the foreground (Near Clip), as shown in the right image. The near clipping plane clips geometry within the distance designated from the camera lens.

If you find that a model or scene you have imported looks odd or is cut off, check to make sure your clipping planes are adjusted to fit the extent of the scene.

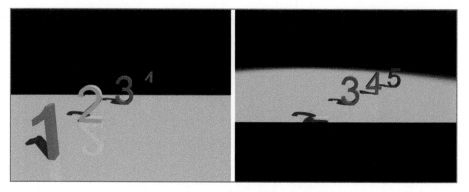

FIGURE 14.10   A far clipping plane cuts off the distant extents of a scene (left). A near clipping plane cuts off the extents directly in front of a camera (right).

To enable clipping planes, click the Clip Manually check box and set the distances needed. Once you turn on manual clipping planes, the camera displays the near and far extents in the non-camera viewports with red plane markers.

Exercise 14.4: Clarifying Safe Frames

Safe Frames allow you to see the portions of your rendered output within a viewport. Safe Frames display a series of rectangular frames in the viewport. This is particularly useful when you are rendering to output that doesn't match the viewport's aspect ratio. Open the c14_ex4_safe_start.max scene file in the scenes folder in the c14_Rendering project folder.

1. In the Camera001 viewport, click the General Viewport label menu ([+]) and choose Configure near the bottom of the menu.

2. In the dialog box, choose the Safe Frames tab. This tab contains settings for frame types, as shown in Figure 14.11.

| | Display Performance | | Regions | | Statistics | | ViewCube | | SteeringWheels |
| | Visual Style & Appearance | | | Background | | | Layout | | Safe Frames |

Setup

☑ Live Area

☑ Region (when Region Rendering)

Percent Reductions

	Both	Lock	Horizontal	Vertical
☐ Action Safe	10.0	☑		
☐ Title Safe	20.0	☑		
☐ User Safe	30.0	☑		

☐ 12-Field Grid   [4 x 3] [12 x 9]

Application

☐ Show Safe Frames in Active View   Default Settings

Apply   OK   Cancel

F I G U R E   1 4 . 1 1   The Safe Frames tab in the Viewport Configuration dialog box

3. The default is to show only the Live Area Safe Frame. To have the other Safe Frames show, you check the Action Safe, Title Safe, and User Safe boxes in the Safe Frames tab.

The Live Area Safe Frame is the extent of what will be rendered. The Action Safe area is the boundary where you should be assured that the action in the scene will display on most if not all TV screens. The Title Safe area is where you

◀

The keyboard shortcut to toggle Safe Frames is Shift+F.

can feel comfortable rendering titles in your frame. The User Safe setting is for setting custom frames, as shown in Figure 14.12.

FIGURE 14.12   Safe Frames shown in the Camera001 viewport

Save the file. To check your work, open the c14_ex4_safe_end.max file in the c14_Rendering project folder.

Raytraced Reflections and Refractions

As you saw in Chapter 9, "Introduction to Materials," you can apply a Raytrace map to a material's Reflection parameter to add a reflection to the object. To get a true reflection of the other objects in the scene, you will need to use the raytracing methodology. There are essentially two ways to create raytraced reflections in a scene:

▶ By using a Raytrace map

▶ By using a Raytrace material

In many cases, the Raytrace map looks great and saves tons of rendering time as opposed to using the Raytrace material.

Exercise 14.5: Creating Reflections with Raytrace Material

In the following steps, you will learn how to use the Raytrace material to create reflections in a scene using the room built in Chapter 3, "Modeling in 3ds Max: Architectural Model Part I," and Chapter 4, ": Modeling in 3ds Max: Architectural Model Part I." Open the c14_ex5_raytrace_start.max scene file in the scenes folder in the c14_Rendering project folder.

> Keep in mind that the amount of control you will have with a Raytrace map is significantly less than with the Raytrace material.

1. Open the Slate Material Editor; in the Material/Map Browser, select Materials ➤ Standard, and drag the Raytrace material into the active view.

2. Double-click on the node title area to load the parameters into the Material Parameter Editor, and change the material name to New Dark Wood.

3. The parameters to create reflections are available through the Raytrace Basic Parameters rollout. Leave most of these parameters at their default values, but change the Reflect color swatch from black to white. This sets the reflection of the material all the way to the maximum reflectivity.

4. In the Material/Map Browser, choose Maps ➤ Standard and drag Bitmap to the Diffuse input socket of the Raytrace material. This will bring up the Select Bitmap Image File dialog box; you should see the images folder of the c14_Rendering project folder.

5. Choose DarkWood_Grain.jpg, and then click Open.

6. Apply the New Dark Wood Raytrace material to the coffee table legs in the scene. Render the Camera001 viewport. The coffee table leg is very reflective; it looks like a mirror, as shown in Figure 14.13.

7. Go back to the Raytrace Basic Parameters rollout, select the color swatch next to Reflect, and change the Reflect color (RGB sliders only) so that R = 20, G = 20, and B = 20, which is a darker gray and will lessen the reflections.

FIGURE 14.13   The Raytrace material with reflections set to the maximum

8. In the Specular Highlight area, change Specular Level to 80 and Glossiness to 70. This will change how clear the reflection appears.

9. Go to the Raytracer Controls rollout and, in the Falloff End Distance area, check the box next to Reflect and change the value to 50. This parameter will fade the reflection over distance, which is more accurate. Select the Camera001 viewport and render, as shown in Figure 14.14.

FIGURE 14.14   More accurate reflections are added to the coffee table legs.

Save the file. To check your work, open the c14_ex5_raytrace_end.max file in the c14_Rendering project folder.

Exercise 14.6: Raytrace Mapping

You use Raytrace maps as you do other maps. This means you can add raytraced reflections or refractions to any kind of material. In this case, you will assign a Raytrace map to the Reflection map channel of a material to get truer reflections in the scene and at a faster render time than when using the material as you just did. Continue with your file or open the c14_ex6_raytrace_start.max scene file in the scenes folder in the c14_Rendering project folder. If you are using the file created from the previous exercises, select the Rug object in the file and right-click in the viewport; from the quad menu, choose Hide Selected.

1. In the Slate Material Editor and in the Material/Map Browser, select Materials ➤ Standard and drag a Standard material to the Active View area. Load the materials into the Material Parameter Editor and change the name to **Hardwood Floors**.

2. In the Material/Map Browser, choose Maps ➤ Standard and drag a Raytrace map into the Reflection input socket.

3. In the Material/Map Browser, choose Maps and drag a bitmap map into the Diffuse Color input socket.

4. From the Select Bitmap Image File dialog box, choose Hardwood_honey.tif from the images folder.

5. In the Maps rollout, change the Reflection Amount to 50.

6. Apply the Hardwood Floors material to the Floor object in the scene by dragging from the output socket to the Floor object in the Camera001 viewport.

7. In the Slate Material Editor toolbar, select the Show Shaded Material in Viewport button (🔲).

8. Render the Camera001 viewport. The floors look good but are too reflective, and a falloff needs to be added.

9. Double-click the Raytrace Map node to load the parameters into the Material Parameter Editor.

10. In the Attenuation rollout, change the Falloff Type to Linear, and then change Ranges: End to 50. Render the Camera001 viewport. The results are shown in Figure 14.15.

FIGURE 14.15   **The reflection map with falloff**

Take a look at the images created with reflections using the Raytrace material and those created using the Standard material with the Raytrace map applied to reflection. They look almost the same. However, there is slightly better detail in the reflections created with the Raytrace material, but with longer render times. Save the file. To check your work, open the c14_ex6_raytrace_end.max file in the c14_Rendering project folder.

Exercise 14.7: Using the Raytrace Material to Create Refractions

Keep in mind that render times are much slower with refractions—so don't freak out.

Creating raytraced refractions in glass can be accomplished using the same two workflows you used for the raytraced reflections in the previous sections. The Raytrace material renders better, but it takes longer than using a Raytrace map for the refraction map in a material. Continue with your file or open the c14_ex7_raytrace_start.max scene file in the scenes folder in the c14_Rendering project folder. This file has the rug unhidden.

1. For this section, you are going to create a new camera. Start by changing the Camera001 viewport to a Perspective viewport:

   a. Select the Camera001 viewport and press P on the keyboard.

   b. Select the wineglass in the scene and then press Z on your keyboard. This will frame the wineglass in the Perspective viewport.

    c. Use Ctrl+C, which is a shortcut, to create a Physical camera from a Perspective viewport.

    d. Name the camera **Wine Glass Camera.**

2. In the Slate Material Editor, drag a Raytrace material from the Material/Map Browser into the active view. Name it **Wine Glass**, and apply the material to the wineglass.

3. Go to the Raytrace Basic Parameters rollout, and change the color swatch for Transparency from black to white.

4. Uncheck the box next to Reflect and change that spinner to **10**. This sets a slight reflection for the material.

5. Take a look at the Index Of Refr parameter. This value sets the index of refraction (IOR) value that determines how much the material should refract. The value is already set to 1.55. Leave it at that value.

6. Go to the Extended Parameters rollout, shown in Figure 14.16. The Reflections section is at the bottom.

Black is opaque and white is fully transparent.

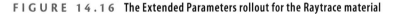

FIGURE 14.16   The Extended Parameters rollout for the Raytrace material

7. Select Additive and change Gain to **0.7**. This gives a bit of reflective brightness for the clear wineglass.

8. Render the Wine Glass Camera viewport. The render shows the Raytrace material on the wineglass refracting and reflecting, but you may notice the jagged edges or artifacts around the reflected objects. What you're seeing is aliasing in the reflections.

SuperSampling is an extra pass of anti-aliasing. By default, the 3ds Max program applies a single SuperSample filter pass over all the materials in the scene.

9. Clone this rendered image by pressing the Clone Rendered Frame Window icon (▓▓), which is found in the Rendered Frame Window toolbar. This allows you to compare the before and after shots of the rendering.

10. Go to the SuperSampling rollout and uncheck Use Global Settings.

11. Check Enable Local Supersampler and keep it set to Max 2.5 Star. Leave the other parameters at their defaults, as shown in Figure 14.17. Render the Wine Glass Camera viewport.

FIGURE 14.17 The SuperSampling rollout

12. Go back to the Raytrace Basic Parameters rollout; in the Specular Highlight group, change Specular Level to 98 and Glossiness to 90.

13. Render the Wine Glass Camera viewport. Figure 14.18 shows these changes.

FIGURE 14.18 The wineglass with the default SuperSampling (left image), and with modified SuperSampling (right image)

You will see a very nice wineglass render. Change the Index Of Refr parameter on the material to 8.0, and you will see a much greater refraction, as shown in

Figure 14.19. That may work better for a heavy bottle, but it is too much for the glass. Now change back the Index Of Refr back to **1.55**. An Index Of Refr parameter between **1.5** and **2.5** works pretty well for the wineglass.

FIGURE 14.19 A much more pronounced refraction is rendered with an IOR of 8.0.

Save the file. To check your work, open the `c14_ex7_raytrace_end.max` file in the `c14_Rendering` project folder.

Exercise 14.8: Using Raytrace Mapping to Create Refractions

Just as you did with the reflections, you will use a Raytrace map on the Refraction parameter for the Wine Glass material. Open the `c14_ex8_raytrace_start.max` scene file in the `scenes` folder in the `c14_Rendering` project folder.

1. In the Slate Material Editor, drag a Standard material from the Material/Map Browser into the view area. Name the material **Wine Glass 1**.

2. Drag the Raytrace map from the Material/Map Browser into the Refraction input slot.

3. Drag the Raytrace map from the Material/Map Browser into the Reflection input slot.

If the Reflection Map setting is enabled, it will take a long time to render the image. If you have a slower computer or perhaps are in a rush, uncheck the Reflection Map box in the Maps rollout of the material.

◄

4. Go to the Maps rollout and change the Reflection Amount to 6. This will reduce the amount of reflection.

5. Go to the SuperSampling rollout and uncheck Use Global Settings. Check Enable Local Supersampler, and keep it as Max 2.5 Star.

6. In the Specular Highlights group, change the Specular Level to 98 and Glossiness to 90.

7. Apply the material to the Wine Glass object in the scene and render as shown in Figure 14.20.

FIGURE 14.20 Use the Raytrace map on the Refraction parameter to create refraction in the wineglass.

8. Go to the Extended Parameters rollout, and in the Advanced Transparency section, change the IOR (Index of Refraction) to 2.5, as shown in Figure 14.21. The higher the IOR, the more magnified the background will look through the glass.

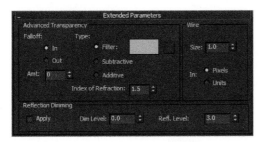

FIGURE 14.21 The Advanced Transparency section in the Extended Parameters rollout

The raytracing reflections and refractions slow down the render quite a bit. You can leave out the reflections if you'd like, but that will reduce the realistic look of the wineglass. Save the file. To check your work, open the c14_ex8_raytrace_end.max file in the c14_Rendering project folder.

Rendering the Interior and Furniture

The Raytrace map calculates reflections as they work in the real world, reflecting the object's environment. You'll need to tweak a few of the scene settings, such as setting the furniture and the interior materials, to have raytraced reflections for maximum impact.

Exercise 14.9: Adding Raytraced Reflections

Open the c14_ex9_raytrace_start.max scene file in the scenes folder in the c14_Rendering project folder.

1. In the Slate Material Editor, at the bottom left of the active view, is an icon of a pair of binoculars. This is a search feature. Click it, and a type-in area appears.

2. Type **Light Wood for Chess** in the type-in area and press Enter. The material will be zoomed in on the active view, as shown in Figure 14.22.

The Zoom To Results feature will frame
the material in the active view area.

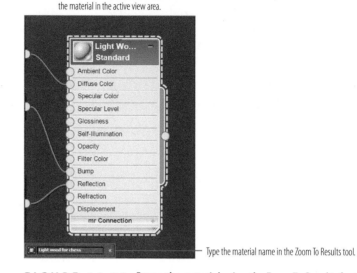

Type the material name in the Zoom To Results tool.

FIGURE 14.22 Frame the material using the Zoom To Results feature in the Slate Material Editor.

3. In the Material/Map Browser, select Maps ➤ Standard and drag a Raytrace map into the input socket of the Reflection map, as shown in Figure 14.23.

FIGURE 14.23 Plug the Raytrace map into the Reflection input socket of the Light Wood for Chess material.

4. Double-click the title of the Light Wood for Chess material to load the parameters into the Material Parameter Editor, and in the Maps rollout, change the Amount value for Reflection to 20.

5. Render a frame, and you should see some reflections of the room.

6. Go through the materials in the Slate Material Editor to add a Raytrace map to any material that would have a reflection.

Save the file. To check your work, open the c14_ex9_raytrace_end.max file in the c14_Rendering project folder.

Exercise 14.10: Outputting the Render

To finish the chapter, we will make a render of the camera move that was created earlier. As you saw with the bouncing ball render earlier in the chapter, rendering out a sequence of images is done through the Common tab of the Render Setup dialog box. Open the c14_ex10_raytrace_start.max scene file in the scenes folder in the c14_Rendering project folder.

1. In the Time Output section, click to select Range and change it to read 0 to **60**, as shown in Figure 14.24.

F I G U R E 1 4 . 2 4   **The Time Output section setup for a range from 0 to 60**

The resolution of the render is set in Output Size. The default resolution is 640×480.

2. Go to the Render Output section of the Render Setup dialog box, and click Files to open the Render Output File dialog box. Typically, animations are rendered out as a sequence of images; but for simplicity's sake, you will render it out to an AVI.

3. In the Render Output File dialog box, choose where you want to store the rendered file and pick a name for the movie (**Room_Raytrace.avi**, for example).

If you want the reflective objects in the scene to have a higher amount of reflection, go back to the Maps rollout and make the Amount value for Reflection higher than 20.

If your computer isn't a powerful one, drop the size to 320×240, half the default size. The render time will be less at this resolution.

Again, it is generally preferable to render to a sequence of images rather than a movie file; however, in this case, an AVI movie file will be best.

4. In the Save As Type drop-down menu, choose MOV Quicktime File (*.mov) and click Save. The MOV File Compression Setup dialog box will appear.

5. In the Compression Settings dialog box, select H.264 for the compressor type, and set the quality slider to Best. This Quality setting applies only to the compression of the MOV file and not to the render itself.

6. Click OK to return to the Render Setup dialog box.

7. Save your scene file. You are ready to render! Just select Render in the Render Setup dialog box.

To check your work, open the c14_ex10_raytrace_end.max file in the c14_Rendering project folder.

Now You Know

Rendering is the way you get to show your finished scene to the world, or whoever will stop and look. Nothing is more fulfilling than seeing your creation come to life, and that's what rendering is all about. In this chapter, you learned how to set up and render your scenes out to files. In addition, you took a tour of raytracing and cameras.

Rendering may be the last step of the process, but you should travel the entire journey with rendering in mind, from design to models to animation to lighting.

CHAPTER 15

mental ray

This chapter will show you how to create materials and render your scene using the Autodesk® mental ray® renderer.

In this chapter, you'll learn to

▶ **Navigate the mental ray renderer**

▶ **Navigate the Final Gather parameters**

▶ **Navigate mental ray materials**

▶ **Use photometric lights with mental ray**

▶ **Use the Daylight System**

Navigating the mental ray Renderer

Mental ray is a popular general-purpose renderer that has fantastic capabilities. One of mental ray's strengths is its ability to generate physically accurate lighting simulations based on *indirect lighting* principles. *Indirect lighting* occurs when light bounces from one object in a scene onto another object. In addition, incandescence or self-illumination from one object can light other objects in the scene. *Direct lighting*, such as from an omni light, is not necessarily required. Another thing to consider is that mental ray's reflections and refractions take on very real qualities when set up and lighted well.

Exercise 15.1: Enabling the mental ray Renderer

Set your project to the c15_mental ray project folder that you downloaded to your hard drive from the companion web page at www.sybex.com /go/3dsmax2016essentials. Open the c15_ex1_assign_start.max file in the scenes folder. You'll render a movie to see the animation. To enable mental ray, follow these steps:

1. Open the Render Setup box by choosing from the Main menu Rendering ➢ Render Setup, selecting the icon in the main toolbar ( ) or use the shortcut (F10).

2. At the top of the Render Setup dialog box, choose the Renderer drop-down menu. Select NVIDIA mental ray, as shown in Figure 15.1.

Once the NVIDIA mental ray renderer is assigned, you can make it the default renderer by clicking the Save as Defaults button on the Assign Renderer rollout. If mental ray is set as the default, the Render Setup dialog box opens with the mental ray controls in tabs. You will not need to do this for the exercises in this chapter.

FIGURE 15.1   Choose NVIDIA mental ray from the Renderer drop-down menu.

Save the file. To check your work, you can open the c15_ex1_assign_end.max file in the c15_mental ray project folder.

mental ray Sampling Quality

Once the mental ray renderer is enabled, click the Renderer tab in the Render Setup dialog box. The following is a brief explanation of the settings that are typically most useful for rendering work.

Under the Sampling Quality rollout, shown in Figure 15.2, are the settings that let you control the overall image quality of your renders.

There are three options to choose from in the Sampling Mode drop-down list. Unified/Raytraced (Recommended) is the default. This mode raytraces the scene using the same sampling method for both anti-aliasing and calculating motion blur. This results in far quicker rendering than the Classic/Raytraced method.

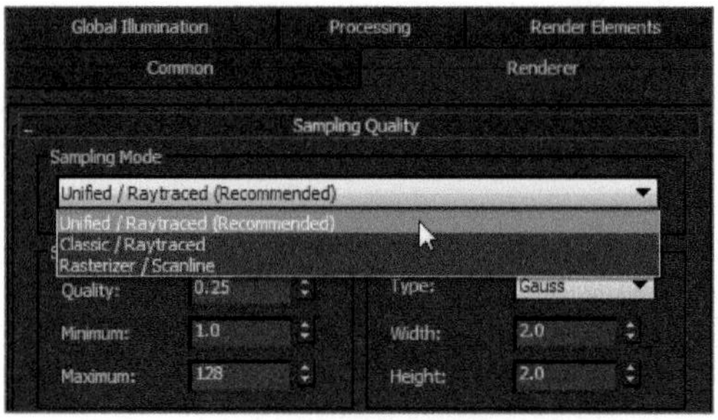

FIGURE 15.2   The Renderer tab shows the Sampling Quality rollout.

Quality essentially sets the "noise level" at which the renderer stops sampling. Higher quality implies less noise. The Quality parameter sets the quality of rendering. The lower the values, the faster the render, but the render is much grainier, as shown in Figure 15.3. The higher value, the smoother the images, as shown in Figure 15.4, but they take longer to render.

FIGURE 15.3 A Quality setting of 0.01 renders a noisy image.

FIGURE 15.4 A Quality setting of 20.0 renders a smooth image.

Navigating the Final Gather Parameters

A popular feature in mental ray is *indirect illumination*—the simulation of bounced light (explained in the next section). Click the Global Illumination tab at the top of the Render Setup dialog box. There are four rollouts, the second of which we will explore further:

▶ Skylights & Environment Lighting (IBL)

▶ Final Gathering (FG)

▶ Caustics & Photon Mapping (GI)

▶ Reuse (FG And GI Disk Caching)

Final Gather is a method of mental ray rendering for estimating global illumination (GI). In short, *global illumination* is a way of calculating indirect lighting. This way, objects do not need to be in the direct path of a light (such as a spotlight) to be lit in the scene; mental ray accomplishes this by casting points throughout a scene. These light points are allowed to bounce from object to object, contributing light as they go, effectively simulating how real light photons work in the physical world.

Figure 15.5 shows the Final Gathering (FG) rollout. Some of the FG options, including how to deal with quality and noise, are explained next.

This type of rendering can introduce artifacts or noise in the render. Finding the right settings to balance a clean render and acceptable render times is an art form all its own and is rather difficult to master.

FIGURE 15.5 The Final Gathering (FG) rollout in the Global Illumination tab of the Render Setup dialog box

Basic Group

These are the most important parameters in the Basic group of the Final Gathering (FG) rollout; they set the accuracy and precision of the light bounces, thereby controlling noise:

FG Precision Presets Slider   Sets the accuracy level of the Final Gather simulation by adjusting settings for the renderer such as Initial FG Point Density, Rays Per FG Point, and Interpolate Over Num. FG Points. Use this slider first in setting how well your render's lighting looks. In the left image in Figure 15.6, three spheres are rendered with the Draft setting for Final Gather, while the right image is set to High. Notice that the right image is a cleaner render, and it also shows more of the background and the spheres than does the Draft quality in the left image. This slider will adjust the settings for several of the values covered in the following list.

FIGURE 15.6   The Draft setting produces a test render of the spheres (left). The High setting produces a better-quality render of the spheres (right).

Initial FG Point Density   This multiplier controls the density for the Final Gather points. This is one of the settings adjusted by the FG Precision Presets slider, but it can also be set manually. This value sets the quantity and density of FG *points* that are cast into the scene. The higher the density of these points, the more accurate the bounced light appears, at a cost of render time.

Rays Per FG Point   This value is controlled by the FG Precision Presets slider but can also be manually set. The higher the number of rays used to compute the indirect illumination in a scene, the less noise and the more accuracy you gain, but at the cost of longer render times.

Interpolate Over Num. FG Points   Interpolation is controlled by the FG Precision Presets slider as well as manual input. This value is useful for getting rid of noise in your renders for smoother results. Increasing the interpolation will increase render times but not as much as increasing the Initial FG Point Density or Rays Per FG Point values.

Diffuse Bounces   The number of bounces governs how many times a ray of light can bounce and affect objects in a scene before stopping calculation. If you set the number of bounces higher, the light simulation will be more accurate, but the render times will be costly. A Diffuse Bounces setting of 1 or 5 is adequate for many applications. Figure 15.7 shows the same render of the spheres as Figure 15.6, but with a Diffuse Bounces value of 5. This render is brighter and also shows color bleed from the purple spheres onto the gray floor.

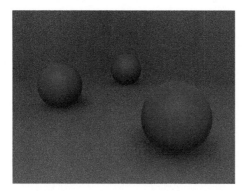

FIGURE 15.7   More diffuse bounces mean more bounced light.

Advanced Group

The Advanced group of settings gives you access to additional ways of controlling the quality of your Final Gather renders. Some of them are described next, in brief. You should experiment with different settings as you gain more experience with Final Gather to see what settings work best for your scenes.

Noise Filtering (Speckle Reduction)   This value essentially averages the brightness of the light rays in the scene to give you smoother Final Gather results. The higher the filtering, the darker your Final Gather simulation, and the longer your render times will be. However, the noise in your lighting will diminish.

Max. Reflections   This value controls how many times a light ray can be reflected in the scene. A value of 0 turns off reflections entirely. The higher this value, the more times you can see a reflection. For example, a value of 2 allows you to see a reflection of a reflection.

Max. Refractions Similar to Max. Reflections, this value sets the number of times a light ray can be refracted through a surface. A value of 0 turns off all refraction.

The mental ray Rendered Frame Window

When you render a scene using the Autodesk® 3ds Max® 2016 program, the Rendered Frame window opens, displaying the image you just rendered. When you render with mental ray, an additional control panel is displayed under the Rendered Frame window, as shown in Figure 15.8.

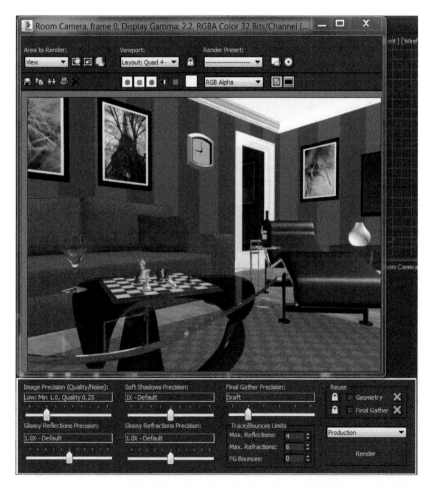

FIGURE 15.8 The Rendered Frame window now shows several mental ray controls.

This control panel gives you access to many of the most useful settings in the Render Settings dialog box so you can adjust render settings easily and quickly.

Navigating mental ray Materials

For the most part, mental ray treats regular 3ds Max maps and materials the same way the Default Scanline Renderer does. However, a set of mental ray–specific materials exists to take further advantage of mental ray's power. The mental ray Arch & Design material works great for most hard surfaces, such as metal, wood, glass, and ceramic. It is especially useful for surfaces that are glossy and reflective, such as metal and ceramic. To showcase these materials, let's retexture a few of the features from the room from Chapter 9, "Introduction to Materials."

Exercise 15.2: Setting Up the Material Editor

Set your project to the c15_mental ray project folder that you downloaded from the web page at www.sybex.com/go/3dsmax2016essentials. Open the c15_ex2_materials_start.max file from the scenes folder in the c15_mental ray project folder. This file has NVIDIA mental ray already assigned as the renderer. The scene includes the room and the textured furniture. There are no lights in the scene, but because NVIDIA mental ray is the assigned renderer, it utilizes the default lights to generate a lighted scene, as shown rendered in Figure 15.9. The materials from the previous chapter are rendered by mental ray; some look the same, but others don't look so good.

FIGURE 15.9 The file rendered with mental ray

1. Open the Slate Material Editor, and then look at the top of the active view. You will see a tab called View 1; it holds all the materials that were created for the scene.

2. To keep the new materials that will be created separate and organized, create another tab for the mental ray materials. To create a new tab, right-click in the blank area next to the tab, as shown in Figure 15.10, create a new view, name it **mental ray,** and click OK.

FIGURE 15.10 **Create a new view.**

Save the file. To check your work, open the c15_ex2_materials_end .max file in the c15_mental ray project folder.

Exercise 15.3: Using Arch & Design Material Templates

In the Material/Map Browser, you will see an additional rollout: mental ray. This gives you access to a whole new set of materials, including the Arch & Design materials. Arch & Design materials have a special feature: templates. *Templates* provide access to already created materials and parameters for different types of materials, such as wood, glass, and metal. These templates can also be used as starting points for material creation. Open the c15_ex3_ materials_start.max file from the scenes folder in the c15_mental ray project folder. You will use an Arch & Design Material to create the material for the tabletop and wineglass in the following steps:

1. Drag an Arch & Design material to the mental ray active view from the mental ray material section of the Material/Map Browser.

2. Double-click the title of the node; this will display the Arch & Design material in the Material Parameter Editor.

3. Name the material **Thick Glass.**

4. From the Material Parameter Editor, in the Select a Template drop-down menu, choose Glass (Solid Geometry), as shown in Figure 15.11.

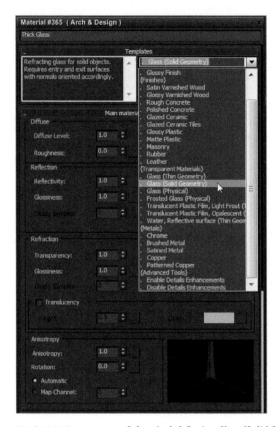

FIGURE 15.11 Select Arch & Design Glass (Solid Geometry) from the template drop-down menu.

5. Drag a wire from the Thick Glass material's output socket to the Coffee Table Top object.

6. Render the Room Camera viewport to see the new material on the coffee table top. There is some blue in the glass; this is from the Refraction color.

7. Select the Refraction Color swatch, and change the color to white to get a clear glass.

8. Render the scene, as shown in Figure 15.12.

Another Arch & Design material template is the Chrome template. You will use it to replace the chrome that already exists on the side table and lounge chair frames.

FIGURE 15.12   Refraction color changed to white to achieve clear glass

9. Press the C key on the keyboard. This will bring up the Select Camera dialog box, which includes a list of cameras in the scene.

10. Select the Lounge Chair/Table camera. Click OK to close the dialog box.

11. In the Slate Material Editor, create a new Arch & Design material and choose Chrome from the template list. Name it **Chrome**.

12. Select the lounge chair and, in the main menu bar, choose Group ➤ Open. This will allow you to select individual pieces within the group. Repeat the same process on the Side Table.

13. Select the pieces of the side table and lounge chair that need to be chrome, which are all the pieces of the table except the glass top, as well as the frame of the lounge chair. When you apply the material, you will get an error message, as shown in Figure 15.13, telling you that a material with the same name already exists. This material is a Standard material that was previously applied.

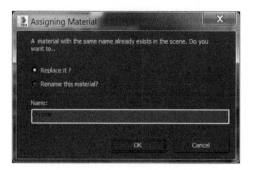

FIGURE 15.13 The message warns you about assigning a material with a duplicate name to an object.

14. Select the *Replace It*? radio button and click OK.

15. Render to see the new Chrome material applied to the side table and lounge chair frame, as shown in Figure 15.14.

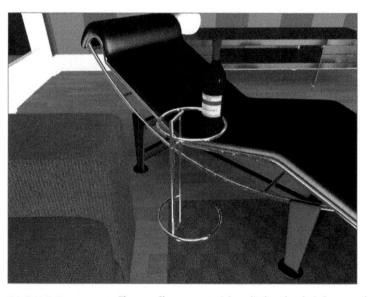

FIGURE 15.14 The new Chrome material applied to the chair frame and side table

Save the file. To check your work, open the c15_ex3_materials_end.max file in the c15_mental ray project folder.

Exercise 15.4: Creating Arch & Design Materials

Using the Arch & Design material, you will create a new material for the floor. There is a template called Glossy Varnished Wood, but you are going to create the floor material from scratch. Open the c15_ex4_materials_start.max file from the scenes folder of the c15_mental ray project folder.

1. Switch from the Lounge Chair/Table camera to the Floor camera by pressing the C key to bring up the Select Camera dialog.

2. Open the Slate Material Editor if it isn't already open, and drag an Arch & Design material from the mental ray rollout of the Material/Map Browser to the mental ray active view.

3. Double-click the title of the node to display the Arch & Design material parameters in the Material Parameter Editor. Name the material **Hardwood Floors**.

4. Drag a bitmap from the Maps rollout to the Diffuse Color Map input socket of the Arch & Design material. This will bring up the Select Bitmap Image File dialog box.

5. Choose the Hardwood_honey.tif file. Leave all the other parameters at their defaults.

6. Apply the material to the floor. You will get an error window telling you that there is a material with the same name already applied. Select *Replace It?* from the dialog and click OK. If the Hardwood Floors material doesn't show up in the viewport, click the Show Shaded Material in Viewport button ( ). Render the Floor Camera viewport. The results are shown in Figure 15.15.

FIGURE 15.15   Floor with the Arch & Design material applied

7. In the Material Editor, in the Reflection group, leave Reflectivity at 0.6 and change Glossiness to 0.6.

8. Render the camera to see the results, as shown in Figure 15.16.

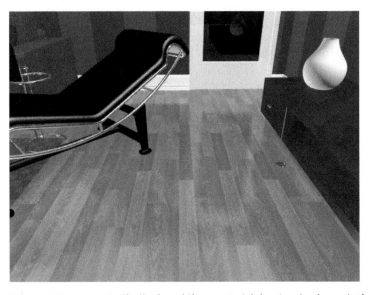

FIGURE 15.16   The Hardwood Floors material showing the change in the reflections

By default, Arch & Design materials have reflection enabled. The area below the Diffuse group in the Material Parameter Editor of the Slate Material Editor is the Reflection group of parameters. Reflections for this material are calculated using the Reflectivity and Glossiness values. The Reflectivity values define the level of reflections. The Glossiness value controls the blurriness of the reflections from sharp (a value of 1) to completely blurred (a value of 0). When you blur your reflections, the blurrier they are, the noisier they will be in the render. You can use the Glossy Samples value to increase the quality of the blurred reflections once you set Glossiness to anything less than 1.

You can use the same techniques for creating Arch & Design materials for the other objects in the scene, like the base of the coffee table and the couch. Save the file. To check your work, open the c15_ex4_materials_end.max file in the c15_mental ray project folder.

Exercise 15.5: Using the Multi/Sub-Object Material and Arch & Design

You can use the same technique for the window that you used in Chapter 9, but the difference is that you will use the Arch & Design material instead of the Multi/Sub-Object material. The window is divided into two materials: shiny white for the frame and a shiny transparent material for the glass. Another way to apply a Multi/Sub-Object material is to apply the material to the selected sub-objects. Open the c15_ex5_materials_start.max file from the scenes folder of the c15_mental ray project folder.

1. Switch from the Lounge Chair/Table camera to the Window camera by pressing the C key to bring up the Select Camera dialog box.

2. Select the FixedWindow001 object and go to the Graphite Modeling Tools > Modeling tab > Polygon Modeling > Convert to Poly.

3. Enter Polygon mode (   ), and select all the polygons for the window frame. The simplest way to do this is to select the Window Glass object, hold down Alt, and click just the window glass; this will deselect the glass. These window objects have "glass" on the front and back; you will need to select both. Switch to a Perspective viewport until you see the outside of the room and backside of the window, and then select the glass on the outside.

4. In the Slate Material Editor, you'll create a shiny white material: Drag an Arch & Design material to the mental ray active view, change the Diffuse color to R = 1.0, G = 1.0, B = 1.0, and rename it **White**

Window Frame. Based on what you know about reflections from the previous steps, the default reflections are too high, especially for the frame on the window.

5. In the Reflection group, change Reflectivity to 0.4 and Glossiness to 0.4.

6. Apply the material to the selected sub-objects using the Assign Material to Selection button (■).

7. Now go to the main toolbar ➤ Edit menu and choose Select Invert; this will deselect the window frame and select the window glass.

8. Back in the Slate Material Editor, drag an Arch & Design material to the mental ray active view.

9. Double-click the title bar of the new Arch & Design material to load it into the Material Parameter Editor.

10. In the Select a Template drop-down menu, choose Glass (Thin Geometry), and select the Show Background in Preview icon (■). This will place a checker pattern behind the sample sphere to make the transparency easier to view. Rename the material **Window Glass**.

11. Apply the material to the window glass using the Assign Material to Selection button.

12. Exit Polygon mode by selecting the Polygon button.

13. Render the Window Camera viewport.

You can see that the window and frame look very similar to the Standard materials, but the coffee table and floor look significantly better than with their previous Standard material. When you're using mental ray, Arch & Design materials are superior. Sometimes the look of a particular object can change depending on the camera angle and lighting. Keep an eye on the window to see if the look maintains the realism you are after.

The Arch & Design material type is an elaborate construct of mental ray shaders, and with proper lighting, it can make any render look special. If you open the c15_ex5_materials_end.max file, you will see several examples of materials beyond what you created in the previous exercise, as shown in Figure 15.17.

Save the file. To check your work, open the c15_ex5_materials_end.max file in the c15_mental ray project folder.

FIGURE 15.17   The final render of the mental ray materials

Using Photometric Lights with mental ray

Photometric lights simulate real lighting by using physically based energy values and color temperatures. Many of the parameters for photometric lights are the same as or very similar to the standard lights you looked at in Chapter 13, "Introduction to Lighting: Interior Lighting."

Exercise 15.6: Using Photometric Lights in mental ray Renderings

In this exercise, you will learn many of the parameters that are specific to photometric lights. To learn about photometric lights, follow these steps:

1. Open the c15_ex6_ light_start.max file from the scenes folder of the c15_mental ray project folder on the book's web page.

2. Create a photometric target light by going to the main menu bar and choosing Create ➢ Lights ➢ Photometric Lights ➢ Target Light to create a photometric target light.

3. When you click on the target light, you will get a Photometric Light Creation pop-up, recommending that you use the mr Photographic Exposure Control, as shown in Figure 15.18. Click Yes.

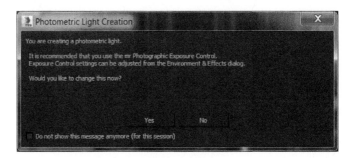

FIGURE 15.18   Select *Yes* in the Photometric Light Creation dialog box.

4. In the Left viewport, click to create the light, and then drag from the ceiling down to the floor. Make sure you stay within the room.

5. You will need to move the light. Both the light source and target need to be selected. The easiest way to select both the light and the target is to select the blue line that runs between the two objects.

6. Switch to the Top viewport, and with the Select and Move tool, move the light and its target so they are above the coffee table.

7. Change the viewport rendering type to Realistic in the Room Window Camera viewport.

8. Select the light source and go to the Modify panel.

9. The first rollout under the modifier stack is Templates. In the Select a Template drop-down menu, select Recessed 75W Wallwash (Web). When you add a template to a photometric light, a new rollout appears. Figure 15.19 shows a photometric light rollout with a "web" distribution essentially defining the light's behavior and the light it casts.

The Templates rollout gives you access to several light type presets to save you time when creating a light.

▶

Lighting manufacturers provide web files that model the kinds of lights they make, so using these distribution patterns as templates will give you a lot of options in simulating real-world lights, such as this 75-watt recessed lamp.

▶

FIGURE 15.19   The Distribution (Photometric Web) rollout

10. You need to take care of some basic stuff now, so with the light still selected, open the General Parameters rollout and check the Targeted box. Checking this box turns the target back on for the light.

11. From the drop-down menu, choose Ray Traced Shadows.

12. Make sure the Window Camera viewport is selected; then in the main menu bar, choose Rendering ➤ Exposure Control, and click the Render Preview button in the Exposure Control rollout, as shown in Figure 15.20.

You originally created a targeted light, but when you used the template, it took away the target. Having a target on a light makes it easier to edit the light's orientation.

The preview may show as either very bright or very dark at first. If so, the preview function will work perfectly once you render a frame for the first time.

F I G U R E   1 5 . 2 0   Exposure Control and mr Photographic Exposure Control rollouts in the Environment and Effects dialog box

13. Under the mr Photographic Exposure Control rollout, select Exposure Value (EV) if it isn't already selected.

14. Set some different values for the EV and see what happens in the Render Preview window. The higher the EV number, the darker the scene will be; when you change the exposure value, the Render Preview window updates. Set the EV to 2 and render the Room Window Camera viewport, as shown in Figure 15.21.

FIGURE 15.21 The room so far

15. You can continue to work with the EV to experiment with the luminance level. When you've finished experimenting, be sure to set the EV to 2 and close the Environment and Effects dialog box.

16. With the 75W light still selected, go to the Modify panel, and in the Color group in the Intensity/Color/Attenuation rollout, click the radio button next to Kelvin and change the value to 5600. This will give the light a bit more warmth by adding more yellow/red.

17. In the Dimming group, uncheck the box next to the 100% spinner under Resulting Intensity to enable the Intensity parameter.

18. In the Intensity group, select cd, as shown in Figure 15.22, and set the cd amount to 200. This will brighten things up a bit.

FIGURE 15.22 Intensity/Color/Attenuation rollout showing the changed parameters

19. Render the scene. The result is shown in Figure 15.23. The scene still looks a bit dark, and the shadows are very dark; they look like black holes. You will use Final Gather to brighten up the overall render.

FIGURE 15.23 The room render with color and intensity changes

20. In the mini panel below the Rendered Frame window, shown in Figure 15.24, change FG Bounces to **7**.

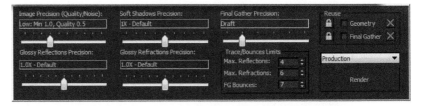

FIGURE 15.24 **This mini panel gives you access to Final Gather controls to adjust your render easily.**

21. Render the scene and compare the resulting render shown in Figure 15.23 to Figure 15.25. Figure 15.25 shows the final render.

FIGURE 15.25 **The final mental ray render of the room's interior lighting**

Save the file. To check your work, open the `c15_ex6_materials_end.max` file in the `c15_mental ray` project folder.

Photometric Light Parameters

Now let's look in the command panel at the photometric light's Intensity/Color/Attenuation rollout for the 75W light.

The Color group of parameters controls the color temperature of the light, which you can set either with a color value or in Kelvin units, just as with real-world photographic lights. In the drop-down menu, there are different color/temp settings. The default is D65 Illuminant (Reference White).

The Intensity group of parameters controls the strength or brightness of the lights measured in lm, cd, or lx at (lux).

lm (lumen)   This value is the overall output power of the light. A 100-watt general-purpose light bulb measures about 1750 lm.

cd (candela)   This value shows the maximum luminous intensity of the light. A 100-watt general-purpose light bulb measures about 139 cd.

lx at (lux)   This value shows the amount of luminance created by the light shining on a surface at a certain distance.

The parameters in the Dimming section are also used to control the intensity of the light. When the Resulting Intensity box is checked, the value specifies a multiplier that dims the existing intensity of the light and takes over control of the intensity.

Using the Daylight System

The Daylight System simulates sunlight by following the geographically correct angle and movement of the sun over the Earth. You can choose location, date, time, and compass orientation to set the orientation of the sun and its lighting conditions. You can also animate the date and time to achieve very cool time-lapse looks and shadow studies.

Exercise 15.7: Using the Daylight System in mental ray Renderings

In essence, this type of light works really well with mental ray and Final Gather. In this exercise, you will use it in the most basic way, using all of its defaults.

1. Open the c15_ex7_daylight_start.max file from the scenes folder of the c15_mental ray project folder.

2. Choose Create ➤ Lights ➤ Daylight System.

3. A Daylight System Creation warning will appear, as shown in Figure 15.26, asking if you want to change the exposure controls to suit the Daylight System. Click Yes.

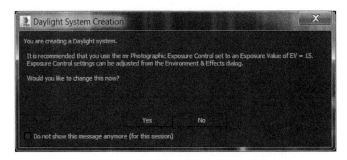

FIGURE 15.26 The Daylight System Creation warning

4. In a Top viewport, click and drag at the center of the scene. This will create a compass that is attached to the Daylight System. Make it the size of the room.

5. When you release the mouse button, move the mouse so the light is placed above the ceiling of the room. The Daylight System is supposed to simulate the sun and sky, so it needs to be outside the room.

6. With the light still selected, open the Modify panel, and in the Daylight Parameters rollout, change the drop-down menus under both Sunlight and Skylight to mr Sun and mr Sky, respectively.

7. When you change the Skylight parameter, a mental ray Sky warning will appear, asking if you want to place a mr Physical Sky environment map in your scene. Click Yes.

The lower the light is to the horizon in your scene, the more it will simulate darker skies at sunset.

▶

8. Also in the Daylight Parameters rollout, in the Position group, select Manual. This will allow you to use the Move tool to move the light to where you want it. The default position represents noon.

9. Move the light so it is going through the window, as shown in Figure 15.27.

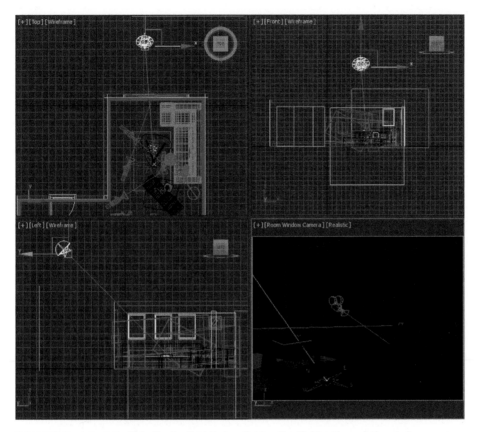

FIGURE 15.27 Move the Daylight System light so it will shine through the window.

10. Select the Room Window Camera viewport and render. As you can see, it is too dark. You are trying to simulate a sunny day, and beyond the direct light coming through the window, it's pretty dark, as shown in Figure 15.28.

FIGURE 15.28 This scene is too dark.

A good tool to use in this situation is mr Sky Portal. It gives you an efficient way of using a scene's existing sky lighting within interior scenes that do not require costly Final Gather or Global Illumination.

▶

▶

A portal gets its brightness and color from the environment already in your scene.

11. Choose Create ➤ Lights ➤ Photometric Lights ➤ mr Sky Portal.

12. In the Front viewport, drag the mr Sky Portal so it fits the window size in the wall.

13. Then in the Top viewport, move the mr Sky Portal back so it is aligned with the opening of the window outside the room. Make sure the arrow is pointing into the room, as shown in Figure 15.29. Figure 15.29 is shown with just the walls, window, Daylight System, and mr Sky Portal.

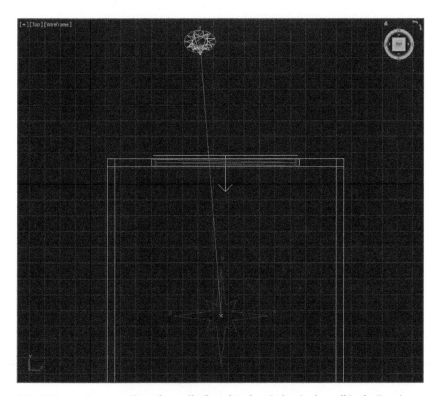

FIGURE 15.29   Move the mr Sky Portal to the window in the wall in the Top viewport.

14. Render the Room Window Camera viewport again. That helps, but it is not enough; it is still too dark, so it's time to play with exposure controls.

15. Choose Rendering ➤ Exposure Control. Click Render Preview.

16. In the mr Photographic Exposure Control rollout, change the Exposure Value (EV) from 15 (the default) to 9. You should see the render preview change to show the update.

17. Render the Room Window Camera viewport again to see the difference. It looks good but is still a bit dark, so it's time to add Final Gather bounces.

18. In the Rendered Frame window, change FG Bounces to **5**. Render the viewport again.

That's it! If you want to play around some more, try moving the light for a more dramatic shadow on the floor. Moving the light can have a dramatic effect on the luminance levels, so be prepared to edit FG Bounces and Exposure Controls. The last render is shown in Figure 15.30. Don't be surprised if it takes a while to render.

FIGURE 15.30 **The final render**

Open the c15_ex7_daylight_end.max file to compare it to your file.

NOW YOU KNOW

In this chapter, you learned the basics of the Daylight System, Sky Portals, and mental ray, which are used for lighting, material creation, and rendering. You saw the quality settings and how they could help you create better renders. Finding the right balance of settings for a clean render is an art all to itself. We introduced the Arch & Design material, and you learned the basics of navigating and applying it. You also started lighting with Final Gather using photometric lights and the Daylight System.

Autodesk 3ds Max Certification

Autodesk certifications are industry-recognized credentials that can help you succeed in your design career—providing benefits to both you and your employer. Getting certified is a reliable validation of skills and knowledge, and it can lead to accelerated professional development, improved productivity, and enhanced credibility.

This Autodesk Official Press guide can be an effective component of your exam preparation for the Autodesk® 3ds Max® 2016 certification exam. Autodesk highly recommends (and we agree!) that you schedule regular time to prepare, review the most current exam preparation road map available at www.autodesk.com/certification, use Autodesk Official Press books, take a class at an Authorized Training Center (find ATCs near you at www.autodesk.com/atc), take an assessment test, and use a variety of resources to prepare for your certification—including plenty of actual hands-on experience.

Certification Objective

Table A.1 is for the Autodesk 3ds Max 2016 Certified Professional exam and lists the topics, exam objectives, and the chapter where the information for each objective is found—and in the chapters, you'll find certification icons like the one in the margin here to indicate where objectives are covered. This book will give you a foundation for the basic objectives covered in the exam, but you will need further study and hands-on practice to complete and pass the Professional exam.

These Autodesk certification exam objectives were accurate at press time. To find the latest information about the exam and what is covered, go to www.autodesk.com/certification. Good luck preparing for your certification!

TABLE A.1   3ds Max 2016 exam objectives

Topic	Exam Objective	Chapter or Appendix
Animation	Create a path animation and evaluate an object along the path	Not Covered
	Identify controller types	Chapters 5, 6
	Identify playback settings	Chapters 5, 6
	Locate the value of keys in the time slider	Chapters 5, 6
	Use a Dope Sheet	Chapter 12
Cameras	Differentiate camera types	Chapter 14
	Edit FOV (Field of View)	Not Covered
	Data management/interoperability	Chapters 1, 14
	Differentiate common file types and usages	Not Covered
	Use the import feature to import model data	Chapter 3
Effects	Use atmosphere effect	Chapter 13
	Identify particle systems	Not Covered
	Identify Space Warp types	Not Covered
Lighting	Compare attenuation and decay	Chapter 13
	Differentiate light functions in a scene	Chapter 13
	Identify parameters for modifying shadows	Chapter 13
	Use the Daylight System	Chapter 15
	Use the Light Lister	Chapter 15
Materials / Shading	Identify Shader parameters	Chapter 9
	Identify Standard materials	Chapter 9
	Use the Material Editor	Chapters 9, 10, 15

Topic	Exam Objective	Chapter or Appendix
Modeling	Differentiate reference coordinate systems	Chapters 1, 2, 7, 8
	Differentiate workflow	Chapters 2–4, 7, 8
	Differentiate standard versus extended primitives	Not Covered
	Identify clone types	Chapters 2–4, 7, 8
	Identify vertex types	Chapter 2
	Use object creation and modification workflows	Chapters 2–4, 7, 8
	Use polygon modeling tools	Chapters 2–4, 7–10
	Use ProBoolean	Not Covered
Rendering	Differentiate renderers	Chapter 15
	Identify rendering parameters	Chapter 15
Rigging	Use Character Studio for rigging	Chapter 11
	Create simple bipeds	Chapter 11
	Use the Skin modifier	Chapter 12
UI/Object Management	Describe and use object transformations	Chapters 1, 2, 5
	Identify selection regions	Chapters 2, 7, 8
	Use viewports	Chapters 1, 2
	Set up and use scenes	Chapters 1, 2

INDEX

Note to the reader: Throughout this index **boldfaced** page numbers indicate primary discussions of a topic. *Italicized* page numbers indicate illustrations.